THE LONG MARCH

TO
NATIONAL FREEDOM, POPULAR SELF-GOVERNANCE
AND
AFRICAN SELF-BECOMING
IN
UGANDA/NILE AFRICA.

THE PROMISE, TASKS AND PROSPECTS

Dr Obyara David Anyoti

Publisher

Alawi Books Ltd.

Publisher: **Alawi Books Ltd.**
125 Second Avenue
Manor Park
London E12 6EN

Website at: www.tboah.com

<u>Contacts:</u> **Email:**   alawibooks@tboah.com

              Tel: [+44] 07983412790

Printed by Create Space – Amazon Books

First Printing, 2017

Book ISBN 978-0-9929462-8-9

Printed hard copies - online order form is available as a hard copy from Amazon Books.

Cover design, Layout and Illustrations: Jack Stevens Alecho-oita.

Contents

Acknowledgement

This publication acknowledges the contribution of Prof. Gregory Maloba (1922 – 2004), a Kenyan scholar and artist who carved his way to fame in Uganda, as the person who designed and built the country's 'Independence Monument.' He sculptured the monument at the invitation of the then Prime Minister of Uganda, Dr Apollo Milton Obote, at independence.

The Geographical Placing of the Nile River in Africa: Uganda/ Nile Africa and the River Nile Question

ABBREVIATIONS

* K.Y.   - KABAKA YEKKA MOVEMENT

* C. P.   - CONSERVATIVE PARTY

* D.P.   - DEMOCRATIC PARTY

* N.R.M./N.R.A.   - NATIONAL RESISTANCE MOVEMENT/ARMY

*U.N.C   - UGANDA NATIONAL CONGRESS

*U.P.C   - UGANDA PEOPLE'S CONGRESS

FOREWORD

"...We never think entirely alone: we think in company, in a vast collaboration; we work with workers of the past and those of the present...

"...In the whole intellectual world each finds in those about him, the initiation, help, verification, information, encouragement that he needs..."

[Antonin-Gilbert Sertillanges The Intellectual Life; Its Spirits, Conditions and Methods (1978 Dublin, Mercier Press)]

This is the story of this publication and communication.

The story is itself an element of the larger story, about the past, present and doubtless – the emergent future in Uganda/Nile Africa.

It is about living history whose fundamental project remains; as the Italian internationalist fighter for freedom and democracy Antonio Gramsci urged; of:

"...an historical, dialectical conception of the world which understands movement and change, which appreciates the sum of efforts and sacrifice which the present has cost the past and which the future is costing the present, and which conceives the contemporary world as a synthesis of the past, of all generations, which projects itself into the future..."

[Harvey Kaye, 1994 Isaac Deutscher Memorial lecture]

Historical sense, and; knowledge of history and obtaining complex reality, holds as indispensable tools in the successful prosecution of the struggles for African liberation.

History indeed, provides insights and questions, but hardly answers to humanity's quest to the future.

Geoffrey Barraclough, in this regard noted the following in his book, *'An Introduction to Contemporary History – London, 1964'*/ at page 1:

"...Merely to recount the course of events, even on a worldwide scale, is unlikely to result in a better understanding of the forces at play in the world today

unless we are aware at the same time of underlying structural changes...
"...What we require first of all is a new framework and new terms of reference..."

Pertinent lessons from the past can in this context be put to the uses of human struggles in contemporary times.

A good grasp of history could indicate to us or tell us what the future portends and, or can bring. However we must as well, take into account the possibilities of historical surprises and accidents that are present in the turbulent unfolding of history.

As active historical players – subjective considerations of human beings about the past, present and future count, and can function either as self-fulfilling or self-negating considerations or points of critical assessment of the possible forward movement of peoples.

The future cannot however unfold, on its own account.

The future remains to be made and constructed by people, including those in conflict, conflagrations and war and, those who strive to design a future they want.

The future that the African masses of people seek to invent is consequently an adventure, with crystallisable objectives, though at times these prove less clear.

When this human adventure begins, as the philosopher noted, there is hardly any turning back. The struggles for an emancipated humanity is the promise of the new future which rises when ways out of the current state of human slavery and catastrophe, and ways forward and upwards from it are, with sacrifices, made.

Uganda, and the Nile African lands, now new colonies of multinational capital and finance interests, have for long existed in a most implosive condition – in the turbulent interregnum between on the one hand the hegemony of dominant multinational capital and finance and their local agents, and, on the other, the rise of a sovereign and free African Africa; an Africa which has recovered its capacities for the self-becoming of its peoples, nations and communities and the powers of African self-renewal.

The slave relations between the peoples of Africa and world imperial hegemons, which have long obtained since the slave holocaust over half a millennium ago, persist in their various forms.

The imperial hegemons continue to sing their old praise songs because Africa is held up, and made to run on the same spot and to mark time in a most implosive situation of apparent *"change without change"*.

This condition of historical paralysis, suffocates African humanity and obstacles Africa's possible forward movement.

Africa's challenge then is to dare seize the wheel of history and turn it forever in its favour.

All peoples, from ancient times have had to face up to this challenge of self-emancipation and reincarnation as subjects of their own history, which is the only way to overcome and transcend imposed relations of slavery.

One Thucydides, an Athenian recorder of historical happenings and events in ancient times, recalled how in 416 BC, the Athenians, who had evolved into the hegemon of their Mediterranean zone of domination – defined with due clarity to their weaker Melian opponents, what constituted the essences and, or fundamentals of asymmetrical relations that exist between; *"...the mighty and the weakened..."* or *"...power and subdued subjects..."* in these most telling words: *"...The strong,..."* he asserted, *"...do as they wish, while the weak have to suffer what they must..."*

The unforgettable Winston Churchill, a celebrant of the slave relations in the then British Empire in a position paper submitted to his cabinet colleagues in January 1914, put forth the British position of hegemony – that was as frank as it was arrogant:-

> *"...We are not a young people with an innocent record and a scanty inheritance...*
>
> *"...We have engrossed to ourselves...*
>
> *"...an altogether disproportionate share of the wealth and traffic of the world...*
>
> *"...We have got all we want in territory; and our claim to be left in the unmolested enjoyment of vast and splendid possessions, mainly acquired by violence, largely maintained by force, often seems less reasonable to others than to us..."*

Uganda, which Churchill baptised as *"The Pearl of Africa"* when he visited that country, was by force of arms, excessive violence and terror, and manipulations of all kinds – made into a British *"Protectorate"* – otherwise a grand name for a colony; a depiction which fits into definitions of a subject of a hegemon as set out by Churchill.

It has been the principal struggle of the Ugandan people to free themselves from the global slave system (whose essences have lived to contemporary times), which Winston Churchill had the courage to define, as the able representative of the British hegemon of his times.

After the 2nd World War, the United States of America (USA) succeeded the British as the global hegemon of a new type, which held sway over most of the world, except the then Soviet Union and the Peoples Republic of China.

Since then, a world capitalist market has come into being.

The powers that rule this turbulent market also rule the world.

One Thomas Friedman, an ideologist and guardian of the US foreign policy aptly depicted the situation in which the USA, has risen as the global market hegemon in these words:-

> *"...The hidden hand of the market, will never work without a hidden fist...*
>
> *"...McDonalds cannot flourish without McDonnell Douglas, the designer of F-15 (fighter aircrafts)...*
>
> *"...And the hidden fist that keeps the world safe for Silicon Valley's technologies is called the USA Army, Navy, and Marine Corps..."*

This reality – fundamentally continues to hold in place, with necessary redesigns.

Many in the world, on the other hand, have disagreed and opposed the position of the world's hegemonic forces as set out by Thomas Friedman.

The former French President Jacques Chirac held the position that:

> *"...The world is not only a market, our societies need rules, and the economy must be in the service of man and not the reverse...*
>
> *"...The freedom of exchange must not impose itself, when the public wellbeing is in question..."*

Another human-centred world, struggles to rise, in tune with the demands and aspirations of the majority peoples of the world – who seek to live deserved lives of dignity, prosperity and happiness as humanity made in the very image of God Almighty.

Even amongst the world hegemons, there has been emergent, a realisation that force or might alone can no longer be considered or taken as self-legitimising.

Henry Kissinger, the former US security and foreign relations expert, and the real politik guru for instance noted that:

> *"...Force might conquer the world but it cannot legitimise itself..."*

The world of slave masters which is everywhere imposed by force upon rebelling freedom seeking peoples, is untenable.

The struggle of the African people of Uganda is predicated on winning political, social and national liberation, so that they can self-empower and build the capacities requisite to invent a humane future in which they can as free African humanity, self-become and relate as equals with free world humanity.

The path to liberation of the African people, which have been and remain difficult and complex, have to be paved no matter what the sacrifices. The African people of Uganda/Nile Africa are faced with the challenge to open up new possibilities for their self-becoming. They also have to face up to resolving the outstanding tasks for the humanisation of society and of the peoples of their country.

THE LONG MARCH TO NATIONAL FREEDOM, POPULAR SELF GOVERNANCE AND AFRICAN SELF BECOMING IN UGANDA/NILE AFRICA, speaks for itself.

It is a programmatic exposition of the salient march and re-entry of oppressed Africans to the mainstream of world history, as well as a proclamation of faith in the ability of the masses of the African people of Uganda to win national freedom and national democratic liberation.

Hitherto, the Ugandan people, whose eyes have for long been set on political, social and national liberation, have repeatedly got sucked into bloody conflicts that only served to prolong the life of neo-colonialism, its militarism and tyranny of which they have suffered as principal victims in their own God given country.

Their proven will to sustain a long drawn-out fight, their courage, and indomitable spirit of sacrifice must never again be channelled into activity which preserves the system of which they are victims. Instead, their boundless energy will have to be directed towards winning for Uganda/Nile Africa, National Freedom, People's Self-rule/Popular

Democracy and the Well-being and Progress of their entire oppressed people.

The people's long march to national freedom in Uganda/ Nile Africa and the march of other oppressed African people towards national democratic liberation from neo-colonial domination, today herald a new stage in the intensification of their efforts for liberation and the genuine redemption of the African continent.

On this long and difficult path, where the African people have won brilliant victories, but have equally met martyrdom and many setbacks, the people's determination to win final triumph over all adversity remains firm and unflinching. Indeed their sacrifices and sustained struggle which continues to confound many in the world, is what reconciles the oppressed African people in Uganda/Nile Africa[1] with the hope that history will be made to bear, at last the fruit of liberation and freedom.

The undying desire for, genuine and unimpaired or unfettered sovereignty, people's self-rule/popular democracy, economic prosperity and overall progress, binds the oppressed African people with all others in the world who share the same aspirations and fight for National Freedom and self-determination of peoples and nations.

The liberty the oppressed African people desire for themselves is part and parcel of global demands of the oppressed people for freedom. The rights the oppressed African people aspire for, stands good for all peoples, for the freedom and liberty of the world's emergent peoples and nations is indivisible.

Ugandan people's recurrent social and political uprisings and insurrections and now their adoption of focused mass struggles as their means of collective self-defence and national salvation, affirm their unrelenting faith and determination to win final political victory over neo-colonialism, its militarism, and tyranny in Uganda/Nile Africa. They stand set to continue on this heroic road of collective self-defence, until the aggression and cruel rule of the 'nyampalas'[2] is overcome, and transcended.

Their now legendary perseverance on this most difficult path, shall indeed overcome the negative political and cultural heritage of colonialism, now compounded by neo-colonialism which has been

---

[1] There is an age-old issue on modern political borders that dismantled ancestral settlements of the nationalities along the River Nile.

[2] agents of neo-colonialism of which the masses of people are the principal victims.

responsible for the dissemination of myths and falsehoods about the root causes of the people's perilous and sub-human conditions of existence, and their alleged incapacities to understand or decide what to do about them.

With the valuable experience gained in unrelenting struggles against the fascist military dictatorship it is now clear that the false final victories claimed by its military regime over the Ugandan people, are mere pauses that the people make once in a while to catch their breath and reorganise so as to continue in their long drawn-out historic struggles for political, national and social liberation.

The Long March to National Freedom, popular self-governance and African self-becoming in Uganda/Nile Africa, is a summary/record of the democratic discussions of the problems facing the oppressed African people in Uganda which were held in the African wild and bushes by a community of Ugandan youths, students, teachers, intellectuals, professionals, peasants, political and community leaders, and other ordinary persons who are participants in Uganda's national democratic liberation struggle.

The fact that they have persevered in the struggle for so long bears clear testimony of the determination of the awakened oppressed African people of Uganda/Nile Africa to persist regardless, in their long and difficult odyssey to national freedom and liberation. It is their resolve that the iniquities of imperialism that have been meted against the oppressed Ugandan people for well over one hundred and fifty years have to be finally ended. The new times for genuine independence, sovereignty, people's self-rule/democracy, freedom, shared prosperity and progress of the world's emergent peoples and nations are now nigh.

In the African continent, from Cape to Cairo and Alexandria, from West Africa across Central Africa to the East African and Horn of Africa regions, across the lands of the Sahel, North of the Sahara in the African lands at the southern Mediterranean Sea shores, from the African Atlantic Ocean coasts to the African Indian Ocean shores and zones, the turbulence generated by a myriad of covert and overt social, political and national liberation struggles continue to buffet the continent.

The African agent and *nyampala*[3] *"Lords of Misrule"* whom the sages of the Ganda nation of Uganda aptly named as *"the Omuzungu Agambye*

---

[3] Ibid 2

Africans"[4], are and hold in consternation, hoping against hope that the intermittent, but continuous uprisings, rebellions and revolts are passing ill clouds. The parasitic African agent and rentier political classes still largely hold in self-denial of the irreversible development of the African mass up risings into popular African transformative forces.

The histories of popular revolts against slave systems, in effect repeat themselves.

Since, the genocidal African slave holocaust over 500 years ago, Africa has witnessed colonial and neo colonial slavery. In contemporary times slavery is now manifested in ruinous processes of globalized naked pillage and plunder of Africa's natural resources endowments and the unadulterated exploitation, repression and oppression of the African masses of people. In this situation the liberatory example of Prophet Moses and the enslaved Judaists in Nile Egypt of the infamous slave master – the Pharaoh, reverberates and finds definitive echo in the communities of oppressed Africans in the ruined and emasculated villages and hamlets, towns/city slums and backyards of Africa.

The idea of liberation from slavery and slave systems, of the need to combine social, political, ideological, psychological contentions and focused actions for social and political liberation; has once again come alive in enslaved Africa which is now nakedly subjected to the rigours of primitive capital accumulation via dispossession, pillage, plunder and open daylight robbery of fabulous natural and bio resources endowments.

The forces; of extreme greed and avarice and naked loot and of ruthless fortune hunters who operate with impunity – have been set loose in Africa.

The cost to Africa and her peoples, communities and nations is incalculable. The oppressed and exploited African – youth, women and men – shall however, not for much longer stand denied.

The African masses of people who find themselves enslaved within political, social, economic systems which deny them their inalienable right to establish systems by which they can work and live creative, productive, prosperous and happy lives without; destructive conflict, conflagrations and war today stand in liberatory anticipation. The subhuman conditions of existence that are imposed on the oppressed African people, which hold them in deep poverty, squalor and want,

---

[4] Ganda language inference *"... the imperial Whiteman's African parrots and copy-cats..."*

amidst endemic otherwise preventable famine and hunger, disease and ignorance, endlessly generate social conflict which can best be terminated by processes of social, political and national liberation.

Another humane world must rise, be built and nurtured in place of the destructive catastrophe that today envelops most of the world of oppressed humanity.

Political, social and national liberation, has hence of necessity to happen in Africa, in order for Africans to open up a new door to a new humane history – in which the masses of the African people work on their own account to duly meet their material, social and cultural needs and the developmental requirements of their various God-given ancestral lands and patrimonies.

This will have to be a new world – of popular, community and national African self-governance, which opens up requisite avenues for their self-becoming.

This shall have to be a world – in which the economy is embedded in society to meet its material, human sustenance and developmental needs, instead of that which has long obtained, where society is driven by the economy and interests of the enslavers of the African people.

This will also have to be a world built on self-motivated labour, justice, culture, and, Africanity – that long aspired process for the humanisation of society, the African youth, woman and man – as a manifestation of '*ubuntu*'[5], and the rise of new human centred African civilisation systems.

This will be a new world of the free, with overall responsible and accountable leaderships that shall no longer exist but free of the controls of local or foreign masters.

It is now abundantly evident that the people of Uganda/Nile Africa have reached a critical and decisive watershed point in their long and protracted historical liberatory struggles. The overwhelming demand for liberatory and transformative change is now more than palpable and, or manifest. It is on its way to becoming a material force.

The emergent leadership and social agency born in these struggles will become manifest and unfold in and from within the liberatory processes themselves – which will be facilitative of the formation and, or construction of a new political bloc that will have to stand equal to

---

[5] part of the Zulu phrase *"Umuntu ngumuntu ngabantu"*, which literally means that a person is a person through other people. **Ubuntu** has its roots in humanist African philosophy, where the idea of community is one of the building blocks of society.

challenges and tasks of assuming the responsibilities incumbent upon them to build requisite political, organisational and practical leadership that is able to guide the masses to successfully effect the political, social and national liberation of Uganda/Nile Africa from the slavery of exploitative and ruinous multinational capital and finance interests, and the destructive fascist rule of their allied and collaborating Ugandan/ Nile African *"Omuzungu Agambye"* Africans or the imperial white-man's stooge, copy-cat and parrot Africans.

At the end of this march of history, the masses of the people of Uganda/Nile Africa shall in fulfilment of their noble objective to re-assert popular independence and sovereignty, the full ownership of their God given land and country, and the maximal control and command of their destiny and that of their country – shall finally declare themselves as the liberated and free people of Africa.

When they get to register this historic milestone and make the deserved new beginning in Uganda's/Nile Africa's unfolding history of the free – the people will once again stand tall and justified to celebrate their popular intervention into the history as free and full subjects of the history they will thereafter make on their own account, and proudly and openly recall the optimistic prophetic words uttered by the late and lamented Dr Martin Luther King – the African American civil and human rights fighter during the historic mass rally – held in Washington D.C., the political capital of the United States of America (USA), on 28 August 1963:

> *"...Free at last, Free at last...*
> *"...Thank God Almighty, we are free at last..."*

The path to liberation and national freedom, popular self-governance, and African self-becoming in Uganda/Nile Africa, indicative of the path to Africa's future.

PROLOGUE

The struggles of the people of Uganda/ Nile Africa for freedom are part and parcel of the freedom struggles of the peoples of Africa and the world.

It is imperative that those who struggle for the common objectives of liberation and freedom work to benefit from the experiences, examples and wisdom of other peoples of the world who fight for similar high objectives.

The story of liberation and freedom of the oppressed and exploited peoples of the world have been much distorted mystified and misrepresented.

This has distorted and complicated the questions of understanding, interpretation and, or appreciation of these historical struggles. The interpretation of historical, liberatory and freedom struggles have always got tied with the question of seeking to establish the truth about, of and in each historical reality.

In the view of Lord John Emerich Acton;,

> *"...Truth is the only merit that gives dignity and worth to history..."*

Lord MacCauly's address to the British Parliament on 22nd Feb 1835 on Africa and its then historical and social realities, stands profoundly instructive in the matter of baring the truth of the then obtaining African condition, and the objective of imperialism towards it.

Lord MacCauly is reported to have said the following

> *"...I have travelled across the length and breadth of Africa and I have not seen one person who is a beggar...,*
> *"...who is a thief such wealth I have seen in this country...,*
> *"...such high moral values, peoples of such calibre...,*
> *"...that I do not think we could ever conquer this country...,*
> *"...unless we break the very backbone of this nation...,*

> *"... which is her spiritual and cultural heritage and therefore...,*
> *"...I propose that we replace her old and ancient education system...,*
> *"... her culture...,*
> *"... for if the Africans think that all that is foreign and English is good and greater than their own...,*
> *"... they will become what we want them to be...,*
> *"... a truly dominated nation..."*

This was a statement of naked truth on the then obtaining wholesome condition of Africa, and the evil objective of imperialism towards the continent.

Other informed relevant opinions have also been made about the complex routes traversed in the effort to seek and establish truth in human history. In this regard Pierre Norza, in Les Lieux de la Memoire, Vol. 1. (La Republique, Paris 1984, p.XIX) noted the following:

> *"...Memory is life. It is always carried by groups of living people, and therefore, is in permanent evolution...*
> *"...It is subject to the dialectics of remembering and forgetting, unaware of its successive deformations, open to all kinds of use and manipulation...*
> *"...Sometimes it remains latent for long periods, then suddenly revives...*
> *"...History is the always incomplete and problematic reconstruction of what is no longer there...*
> *"...Memory always belongs to our time and forms a live bond with the eternal present; history is a representation of the past..."*

Zachary Karabell, author of 'The people of the Book – The forgotten history of Islam' (John Murray Publishers – 2007), looking into the larger question and context of truth noted at page 3, the schemed presence and absence of certain facts and themes in history thus:

> *"...There is known history and forgotten history...*
> *"...History that supports our sense of the present...*
> *"...And history that suggests other ways..."*

In the given situation, it is necessary if not imperative to prod particular African histories so as to seek out the truth of the contemporary setting of things.

One has to prod into multiple explanations and historical materials in order to seek out the truth. Today's powers in the world routinely distort and mystify truth in history.

There is indeed no easy way to seek out and, or access the truth. Jesus the Christ who recommended the search for the truth as a liberatory path, set this quest as a riddle:

> *"...Seek ye the truth...*
> *"...And the truth shall set thee free..."*

History is of complex characteristics, depictions and interpretations. And *"History"* noted T.S. Eliot, *"has many cunning passages."*

> *"...Along any such passages...*

noted Professor Amit Bhaduri[6], the Indian political economist,

> *"...we might hope to travel in one direction only to end up in the opposite direction, and the irreversibility of time would prevent us from returning even to our initial position to correct the mistake...*
> *"...History is not merely unpredictable...*
> *"...It has almost magical quality to create illusion that takes at times bewilderingly strange turns..."*

Karl Marx – the renowned political economist and philosopher of proletarian revolution, however, critically noted that:

> *"...History does nothing, it possesses no immense wealth, fights no battles. It is rather man who does everything, who possesses and fights..."*

Geoffrey Till, a maritime historian held the viewpoint that;

> *"...because humans are active historical players, their beliefs about the future can function either as self-fulfilling or self-negating prophesies..."*

In short, their active interventions into history, based on their given beliefs, influence its unfolding.

To E.P. Thompson – it is best

---

[6] The Face You were Afraid to See - Amit Bhaduri, Essays on Indian Economy

"...to look at history as history..."

- with

*"...man placed in actual conditions which they have not
chosen, and confronted by indivertible forces, with an
overwhelming immediacy of relations and duties and with
only scanty opportunity for inserting their own agency ..."*

What is here to be noted in historical processes, according to T.S. Eliot, is the dynamic kick in place by

"...vast impersonal forces..."

These nameless millions are individuals acting more or less unconsciously, while together constituting a force.

The role that the individual plays in history, is hence influenced by a confluence of many factors and in complex situations of social processes and contentions, in which individuals get engaged as social beings.

Yet as Professor H. Butterfield[7] one noted,

*"...There is something in the nature of historical events
which twists the course of history in a direction that no man
ever intended..."*

Overall, however E.H. Carr[8] noted,

*"...the past is intelligible to us only in the light of the
present; and we can fully understand the present only in the
light of the past...*

*"...To enable man to understand the society of the past and
to increase his mastery over society of the present, is the
dual function of history..."*

In visualizing the past in Uganda/Nile Africa, there is need to look at matters from all angles. And, it is most delimiting to take the position that facts speak for themselves, that particular issues are to be debated *"on their own merits"*, that specific themes, episodes, periods, etc. are to be isolated for interrogation in the light of some undeclared and probably unconscious standards of reference.

Our attempt here to interrogate the history and historical realities of Uganda/Nile Africa must be to endeavour to visualize parts with reference to the whole, to the given facts with reference to their significance, to visualize given events with reference to their causes or

---

[7]   H. Butterfield - The Englishman and His History (1944), p.103
[8]   E.H Carr What is History (With a new introduction by Richard J. Evans), Palgrave 2001, p.49

consequences and to look at the given or particular crises with reference to the general situation of things.

Interrogating the Ugandan/Nile African recent colonial and post-colonial history and issues are hence best done from the larger perspective, and indeed whenever humanly feasible from all angles.

The question of winning National freedom in Uganda/ Nile Africa is best visualized with the aid of historical sense.

Uganda as a polity is not well understood by many observers and even Ugandans themselves. This difficulty of understanding, owes much to the country's complex history and its geostrategic placing in the Nile River valley lands. The culture and practices of the interpretation of its history largely through the characters and experiences of political and historical personages uncontexted, further befuddles the matter of the rise and being of the country's realities.

The foregoing is a compounded reality, which is not easy to understand and explain.

History and its locomotives in this regard, are critical factors in drawing up necessary explanations of the story of the Nile River valley lands (of which Uganda is a vital part), their ever reconfigured being and in the backdrop of past civilisations that sprouted in the valleys and banks of the great Nile River.

Since ancient times, threads of concern constructed around the matter of the security of the waters of the Nile River, have continuously registered its salient, covert or even its overt presence.

In disputes with ancient Egypt, the rulers of ancient Ethiopia, even when they lacked the necessary technical capacities at the time, to do so, threatened to stem the flow of the Blue Nile (which has its source in the Ethiopian highlands) as the means by which to reduce Egypt and the Egyptian delta region into a wasteland.

While such a feat at the time, stood beyond the skills and resources of ancient Ethiopian authorities, it has become feasible in modern times - given the higher technologies that can now be collated for the purpose.

Yet, even as a phobia alone, the effect of this threat on the process of the 19th century European colonial scramble for Africa, proved significant.

Sir Evelyn Baring, later to become Lord Cromer, the de facto/ shadow British ruler of Egypt at the time of Ethiopian-Italian agreement in the 19th century, held the opinion, expressed in his communication to the then British Prime Minister that;

> *"...were a civilised European power to be established in the Nile River valley, they would so reduce the water supply as to ruin the country [Egypt]..."*

And further that,

> *"...Whatever power holds the upper Nile Valley, must by mere force of its geographical situation, dominate Egypt..."*

To Britain and her allied powers then in control of Egypt, denial of access to; its quality cotton for British textile industries, and wheat production to feed the British and European proletariat but above all, the control and management of the strategic Suez Canal, the shortest waterway to India and the East, would be devastating.

Consequently, Egypt, the Sudan, Uganda, and Ethiopia were best to be directly or indirectly taken into the British imperial control zone.

The phobia of the security of the Nile River waters has lived into contemporary times and continues to generate bad blood amongst countries of the Nile River riparian lands and a myriad of intrigues amongst foreign powers that hold interest over the Nile River waters and valleys.

As recently as in 1985, the otherwise well considered late Dr Boutros Boutros Ghali[9], the then Egyptian minister of state for Foreign Affairs warned that:

> *"...The next war in our region will be over the waters of the Nile, not politics..."*

The late Egyptian president Anwar Sadat, even issued threats to wage war against and bomb back to the Stone Age, any Nile River riparian land and country that interfered with the flow of the waters of the Nile and would cause untold damage to the vital interests of Egypt!

The same approach washed over to his successor as state president – Hosni Mubarak.

The Nile River water security interests, constituted a first structural constraint on Uganda at the time it won political independence on October 9, 1962. By force of the 1929 and subsequent 1959 Nile water *"agreements/treaties"*[10], Egyptian physical presence has been

---

[9] later Secretary General of the United Nations Organisation.
[10] Ibid 1

established to hold in Jinja where the Lake Victoria waters exit to the Nile River.

By October 9, 1962, the state of Israel which holds much interest in the Nile River waters had already with the salient agreement of the British colonial power, established a representative office in a building directly opposite the Ugandan Parliament and the Ugandan Prime Minister's office in Kampala.

Britain and the State of Israel, have since directly or indirectly, saliently or overtly, continued to dig in deep into the Ugandan vital geography and political space.

The continued structural assertion of their interests and presence, much explains their involvement with the first elected Ugandan government under the then Prime Minister, now late Dr Apollo Milton Obote, who was a man of deep Africanist and Pan-Africanist mould.

The relations between Uganda government under Dr Milton Obote, and Britain and the state of Israel in the 1960's – was that of contentious engagement and co-operation.

The record and experience of these relations, is itself a long murky story.

President Gamal Abdel Nasser of Egypt, Dr Milton Obote's personal friend and political ally – cautioned him against generating adventurous contentions with the two power systems.

As a Colonel, Nasser had learnt much from the 1956 British-French and Israeli aggression in their attempt to forcefully retake the Suez Canal and place it under their control, and in the 1967 Egypt/Arab war with the state of Israel. As President, Nasser advised Dr Obote to play along with Britain and the state of Israel – but to always, keep his eyes on the prize of independence and sovereignty of the Nile Valley lands and Basin.

The two power systems instead – sought hegemonic big brother relations with the government and state of Uganda.

The internal situation in Uganda, however, got increasingly compounded in the 1960's; with the outstanding unresolved National and Social Questions generating heat in its polity.

Foreign capital interests in banking, plantation agriculture, agricultural products processing and trade, mining, tourism, etc., was at the time also digging deep into Uganda's economy from which they made fabulous gains.

The Obote government sought to hold on to its economic spaces by intervention in the economy via the Uganda Development Corporation (UDC), peasants and farmers co-operatives, state development finance institutions, agricultural products marketing boards, etc.

The stage for open and acrimonious contentions between state/ national interests and foreign capital was set in place by the mid 1960's.

Dr Obote meanwhile, had visited and engaged the Soviet Union and People's China; from where he sought for alternatives in economic and technical development, military and security co-operation and support.

Following upon these visits, the Chinese – among other things worked with Ugandans to systemise rice production at several key places in Uganda. Uganda had at the time minimal experience in rice production.

The Soviets built a noted multi-purpose agricultural technical college to train technical personnel for the mechanisation of agriculture in the country.

The United States of America (USA) got engaged in women's education and built a magnificent, then state of the art, secondary school as a basis from which to progress to later build a university for women.

The state of Israel, engaged in building experimental stations for dry land agricultural developmental projects, programmes and sciences.

These concerns were all established within a radius of less than 80 kilometres from each other on Uganda's main road and rail access to Kenya.

Dr Obote at the time was scheming to customise the policy recommendations of the Bandung 1955 Non-aligned Movement Conference, the preceding London Pan-African Conference (PAC) resolutions of 1945 and those of the All Africa Peoples Conference (AAPC) of 1958 at Accra, Ghana.

The British who were left out of the said notable developmental co-operation projects were not amused.

The renowned French philosopher, François Marie Arouet Voltaire, had in his time aptly noted that:

> "...It is dangerous to be right in matters on which established powers are wrong..."

Dr Obote doubtless understood the unease of the British in the situation. But their known practices to put self-gain and profit before all else could not be permitted to override the all-else.

The days of open loot of Africa's natural and bio resources bounties and the fruits of labour of her people were yet, however, to be brought to an end.

Africa has come quite far from the days of the slave holocaust, when virile African labour was abducted for chattel slavery in the Americas.

The late lamented Prof Ivan Van Sertima[11], an African from the Caribbean, nut shelled the effect of the slave holocaust on Africa succinctly:

> *"...No human disaster, with the exception of the flood (at Prophet Noah's time, if that biblical legend is true) can equal in dimension of destructiveness, the cataclysm that shook Africa...*
>
> *"...We are all familiar with the slave trade and the traumatic effect of this on the transplanted black, but few of us realise what horrors were wrought on Africa itself...*
>
> *"...Vast populations were up-rooted and displaced, whole generations disappeared; European diseases descended like the plague, decimating both cattle and people, cities and towns were abandoned, family networks disintegrated, kingdoms crumbled, the threads of cultural and historical continuity were so savagely torn asunder that hence forward one would have to think of two Africas: the one before and the one after the holocaust..."*

At Africa's subsequent colonisation, about two centuries later, by European capital and trade interests, Africans still visualized slavery as a continuity of rapacity that continued to oppress, exploit and derelict African humanity.

The Gold Coast Aborigine of 31st August 1900 aptly summed this situation thus:

> *"...The old slavery is dead, but a more subtle slavery may take its place...*
>
> *"...The demand of the capitalist everywhere is for cheap and docile labour ..."*

---

[11] Holocaust: Ivan Van Sertima, New Brunswick and London, 1984, p.8

The Africans noted that they were openly robbed of the fruits of their labour. The Pan-Africanist Congress held in Manchester in 1945 took the position that;

> *"...Africans were unwilling to starve any longer while doing the world's drudgery..."*

It went further,

> *"...We condemn the monopoly of capital and the rule of private profit alone...*
>
> *"...We welcome economic democracy as the only real democracy...*
>
> *"... Freedom and Africa for Africans..."*

went their cry.

[De]colonisation got adopted by the late 1950's as a process to a new way to colonise Africa at political independence.

Imperialism, the system of global primitive capital accumulation in the sad Third World, closed for Africa the path of auto-centric capital accumulation for popular and national development - i.e. the goals and positions of the original Bandung Non-Aligned Movement Conference (NAMC), and the 1945 Pan-African Conference (PAC).

Africa despite political independence was subjected to naked and unprotected, integration into the global systems of capital accumulation.

Internal integration of African polities was continually disrupted.

The powerful interests that run the processes of global capital accumulation cast the African demands for political and economic independence - as a pipe dream.

Primitive accumulation has since prevailed, co-opting the imperial Whiteman's Africans in its processes as mindless, callous and cynical agents, satraps and pawns.

Under the globalised systems of primitive accumulation, multinational capital freely plunders Africa's natural and bio resources and out rightly robs the fruits of labour of African labouring people.

The rest of the African masses of people - stand subjected to rigorous all round marginalisation and emasculation.

As one observer noted;

> *"...'slavery' under open primitive capital accumulation, has not died in Africa, it has been customised..."*

Africa is now caught up, entrapped in the net of multinational capital.

They have taken the chains of slavery from the African legs, and transferred them to the shoulders and necks of African masses of people.

What have been the possibilities of negating and transcending these systems of slavery in Uganda after political independence and effecting necessary transformative change?

Historical change can best be effected by historical forces on the basis of the struggles for social, political and economic transformation to meet the wider wants and necessities of the people and country.

In the Uganda of the 1960's these liberatory forces needed to be forged within popularly appreciated political perspectives.

These are the challenges that post-colonial Africa had to face up to. Dr Obote, as political leader in Uganda, was faced with similar challenges in the specifics of his country.

Until the socio-economic and political developments of the late 1960's in Uganda, Dr Obote was tolerated as a necessary political inconvenience by British and associated interests in the governance of Uganda.

But Dr Obote who until then, ran an *"open"* capitalist economy, got to set out the policies of his administration in tune with the principles of the Uganda People's Congress - the political party he led - which got encapsulated in the Common Man's Charter[12] Dr Obote wished to;

➤ further strengthen and bolster African political independence,

➤ work for African integrity, dignity, unity, and forge fraternal cooperation with other African peoples including those in diaspora (particularly the exiled Africans in the America's and Caribbean),

➤ follow a non-aligned foreign policy course,

➤ increase and distribute wealth created in the country particularly to the deserving exploited and impoverished African masses of people,

➤ work to create on the basis of economic prosperity and social justice a new non-polarised society, and responsible and accountable democratic system of governance,

➤ develop the Ugandan polity into an Africanist instrument that could make necessary contribution to free the African and other peoples

---

[12] see Appendix for details.

still colonised, and rally African peoples to defeat evil apartheid and thus open the way to larger and more meaningful Africanist cooperation, collaboration and solidarity in all fields, as Africa rose to assert its place of dignity among the free of the world and in the comity of nations of the world.

Dr Obote subsequently rationalised these positions in his policy declarations and in a major political document: The Move to the Left/The Common Man's Charter[13].

These were critiques of the socio-economic and political state of Uganda at the time.

Dr Obote rapidly followed them with nationalisation of finance institutions, manufacturing, agricultural and trade concerns, road transport enterprises, etc.

This move was a bolt from the blue.

British and foreign economic interests who then dominated the Ugandan economy were taken by surprise, shocked and profoundly shaken.

These nationalisation measures forced the British and foreign economic concerns into economic partnerships with the state.

Dr Obote announced on May 1, 1970, legislation whereby the Uganda government would take over all foreign import and export enterprises and, or businesses and acquire 60 per cent of the shares of oil companies, manufacturing industries, banks, insurance companies, and other business and trade sector concerns. Compensation was to be paid over a period of up to 15 years out of the profits received by the Uganda government from the nationalised enterprises.

The British recognised that these measures were entirely legal, but a direct challenge to British business interests. Britain had similarly carried out a huge nationalisation programme in its own economy after the 2nd World War.

Dr Obote, like other African leaders of politically independent countries that alien capital dominated, had to face up to the quandary of overseeing economies that generated *"economic growth without development"*. Older countries such as Liberia, Ethiopia, Egypt, Morocco, etc. suffered from a similar situation and would as a result, without the matter being addressed, implode.

---

[13] Ibid 2 & 4

In 1962, during the political tenure of President William Tubman, a team of highly qualified American economic experts were sent by *The United States of America International Development Agency (USAID)* to examine the Liberian economy and its development problems.

The team noted that the overall economic system of Liberia had not in its fundamentals changed, despite the high growth rates it had registered for quite some time. "...*Liberia*...," they ruefully noted in their report: "...*is not developing*..."

If Liberia's money incomes had quadrupled, so had its imports! If government revenues had octupled, they had for most part, been spent in ways that did not apparently increase the productive capacities of the nation.

The American experts[14] could hardly hide their disappointment with the sad economic situation in Liberia.

An essential reason for this absence of development they explained, was that an enormous growth in primary commodities produced by foreign concessions (rubber, iron, forest exploitation, etc.) - had been unaccompanied either by structured changes to induce contemporary growth or institutional changes that are necessary to distribute real gains in real incomes among all sections of the population.

Liberia, for more than a century, was a colony of black settlers/ former slaves living from the enterprise of large companies, which the settlers however, in no sense controlled.

These settlers constituted an elite who were expected to become agents of constructive change, and beyond any doubt, it was well endowed with a *"values system"* conformable to capitalism.

Yet no local capitalist system appeared or even began to emerge in Liberia as a fully-fledged system.

All that happened is that the Liberian elite became the agent of its foreign or alien economic regulator, i.e. in Liberia's case: North American capital.

Over time, even when Liberia acquired some coherence as an entity of its own, its basic socio-economic relationships with alien capital, in which it was its minor agent and appendix, continued unabated.

---

[14] Professor R.W. Clower, G. Dalton, M. Harwitz, and A.A. Walters; authors of *"Growth Without Development"* (Evanston: North Western University Press, 1966),

Liberia, wittingly or unwittingly, remained within the same system, within which its elite continued in substance to act as the local intermediaries of foreign capital and finance interests, or enterprise.

This partnership between dominant economic and financial interests and convenient local elites enclosed within international capitalist structures and relationships, has continued to hold in Africa, since their inception; during the slave holocaust that was meted against African peoples.

These African elite cannot grow into an independent bourgeoisie because they cannot do so.

They remain structurally, ideologically and culturally, the junior partners of an external system upon which they must continue to depend.

They are held up, entrapped in positions similar to those of older African elites – kings, queens, chiefs and traders who had thrived on the long distance trade or the Atlantic slave trade gains of pre-colonial times.

At the rise of the Atlantic slave *"trade"* – i.e. the times of the abductions of African labour for export to the America's - the African elite - kings, rich men and prime merchants – engaged themselves in a partnership chiefly concerned with the export of African captives to which they became addicted to the ruin of African societal formations.

These elites saw themselves grow rich as their economies too were quantitatively grown, but this growth was without systemic development, because they could not transform their financial or commodity accumulations to independent capital of their own which they would have had the freedom to deploy.

The same quandary was to be faced by their later successor elites.

It is against this background, that Africa's attempts to escape its ruinous entrapment in the globalised economic system should be visualised, including the nationalisation of foreign enterprises in Uganda in 1970.

British Foreign Office saw this as a programme with, 'serious implications for British businesses in Uganda and Africa generally.' The Foreign Office expressed their worry that;

> *"...there is a danger that other countries will be tempted to try and get away with similar measures with more damaging consequences for British investment and trade..."*

British foreign office took note that three weeks after the announcement of the Ugandan measures, the Sudanese government had also nationalised foreign businesses;

"...in an even more unacceptable way..."

The fear that Dr Obote's nationalisations would get promoted elsewhere particularly in Africa, shook British business to the core. The East African and Mauritius Association told British foreign office:

"...the end result is the loss of British investment overseas
and the establishment of precedents which could involve
similar action by governments of other territories with
adverse repercussions on the British economy..."

The fear was the acceptance and repeat of such a replicable example and hence *"...the emergence of a pattern in Africa..."*

The socio-economic restructuring that the Obote government had projected and was beginning to put into effect, was to be as expected, resisted by British interests at all possible levels.

The British pulled out every possible trick from the bag to discredit the Obote government actions before the popular measures it was taking and putting into effect could fully radiate in impact to other parts of Africa where British capital held significant interests.

At about the time of the 1970 pronouncements on nationalisation of foreign enterprises in Uganda, a British diplomat in charge of immigration at the British High Commission in Kampala organised a fake kidnap of one of their members of staff in charge of immigration, one Brian Alastair Lea, in the desperate effort to tarnish the image of the Uganda government before the world, and above all divert excited supportive public opinion in Africa from embracing the import of the question and matter of nationalisation of, and, or forced partnership in ownership of capitalist foreign enterprises with African countries.

The British diplomat's faked kidnap story as expected, hit media headlines in the world and temporarily diverted the attention of the Uganda government, to attend to and address the alleged kidnap of the British diplomat.

In the unfolding drama, Brian Alastair Lea, proved to be a real star performer and centre of attention.

President Obote, most astutely took the matter to the Uganda Parliament, which constituted an independent commission of enquiry on the kidnap affair. A reputable judge of the High Court of Uganda, Robert Ernest Gordon Russell, who was of British nationality, chaired it. Counsels Godfrey Binaisa QC[15], then Attorney General of Uganda, and Gurdial Singh[16], a leading advocate of the High Court of Uganda, represented the government of Uganda at the Commission of Enquiry.

The British request to send, a high level investigative team of their own to Uganda, was given a nod or accepted. They sought to carry out their own assessment of the alleged kidnap affair.

Across board, the kidnap affair was seen to be a vulgar and the British diplomat conveniently mounted that crude self-made hoax. His mandate covered matters of immigration in the British High Commission in Uganda where he held clout.

The hoax had involved a number of British protected persons of Asian origin who were seeking to have their immigration applications to enter Britain expedited. Diplomat Brian Alastair Lea, took undue advantage of them and their predicament.

The kidnap hoax was outright amateurish and a terrible embarrassment to all.

It had however done the intended damage to distract Africa from the import of this one of Africa's valid endeavours to take charge of the command points of the capitalist economies that Africa had been forced to host since colonisation.

Diplomat Lea was recalled to London, without much ado, to save face.

He had undoubtedly been caught in the act. As in all such cases, His Excellency Brian Alastair Lea, became the sacrificial lamb in the much-bungled affair.

The kidnap hoax and affair should however have acted as a wakeup call to the Obote government that no stone would be left unturned in the effort to defeat the emergent socio-economic programme that the Uganda government was in the process of prosecuting.

The British had fired the first, but not the last combat shot, as subsequent events would show.

The East African and Mauritius Association saw it as imperative, that the British government had to make clear to the other African and Third-World governments;

---

15 Later President of Uganda 1979/80
16 Later Uganda High Commissioner to India 1981-1985

> *"...their very grave concern at recent developments in Uganda..."*

About fifty British firms were on the nationalisation schedule – including Grindlays, Standard and Barclays banks, Shell BP, British American Tobacco (BAT), Dunlop, Brooke Bond, Mackenzie Dalgety, etc.

By the end of 1970 – only Shell BP, using its accumulated oil wisdom, had signed a compensation agreement with the Uganda government.

The British High Commissioner Richard Slater, an envoy with intense visible pathological hatred of Dr Apollo Milton Obote, held the opinion that;

> *"...British interests suffered more than any other..."*

from the recent nationalisation measures. However, he also noted that;

> *"...to the extent that non-Ugandan interests were liable to be hurt, the measures were popular..."*

More so that;

> *"...for the vast majority of what I can only describe as the 'elite' of Uganda, the implications were deeply disturbing..."*

This was the native 'elite' that the British nurtured in the country in their image. These copycats and imperial Whiteman's Africans, whom the sages of the Ganda nation of Uganda named, *"...the Omuzungu Agambye Africans..."*[17] were hated caricatures of the imperial European.

In the USA and the Americas, the oppressed know these human caricatures as *'Uncle Toms'*[18]. In former Portuguese colonies, they are called *'Assimilados'*[19], while in former French colonies they are known as *'Assimiles'*.

These elite, the Whiteman's Africans, whom the sages of the Ganda nation aptly named *"...Omuzungu Agambye Africans..."*[20] were also in great fear of the stringent anti-corruption legislation enacted by Uganda government in June 1970. To the British High Commissioner Slater – the British interests were designed to protect;

> *"...the native 'elite' from the effect of popular measures..."*

Eric le Tocq, another foreign office analyst and operative noted that;

---

[17] Ibid 4
[18] Ibid 4
[19] Ibid 4
[20] Ibid 4

> *"...We are prepared to believe that the policies which he (Obote) is pushing through may well prove, in time, to be in best interests of Ugandans..."*

as there was also the

> *"...inequity of pre-nationalisation arrangements under the East African Community (E.A.C.), where many companies (largely British) remitted their profits to Nairobi, Kenya, instead of re-investing them in the country in which they were earned (Uganda)..."*

Under Dr Obote;

> *"...Capitalism has become a dirty word and the well-to-do are wondering whether it might not be wise to turn the Mercedes Benz for something more modest and sell off a house or two...",*

the British spokesman opined.

Dr Obote, had to be contained by any means necessary; hence the Gen. Idi Amin-Dada coup of January 25, 1971 which was immediately welcomed by British officials. There had been an assassination attempt against Obote at Lugogo stadium in Kampala after the Uganda Peoples Congress (UPC) party conference in December 1969. The British were aware of the difficulties that Gen. Idi Amin was projected to face with the law. The British and the state of Israel, courtesy of Col. Baruch Barlev, conveniently took advantage of Maj. Gen. Idi Amin-Dada's personal difficulties to persuade him to mount self-serving action, via a most destructive military coup d'état.

History shall hardly absolve them.

They had involved Gen. Idi Amin-Dada in covert intelligence activity in Southern Sudan, where they acquired spaces to train for him the coup strike-force. The man leading the coup preparations was an experienced MI6[21] officer, one Beverly Gayer Bernard, who worked together with an Israeli Mossad[22] officer, the then military attaché in Uganda – one Col. Baruch Barlev. A declassified cable from London, records a situation report sent by the British High Commissioner to Uganda, Richard Slater, which stated that;

---

[21] The Secret Intelligence Service (SIS), commonly known as **MI6**, is the foreign intelligence service of the government of the United Kingdom.

[22] **Mossad**: (Hebrew: "Central Institute for Intelligence and Security"), one of the five major intelligence organizations of Israel, being concerned with espionage.

*"...In the course of last night, General Idi Amin-Dada caused
to be arrested, all officers in the armed forces sympathetic to
Obote..."*

Slater and the Mossad Col. Baruch Barlev were together that night with MI6 Beverly Gayer Bernard. They were the foreign technical arm and managers of the Amin military coup d'état. The Mossad had paid big commissions for every resource that Gen. Idi Amin facilitated to be delivered to the Mossad/Anyanya[23]/South Sudanese armed project against the then Sudanese central government.

British Prime Minister Edward Heath, who was the high reference point in the Idi Amin military coup d'état, openly mocked Dr Obote, who was the lead campaigner in the condemning and working to estop the implementation of the British decision to renew arms sales to apartheid South Africa. He is reported to have wagged his finger at Dr Obote and said;

*"...I wonder how many of you will be allowed to return to
your countries from this conference..."*

The MI6's Beverly Bernard plan of the coup was successful. Gen. Idi Amin-Dada's strike-force trained in Southern Sudan rebel area, went into action with Israeli Mossad Col. Baruch Barlev in close supervision of their action.

The rest is history.

*"...It is also imperative that Britain canvasses other
'moderate' pro-British governments in Africa, who we judge
likely to be sympathetic towards General Amin to recognise
the new regime...*

*"...We are hoping that we can discretely let General Amin
know of these efforts which we are making on his behalf..."*

noted the British foreign office.

To Harold Smedley, the Under Secretary of State at the foreign office;

"...We have no cause to shed tears on Dr Obote's departure...

*"...At long last we have a chance of placing our relations with
Uganda, on a friendly footing..."*

As for British High Commissioner Slater;

---

[23] Refers to the South Sudan separatists rebel army formed in 1955.

"...Anglo-Ugandan relations can only benefit from the change...
"...Amin is deeply grateful - as I am - for the promptness with which Her Majesty's government recognised his regime..."

The British welcomed the overthrow of a government recognised by British officials then to be promoting many policies;

"...in the best interests of Ugandans..."

In its place they promoted a most vicious military dictatorship, from whose destructive tenure the country has never fully recovered.

Soon after the Gen. Idi Amin-Dada military coup – Gen. Idi Amin, was invited to have tea and sandwiches with Her Majesty Regina/Queen Elizabeth-II of the United Kingdom of Great Britain. They also let the general take a walk thereafter over the green at Buckingham Palace!

Richard Slater, Her Majesty's High Commissioner to Uganda was a convinced British diplomat and envoy – in whose assessment, to quote;

"...despite his limitations he (Amin) has considerable dignity and more the air of a leader than Obote..."

To Eric le Tocq, of British foreign office, Gen. Idi Amin-Dada's example was best visualized as an asset.

The 1971 Ugandan military coup could be replicated in Africa, to the best interests of Britain, further noted the intelligence analyst – Eric le Tocq – then of the British foreign office's South-East Asian Department:

"...Gen. Idi Amin-Dada removed from the African scene one of our most implacable enemies in matters affecting South Africa ...

"...Our prospects in Uganda have no doubt been considerably enhanced ...

"...If Amin-Dada's coup is successful, in that it remains firmly entrenched in power, and eventually gains acceptance ...

"...of the other black African governments, this will no doubt enhance the temptation in other African military leaders to follow his example...

"...Events in Uganda will have been noted in Kenya military circles, though there seems little likelihood of any military move until President Kenyatta leaves the scene...

"...This could conceivably produce a government better disposed to Britain than Kenyatta's political heirs..."

Britain consciously supported and connived in the rise of Gen. Idi Amin-Dada because of the urge of the long standing British interests to get rid of governments like that of Obote who were challenging – the African parasitic *'elite'* and promoting popular policies and measures.

Gen. Amin was used to reverse the entire Ugandan nationalisation plans and programmes, noted Eric le Tocq:

> *"...Many firms were saved from a nasty dose of nationalisation by Amin-Dada's seizure of power..."*

The policy of private investment by foreign capital was broadly welcome to British companies and should go a long way towards the restoration of foreign investment confidence in Uganda, noted British foreign office. Further to this that;

> *"...The new regime was showing an encouraging attitude in economic and financial spheres...*
> *"...We expect its policies to be more pragmatic and less ruled by somewhat rigid doctrines of the Obote regime..."*

The cost to Uganda of British support to the military regime remains staggering.

They had connived with other imperial powers to hoist into a position of state and power responsibility, a man of lumpen character and world outlook.

The military regime went headlong to massacre not only civilians, but also one of the best professionally trained army officer corps in the British Commonwealth.

But, there were British armaments to be marketed to the military regime, including – Saladin, Saracen and Ferret armoured vehicles, StrikeMaster and Jaguar aircraft, perhaps Harriers, helicopters, radars and light guns, etc.

This show of willingness to sell arms to Uganda was a necessary act not only to prevent the military regime from going elsewhere for arms purchases, but also to discourage the regime from purchases, which were over, to which Eric le Tocq commented;

> *"...ambitious, militarily, technically or financially..."*

The political desirability of supporting the military regime became more critical, after the world came to take note of the massacres the regime occasioned in Uganda, and its utter recklessness.

The skeletons in the British cupboards in its relations with Uganda – were not to be exposed.   This danger had to be averted ahead of schedule.

The late Edward Heath, then British Prime Minister, could not hold his excitement when Gen. Idi Amin sought to pay a visit to Britain. Peter Moon, his personal advisor wrote thus;

> *"...in the projected visit the 'PM' would like the welcome to be of high level, so that Gen. Idi Amin-Dada is made to feel that he was being highly honoured..."*

Prime Minister Heath had in Singapore mocked Dr Apollo Milton Obote that, loud-mouthed leaders like him may not be able to freely return to their homelands, let alone in power.

Dr Obote had led a virulent arms embargo campaign against sale of arms to South Africa by Britain and Europe, which had unnerved the British.

With, rather meagre gains and results from the British/Uganda relations, Gen. Idi Amin-Dada in 1972 – exploded a political bomb on his British friends.

Gen. Idi Amin directed that British protected Indians in Uganda were to leave Uganda, within 90 days. It was the responsibility of the British authorities to see to their facilitation and travel to Britain.

Slater's bribery schemes had failed to bear positive results for the British.   Gen. Idi Amin-Dada had scored a feat in effecting modern ethnic cleansing of British protected persons of Indian/Asian origin.

Ever since, the grave social crisis thereby triggered, has continued to engulf the country, expelling thousands of young people from Uganda. The effect is the continued expulsion of young intelligent Ugandans from the country into the four corners of the world and diaspora. Like other investible capital that is created by Ugandan labour – the bleeding of the country of its virile youths with developable skills, depletes the country of its otherwise necessary labour with which to generate productive activities.

The Israeli too in 1972, were to be abandoned by Gen. Idi Amin-Dada. They had refused to supply him long distance aircraft to bomb Obote and Nyerere in Dar es Salaam, Tanzania, despite his travel to the state of Israel for conversations with Prime Minister Mrs Golda Meir. From Israel, Gen. Idi Amin-Dada flew straight to see Col. Muammar al-

Qaddafi with whom he pledged to fight for the eradication of Zionism and imperialism.

Gen. Idi Amin-Dada was well recompensed with substantial resources by Col. Muammar al-Qaddafi. For the British, their tropical fruit had turned sour.

Richard Slater remained unrepentant to the end on the appropriateness of British power and political intervention in Uganda. As for Gen. Amin-Dada's destructiveness, Slater was of the opinion that;

> *"...We cannot tell him (Amin) to stop murdering people and my plea is business as usual with the General..."*

As for Obote, Slater was conclusive in his judgement that;

> *"...Obote in my opinion has never been and never will be a friend of Britain..." [1972]*

Dr Obote had not only violated the fundamental prescribed rules of behaviour of the Garden of Eden, eaten the forbidden fruit of freedom, but had also crossed the Rubicon. Slater was convinced that the British had in Gen. Idi Amin-Dada, acquired a willing and pliable tool, if not pawn or satrap. They were grossly mistaken.

After the tenure of the Conservative government of British Prime Minister Edward Heath, came the Labour administration of PM James (Jim) Callaghan and his foreign secretary, Dr David Owen. The latter held a pathological personal hatred of Dr Milton Obote, whom he thought was a black African Machiavelli, an evil genius – who needed to be politically buried alive, before he caused the sure destruction of British interests in Uganda and the larger Eastern African region.

He was instrumental in sabotaging Obote's deserved return to government in Uganda, after the fall of the British darling General, the Field Marshal Idi Amin-Dada[24]. Instead, Dr Owen promoted the installation of Prof Yusuf Kironde-Lule, a former colonial minister and a man of provincial and limited world outlook, as the new President of Uganda.

There was great fear that, if Dr Obote assumed power again in Uganda, the *"skeletons in the cupboards"* left by the British in Kampala

---

[24] By the time of his overthrow in 1979, the penultimate titles with accompanying medallions were '...Field Marshall, Conqueror of British Empire (CBE); Victorious Cross (UVC); Distinguished Service Order; Distinguished Conduct in the Field (DCF); Distinguished Service to the State (DSS); King of Scotland...'

during the Gen. Idi Amin-Dada's tenure, could be brought out into the open by Dr Milton Obote.

This was yet again another fundamental misreading of things and the character of Dr Milton Obote, whose level of understanding of the political world and global politics was undoubtedly much higher than that of Dr David Owen; the brain and neuro-surgeon.

That sad period in the Uganda-British relations has now passed.

In the unfolding of events since; Dr Apollo Milton Obote, now deceased, can neither have his revenge against his British detractors nor will he get his reward for resisting the imposition of slave relations; upon Africa by British and associated capitalist world powers.

On the foregoing, history will have its say.

In 1963, Apollo Milton Obote was awarded an honorary doctoral degree from Long Island University in the United States of America. He chose to give his acceptance statement on the struggles for cultural and racial equality and non-discrimination. Dr Obote in this regard had adopted the position that the **Pan-African Congress (PAC)** manifesto of 1923 had proclaimed on these matters:

> *"...In fine, we ask in all the world, that black folks be*
> *treated as men..."*

James Baldwin, the African-American writer, had encapsulated that resolution in his writings.

What Dr Apollo Milton Obote sought to achieve was the realisation of the goals that the brilliant African American writer, James Baldwin, a man of utter innocence, had restated in his essay (Fifth Avenue, Uptown) in the June 1960 Esquire journal: *"...Negroes* [meaning black Africans in Africa and diaspora] *want to be treated like men..."* a perfectly straightforward statement containing seven words;

> *"...People who have mastered Kant, Hegel, Shakespeare,*
> *Marx, Freud and the Bible, find this statement*
> *impenetrable...",*

observed the great African writer, Chinua Achebe in 'Postscript: James Baldwin (1924 – 1987)'.

The words of the departed and lamented intellectual African-American, James Baldwin, on basic human equality, have lived into contemporary times and will remain to bear witness, inspire and uplift the spirit of the struggles for freedom of oppressed African humanity and enthuse it in its movement towards African self-becoming and self-determination. In this regard, the memory Dr Apollo Milton Obote, which is best visualized in his efforts and struggles to win due dignity and respect for African humanity, will in history perhaps live longer than that of his detractors like Dr David Owen.

James Baldwin further summed up the very desperate situation of the much tribulated African humanity in the America's and the cruel subhuman conditions in which they have been marginalised to exist in the following words:

> *"...The most dangerous creation of any society is the man who has nothing to lose. You do not need ten such men...*
> *"...Only one will do..."*

A friend of Milton Obote who shared with him the birth date of December 25, Malcolm X, El-Hajj Malik El Shabazz, leader of the African American freedom and liberation struggle - one born, son of an African chief in a colonised country, the other grandson to an African slave – amplified the core of African freedom and liberation struggles thus[25]:

> *"Human Rights! Respect as human beings! That's what the black masses want...*
> *"...That's the true problem...*
> *"...They want to live in an open, free society where they can walk with their heads up, like men, and women."*

At another time Malcolm X boldly stated his stand in the long struggle for the liberation of humankind in the following words[26]:

> *"...I'm for the truth, no matter who tells it...*
> *"...I'm for justice, no matter who it is for or against...*
> *"...I'm a human being first and foremost, and as such I'm for who and whatever benefits humanity as a whole..."*

Malcolm X had aptly stated in summation the essence of the freedom struggles of the oppressed peoples of the world.

In the age of imperialism, it is apparently an unforgivable crime to even hold a mirror to reflect and show, and, or take a position against the history, and, or realities of the unspeakable criminal suffering that

---

[25] P.378 - The Autobiography of Malcolm X/ with the assistance of Alex Haley.
[26] P. 483 - Ibid 24

the imposed terrible situations of slavery have occasioned on African humanity throughout the world.

Many amidst this oppressed humanity which lives tormented and dehumanised lives, were, have been or get embittered throughout their lives of suffering.

In the year, when Apollo Milton Obote of Uganda/Nile Africa was born, Marcus Mois Garvey, then leader of the human and peoples rights struggle in the USA, who was then held and imprisoned at the Atlanta Penitentiary, penned a poem that can be taken to be representative of the feelings of many of the African freedom struggle leaderships who existed at those difficult times of the sad social relations that has pitted humanity against humanity; in which the oppressed has suffered most profoundly at the margins of heartless and in effect soulless conditions, thus:

> *"...In death I shall be a terror to the foes of Negro liberty...*
> *"...Look for me in the whirlwind or the long storm...,*
> *"...Look for me all around you..."*

Marcus Mois Garvey passed on in 1940 in the UK of Great Britain.

Five years after Dr Obote won hard fought general elections in December 1980, following the fall of Gen. Idi Amin in April 1979; the Christian Democratic International sponsored the **Democratic Party (DP)** in Uganda which worked under the guidance of the then Papal Pronuncio[27], the then US Ambassador Clayton Davis (an expert at regime change) and the then Ugandan Catholic Archbishop, Cardinal Emmanuel Nsubuga, to facilitate another military coup d'état on 27th July 1985, using a set of old military officers (Catholic-led), who had been part of the 1978/79 liberation war. The country had by then been inducted into processes of reconstruction, which had thus begun to move forward full steam.

The old military officers did not have a clue on administering a modern state, let alone run a capital driven economy.

Their short, but tragic tenure in office, was a catastrophe.

It presented their successor, the National Resistance Army/Movement (NRA/M)-military regime, with a chance to destroy, ruin and desolate the entire Northern, Eastern and North-Eastern regions, and other areas of Uganda.

---

[27] Infers to the Vatican Representative

These areas and regions that had been transformed into looting and killing fields by the fascist neo-colonial state military and war machine in Uganda, are today cynically classified under the epithet - *'former'* war destroyed areas and regions of the country.

The operational policy of the war machine of the fascist neo-colonial state was that of predation, scorched earth; open robbery and spoliation.

This genocidal, predatory and spoliatory method of war, found reflection as well in the expeditiary wars carried out in other areas of the Great Lakes region, particularly in the Democratic Republic of Congo (DRC) and the Republic of South Sudan where the Ugandan fascist neo-colonial state's war machine operated in its unfortunate intervention in the affairs of these countries - as hirelings of alien un-African interests and imperial powers.

The fascist Ugandan/Nile African political and military leadership came out, in these catastrophic military projects, as both unrepentant authors and direct perpetrators of aggression, genocide, crimes against humanity, spoliation and plunder in the African region of Nile Africa's placing.

These criminal aggressions against the neighbouring countries, their clusters of African peoples, communities and nations - shall for ever sully the name of Uganda/Nile Africa as a fascist neo-colonial state.

The deeply profound sufferings of the victims of these criminal fascist military aggressions which have their roots in actions meted within Uganda/Nile Africa against her people, before they were externalised to the Great Lakes region - shall only become atoned when the authors and perpetrators of genocide, crimes against humanity and spoliation get duly subjected to measures of justice, so that beyond the culpability of those found guilty such as in the International Court of Justice (ICJ) case holding of *'the Democratic Republic of Congo vs. Uganda,'* - due reparations, compensations and measures of atonement have to be imposed against and made good by the said military aggressors.

The fascist military regime was facilitated into governance of Uganda in 1986 by governments of neighbouring countries that on the face of it, feared the return of Gen. Idi Amin-Dada's forces to government in the country.

In extending this support to facilitate the rise of the fascist dictatorship in Uganda, the regional East African governments, perhaps for other different reasons as well, synchronised their support for the National Resistance Army (NRA) with those of multinational capital and finance, in whose interests the country has had to be held as prey.

The popularly resisted cruel rule of the fascist military dictatorship and its tragic record in Uganda/Nile Africa is yet another proof that the rule of minority political forces can never be accepted by political majorities in non-transformed societies.

The law, rules and practices of military governance of the Nile River valley lands once again came into full bloom in the late 1980's.

Foreign economic interests, multinational corporations and finance - subsidised and supported local forces in the Nile River valley lands that ensured the imposition of the *'order'* requisite for their free activities of plunder of natural and bio resources, and open robbery of the fruits of labour of the peoples of these lands.

In this age of open plunder of African resources, forces of extreme greed and avarice, pillage and spoliation, grand thievery and corruption - have been set loose on the African continent.

There have been projections in Africa, to organise a number of militarised hubs around which to dominate the African continent and hold it in subordination to imperialism: Egypt for North Africa; Nigeria for West Africa and South Africa for Southern and central African zones. The East and Horn of Africa zones have been placed under ad hoc military arrangements. The sub-zone centres of Kenya and Ethiopia, have had first to deal with their own difficult internal problems and the ripple effects on them of the long-standing Somali political imbroglio or problem.

An East African military intervention force has been formed. It is meant to be a mercenary force funded by external finance/aid and working as a subordinate of the stronger imperial military forces such as the US Africom or the USA African Command, and other mobile NATO/European special forces.

The imperial idea and scheme here is to soften the African ground and spaces to ease the institution therein of more ruthless programmes and projects of primitive accumulation by multinational capital and finance interests.

Social marginalisation, dispossession of African ancestral lands and capture of the livelihood habitats of the African masses of people by coalitions of ruthless fortune hunters (foreign and local) - have deeply impoverished and derelicted the African masses of people who have in their millions been pushed to exist amidst the most subhuman conditions, utter destitution, squalor and want.

One of the forgotten wise men of African history, who was the Egyptian finance minister (pre-revolt government), Abdel Galil El-Emary, described in a nutshell the nature and character of the Egyptian economy which is similar to many African economies – as being in the like of;

> *"...A cow grazing in the pastures of the country (Egypt); with its udders, being sucked dry of its milk from the outside..."*

These economies are on a continuous basis haemorrhaged of their investible resources with little or nothing left to institute new production sectors or units with which to create necessary sustenance and wealth (surpluses) to generate new productive investments or re-develop the older economic sectors.

It is hence no surprise that Africa gets held up and stranded within a state of compounded socio-economic backwardness and stagnation.

The oppressed and exploited and increasingly disinherited masses of people in Africa, have of necessity and are compelled in the circumstances, to rise and self-defend.

It is in these circumstances that gross authoritarian and military governance has proliferated in Africa, and in particular in the lands of the Nile River valleys.

Primitive capital accumulation, whose major mechanisms of operations are spoliation and robbery, are as systems; run primarily by force.

Its victims are compelled in the situation to seek ways out, forward and upwards from the slavery it imposes on them.

This march to social, political and national liberation calls for the crystallisation of an alternative bloc of all those societal elements who have little choice, but to free themselves from this slavery of ravenous globalising capital.

It is the duty and responsibility of each victim people to coalesce the African oppressed, exploited and disinherited into requisite liberatory forces.

This bloc is the locomotive, drive and striking force for political, social and national liberation, and the realisation of national freedom.

These liberatory elements are present in the impoverished, derelicted and desecrated African rural areas, amongst the rural and urban impoverished dwellers of petrifying and festering slums in towns and cities, amongst the rural and urban marginal, exploited informal and formal labour, impoverished marginalised intellectuals, small producers, artisans, small marketeers and traders, stranded youths without a future, multiply oppressed African women, the millions of unemployed and the underemployed, the millions amongst the African masses of people – who exist in hell on earth and ever struggle to keep soul and body together, amidst destitution, squalor and want, etc.

Given the vision; of liberation and national freedom, for an alternative developmental process and humane world of justice, the wellbeing and welfare, and integrity and dignity of the African – who has hitherto been held as an unprotected victim of oppression, exploitation, the outstanding obligation, is to mould – the requisite political instruments and organisations for the struggle to win this new liberated and free Africa. This Africa shall be of popular self-governance, free from the clutches of corrupt elite factions, free from the grip of multinational capital and with an organic leadership of the masses that is able to guide the struggle to generate autochthonous and beneficial development and to secure and ensure equity and equality of all.

In this Long March to National Freedom, many amongst the oppressed and exploited African masses of people, are being drawn in to engage in the liberatory process; to win for themselves and their communities and nationalities the right to self-govern as the means to pave ways and means for their collective self-becoming.

In late 1980's – at the beginning of the formation of the Society of the Long March to National Freedom, Popular Self Governance and African Self Becoming in Uganda/Nile Africa – after the advent of new military dictatorships in the country; a poor peasant Uganda Peoples Congress (UPC) party branch chairman, Compatriot Lokeris, from the North-Eastern Karamoja region of Uganda, saw the new processes of African national liberation as being akin to the past liberatory processes of the enslaved Judaists in ancient Egypt, led by Prophet Moses – which was a historic mass liberatory act of the enslaved who leveraged themselves from slavery in Egypt to freedom in Canaan.

To Compatriot Lokeris – the advent of military dictatorship in Uganda inaugurated a necessary beginning for an African Passover from modern slavery to freedom and the eventual defeat of the treacherous and parasitic political elite of the country that utilised military dictatorship to plunder Africa's natural resource endowments and wealth together with alien economic and finance interests.

To Compatriot Lokeris, it came as no surprise at all that the imperial Whiteman's African had once again organised the overthrow of the elected government led by his Africanist party leader – Milton Obote – given his relentless quest to secure the wellbeing, welfare and dignity of the ordinary/ common African people.

Though liberation, Compatriot Lokeris noted, would take time; it was sure to succeed if the root causes of the problem of Uganda could be accurately assessed and hence accordingly addressed.

Dr Apollo Milton Obote, his party leader, he stated with visible pride; "...*has balls...*" to be able to hold unperturbed and unfazed the audacity he had demonstrated in the struggles against the endless evil schemes of foreign interests and their mercenary Whiteman's Africans to enslave Africa and her people.

To the late lamented Compatriot Lokeris – there was little need to justify the struggle for liberation in Africa; it was a necessity without which the Africans would remain enslaved and hence incapacitated to hold in hand and maximally command and control their destinies particularly in the new emergent world of extreme greed and impossible avarice.

Compatriot Lokeris held the view that the African people are in the like of bees that are caught in the trap systems that the predator spiders have weaved in place.

They have to free themselves by breaking out from these web traps, which have held and constrained them in slavery, or else they cannot avoid being eaten by the predator spiders.

This entrapment of the African people and their continent by alien predatory and spoliatory interests that prey on Africa's bounties, leaves the African people only with the options of freeing themselves by all and, or any means necessary – so as to access a future of open possibilities within which they can in freedom, live in prosperity and happiness, and create the necessary conditions to self-become.

Without resolving the extant problem of captivity, all else, Chairman/Compatriot Lokeris noted, would be in vain.

The reality of Africa's extant slave condition has borne out this position.

Honour and homage has to be paid to the late lamented liberation and freedom fighter, Compatriot Lokeris and his fellow compatriots and comrades for their profound perception of the new modernised African slave situation and their unbending resolve to defeat it.

Indeed as the oppressed and exploited African masses of people set to mount focused struggles to defeat the social, political and economic systems of new slaveries now imposed over the continent through the imperial Whiteman's Africans – it is evident that genuine lasting peace shall only emerge in Africa when justice and shared prosperity rise in the continent as the processes that secure African peoples wellbeing, welfare, integrity, and open up necessary spaces within which the dignity of the African person gets nurtured in the context of Africanity, which is the realisation of the quest for *'UBUNTU'* – or the humanisation of the African person and society.

The realisation of the foregoing will enable Africa, to once again create for the continent and the African people, the long aspired for rights; to popular self-governance, to self-become and regain the historical powers of African self-renewal.

INTRODUCTION

The rise and the global spread of European economic and capital interests generated dramatic transformative change and impact that has touched on most areas of the world, and in finality spread to 'the four corners of the earth'.

Adam Smith[28], the renowned British political economist, at his time noted that,

> *"The discovery of America and that of a passage in the East Indies by the Cape of Good Hope, are the two greatest and most important events recorded in the history of mankind...*
>
> *"...Their consequences have already been great..."*

Marx and Engels, German political economists of repute, in similar vein were later to note the following[29]:

> *"...The discovery of gold and silver in America, the extirpation, enslavement and entombment in mines of the aboriginal population, the beginning of the conquest and looting of the East Indies, the turning of Africa into a warren for the commercial hunting of black skins, signalled the rosy dawn of the era of capitalist production...*
> *"...The idyllic proceedings are the chief momenta of primitive accumulation...*
> *"...On their heels treads the commercial war of European nations, with the globe for a theatre..."*

Capital was to transform from the mercantile to its industrial form, when labour under the slave plantation production systems – generated investible surpluses which were used to trigger the industrialisation of Europe. Thereby, within Europe for instance, the factory system of production was established. The slave as a source of labour power was replaced by the wage earner who became the victim of exploitation.

---

[28] Adam Smith, An Inquiry into the Nature and Causes of the Wealth of Nations – ed. Edwin Cannan (Library of Economics and Liberty) 1904
[29] Karl Marx, "Genesis of Industrial Capitalist", Capital: Vol. 1 (1867)

And Marx and Engels would later observe[30] that as a consequence, raw materials for industrial production were;

> *"...drawn from the remotest zones; for industries whose products are consumed, not only at home, but in every quarter of the globe...*
>
> *"...In place of the wants, satisfied by the production of the country, we find new wants, requiring for their satisfaction the products of distant lands and climes.*
>
> *"...In place of the old local and national seclusion and self-sufficiency, we have intercourse in every direction, universal inter-dependence of nations..."*

Since the times of Karl Marx and Fredrick Engels – and the notable further development of capitalism in modern times, the reign of multinational capital and finance, has been visibly globalised, a process to which Africa, the lands of the Nile River valley and Basin, which includes Uganda/Nile Africa have been to various degrees subordinated.

The consequences of this on Africa and Uganda/Nile Africa stand incalculable.

The situation which has arisen since, has shaken the African peoples, nations and communities of Uganda/Nile Africa to their very roots.

The question of what is to be done in this situation, to effect the resolution of the multiple problems that have arisen in Uganda/Nile Africa on a lasting basis, has persisted.

Many who have faced similar situations in other parts of the world – have had to face up to the challenges to resolve the problems that have held them in terrible slavery of ravenous globalised multinational capital and finance interests.

One of the eloquent leaders and sterling voices of the struggles that have arisen in a similar situation, the "Mahatma Gandhi" – contexted the dilemma of those involved in the freedom struggles of their peoples and countries from colonialism and alien rule in the following manner:

> *"...First they ignore you...;*
>
> *"...then they ridicule you...*
>
> *"...Then they fight you, and*
>
> *"...then you win..."*

[Mahatma Gandhi]

---

[30] Karl Marx and Fredrick Engels' "Bourgeois and Proletarians" – in The Communist Manifesto: A Roadmap to History's Most Important Document, ed. Phil Gesper (Chicago: Haymarket Books, 2005)

The recurrent social and political uprisings, rebellions, revolts and conflagrations taking place in Africa are primarily a reflection of the new phase of the very grave political and social crisis that grips the continent. Amidst struggles for their self - defence, the African people have been fighting to overcome both the legacies of the past and the violent imperialist domination of the present.

In these circumstances, successes of the African people's social and political mass struggles constitute the only remaining hope to win freedom. This phase of crisis, which now pervades the entire socio-economic and political fabric in Africa, has brought to the surface a number of questions, which had been hitherto confusingly formulated. These questions concern the nature and character of the crisis and *'What Should Be Done'* by the oppressed African people so that they can at long last get to grips with this perilous situation and take their destiny in hand.

In the case of Uganda - a Nile African country - the present period of crisis has its roots in the recent colonial past and the immediate post-colonial period. It is in those earlier periods of the country's formation and skewed development that the seeds were sown for today's military and tyrannical regime and its reign of genocide, plunder and spoliation.

Uganda's on-going problems have to be traced from these roots so that realistic and lasting solutions to them can be found.

The process of colonisation of Uganda fully inducted the country into the world capitalist division of work and market and subjected Uganda and her people's labour to the most negative forms of control and exploitation.

As a result, the Ugandan people lost control over their vital affairs as colonial capital and its power systems subjugated all previously independent economic and political structures in the country to their dominance. This negative induction by force unprotected into the world capitalist system is the single critical factor, which has qualitatively changed the trajectory of the Ugandan people's historical development.

It transformed the people from authors of their own history as a free people to mere objects of history, as an enslaved people. Since then, it has effectively prevented them gaining control of their own destiny.

British colonisation of Uganda was originally embarked upon by the armed forces of the Imperial British East African Company for economic, strategic and military interests. As far back as the mid-19th century, Britain regarded Uganda's colonisation as being crucial to the defence of her interests in Egypt, the Suez Canal, India and the East. It was believed that whoever controlled Uganda and its source of the Nile River waters could control Egypt, with its Mediterranean access to the Indian Ocean.

Old Uganda, which was a component of British East Africa, also constituted a landmass with which the Sudan and Egypt were enjoined to the Indian Ocean. The shaping and reshaping of Ugandan territory under British interests and control continued to go through very many phases and only ended at the eve of the year of Uganda's political independence in 1962, i.e. at the time British imperialism conceded governance of Uganda to a local political alliance of Ugandan nationalists, the country's false-bourgeoisie, pseudo-feudals and local land propertied interests.

The process of Uganda's colonisation thus unfolded amidst conflicting interests of rival foreign powers in the strategic setting of Uganda in the African continent. These considerations continue to assume varying importance in our times, in circumstances where foreign forces have now established deep economic and political interests not only in the countries of the African region of Uganda's placing, but throughout the Nile River valley lands and the middle Eastern lands beyond.

As a result, Uganda's geo-strategic placing lays it open to the varied influences from foreign forces who continue to have strategic interests and other vital investments in the East African region, as well as in the Nile Valley and the adjoining energy resources in the rich Middle East.

The institution of colonialism in Uganda established an overriding socio-economic and political structure that was designed to dominate and plunder the mosaic of agricultural and pastoral societies and nationalities that lived across state and non-state formations. The state formations i.e. various kingdoms, chieftainships, and their ruling circles provided fertile ground for the institution of *"indirect colonial rule"* which has been the harbinger of neo-colonial rule in post-colonial Uganda.

Indeed, there has been no lack of agents for foreign domination of Uganda since the advent of colonial rule in the country. Its policies of *"divide and rule"*, political repression and exploitation of the Ugandan people and country were implemented in conjunction with the locals it co-opted and nurtured to facilitate its rule. This is the crucial factor which imperialism has used to build roots in the country.

It explains why Ugandan patriots have to fight other Ugandans who are allied to imperialism. They constitute the local component of the system of oppression, exploitation and dehumanisation from which the people seek to win their Independence and National freedom.

The country's affairs are therefore both, local because they occur and are given a concrete manifestation in Uganda, and, global in perspective, because they occur as part of the global chain of events into which imperialism has entangled the Ugandan people ever since Uganda became inter-linked to it, through colonialism.

The struggle of the people of Uganda then, revolves around the question of overcoming the country's imperialist domination in all its guises.

It is similarly a struggle for building a sovereign personality for the country.

An accurate appreciation of the tasks of national emancipation requires an examination of the historical rise and the contemporary character of the chronic conditions of economic, social, political, and overall instability of Uganda. It is only on the basis of such appreciation that her people can realistically tackle the question of *'What Is To Be Done?'* for the salvation and national emancipation of Uganda.

The attempt made by the militarist regime to hold on to the governance of Uganda regardless of the consequences is futile. Its efforts to manage the country's social and political crises through force, has aggravated the situation and generated bloody conflagrations of unprecedented scale. The depth of the obtaining crises is now such that they require an equally profound solution.

It is thus from historical experience and the reality of today's perilous existence of the Ugandan people, that ways and means for the resolution of Uganda's crisis will have to be sought.

Yet, the on-going participation of suffering Ugandan people in their own liberation through civil, political, and focused mass struggles is already determining the direction and character of the peoples Long March to Ugandan (National) Freedom, Popular Self-governance and African Self-becoming. The ordinary Ugandan people have come to understand that moments are arising for them to free themselves and their country for ever from oppression, exploitation and imperialist dominance.

They have through their numerous uprisings and direct struggles against the military dictatorship, understood that it is their duty and absolute right to render themselves masters of their own destiny for the good of all in their motherland. These heroic attempts at winning national freedom constitute a new point of departure and a basis for evolving a national liberation movement of the people.

These watershed developments, culminating in the people's political, and general resistance and struggles are causing great alarm among those local and foreign interests, who continue to profit from a neo-colonial Uganda which the people are now set to dismantle.

The new phase of crisis which the regime of genocide, plunder and spoliation has triggered in the country provides an opportunity for her people to seek a permanent solution to the chronic problems of Uganda which have now been escalated into a real threat to the very existence of the country.

The Ugandan people have to continue to take care not to be misled by self-seeking warlords inside or outside the regime, who wish to squander the people's courageous sacrifices in self-serving projects that provide mere palliatives rather than a permanent cure for the country's underlying political disease.

Indeed, the gross suffering and misery in which neo-colonialism entraps the oppressed, and the trials and tribulations of the national liberation struggle, create circumstances where the urge for a quick solution to the crisis becomes overpowering and false solutions are propagated by all types of political characters and opportunistic warlords spawned by the crises of neo-colonialism in the country.

The accumulated wisdom and experience of the common Ugandan people puts them in good stead to see through these false solutions. After a century and a half of suffering great distress, the Ugandan people stand determined to put to a permanent end their continuing torment. They are determined to win genuine national freedom (a People's 'Uhuru'[31]) from imperialism to be able to create conditions suitable to evolve a new, democratic, just, and prosperous Uganda. Upon this foundation, it will be possible to transform Uganda into a modern, developmental, progressive, and peaceful country that accommodates all its diverse nationalities that shall live in fraternity as free people in their motherland and the world.

---

[31] Swahili language meaning '...FREEDOM...'

This is the meaning of the long march to National freedom and Independence. It is what explains the oppressed people's continuing civil, political, and mass struggles and the objectives of their oncoming inevitable victory over the negative foreign and local interests, which continue to enslave Ugandans.

It is in the context of National Liberation and Freedom that conditions shall be created to enable the entire people to democratically and collectively forge a path, which is underpinned by their own effort for Uganda's autonomous and beneficial development. Such is the Uganda for which her oppressed people continue to make sacrifices. It is also the Uganda for which many have been martyred.

It is the Uganda, which her people aspire to construct with their own effort in order to live in security, prosperity and happiness.

The principal task is to win and secure national freedom and thereby put an end to plunder and spoliation, naked militarism, terrorism and the poverty spawned by ruinous neo-colonialism in the effort to pave the way for a new, just, democratic and prosperous Uganda to emerge. In discharging these historical and great tasks, the oppressed Ugandan people will have to forge a national liberation movement which is a necessary vehicle with which they shall achieve a greater understanding and appreciation of their placing in the world imperialist system and hence map out appropriate strategies to win National Freedom. It shall be its responsibility to organise, unite, inspire, and guide the oppressed Ugandan people in the glorious struggle for national freedom and national democratic liberation of Uganda.

The peoples, Nations and communities of Uganda/Nile Africa, have in the result correctly come to visualize themselves to be the liberators of their own destinies.

Faced with the need to seek a different and another world, outside that of their obtaining enslavement, oppression and exploitation, one within which - they can live and flourish as the communities of the free - they confront an array of problems in the effort to forge necessary political, organisational, practical, ideological and ethical means with which to navigate their way forward to liberation, and hold in hand their destinies and that of their lands.

This publication presents an overview of these valid efforts.

The prologue is an attempt to present the tribulations met in the immediate decade since political independence - on 9 October 1962. It makes the effort to set out the outlines of what took place then, in the country's political development - which involved specific political and historical personages. An attempt is here made to depict the complex array of the push and pull factors that had been generated by the contentions of multiple foreign and local interests in the context of the situation then obtaining at the said first post-colonial decade.

Given the fury of events that occurred then, one cannot, but be in agreement with - author Henry Fielding[32] who once observed that:

> "...It is trite, but true observation that examples work
> more forcibly on the mind than precepts ...."

Professor Antony Chase in his book[33] affirms that:

> "...Abstraction unaccompanied by concrete images is perhaps
> the most striking symptom of everything that is wrong with
> contemporary writing in the social and human sciences...
>
> "...Not that writers with something difficult or conceptually
> elevated to say should refrain from writing, but even serious
> readers pray for something solid to hold on to, like a picture
> or diagram, a figure in their landscape, something with real
> shape and dimension...
>
> "...There should be something concrete in theory to which
> one is drawn, as in music or the ocean one is drawn to
> rhythm..."

Active historical players with given visions and hopes, even mistaken ones, are often thrust into the turbulent flow of history to play specific roles.

The prologue - is meant to introduce the reader to the past which cascades into the contemporary times in which new political and historical personages today play various roles in the political drama and struggles of the peoples of Uganda/Nile Africa.

The Introduction - presents a severe summation of the path of the country from the genesis of the modern political development of the problem of Uganda, that the imposition of British imperial hegemony triggered into being, and, the resultant local African resistance to it which is reflected in the risen hopes of the Ugandan/Nile African

---

[32] The History of the Adventures of Joseph Andrews and His Friend . Abraham Adams (London: John Lane The Badley Head - 1929) at p.3

[33] *Law and History" - The Evolution of the American Legal System*, p.2, The New Press/ NY, USA/ 1997 -

peoples, nations and communities to reclaim their African freedom and sovereignty.

Chapter I – takes the reader back to the rise of the political drama of Uganda as part of the general struggle experiences that unfolded with the imposition of the hegemony of imperialism in the lands at the Nile River valleys and Basin. The evolution of the local social and political forces that thereby developed and got into political contentions in Uganda/ Nile Africa is here given a sketch analysis and exposition.

Chapter II – examines the then evolving dynamic of the contention of these social and political forces and the roots and basis of the formation of political parties in the country.

Chapter III – is an attempt to visualize, the essence of the complex political problem of Uganda/Nile Africa in terms of its effect on various social classes that evolved in the country since colonisation.

Chapter IV – sets to examine the rise and essence of the politics of new fascism in the country and the nature and character of the agent and rentier class rule – therein established. The chapter also makes inroads into examining the consequences of the politics of fascist rule that emerged in the country and its impact into the African environs of the country's geographical placing.

Chapter V – is an attempt to probe into and visualize the possible consequent road to a new, just and national democratic Uganda/Nile Africa – its prospects as well as the odds against it.

Chapter VI – probes into the possibilities that may unfold after the political defeat and demise of the fascist dictatorship in Uganda/Nile Africa. It examines and theorises the question there arising of transition to popular self-governance.

Chapter VII – is an attempt to peep into the possible future that may unfold or may be induced or made to emerge out of the political drama occurring in Uganda/Nile Africa, and postulates what could be the requisite guarantees to ensure and secure sustainable national freedom and the construction of Nile Africa's popular national democracy within which African self-becoming can be nurtured and developed.

The Appendix – presents the Common Man's Charter (1968/9) for the purpose of its interrogation and rereading – for a rethinking that may assist in establishing and theorising a path to win a more beneficial and inclusive popular democratic alternative system of development for Uganda/Nile Africa after the political defeat of fascist rule.

CHAPTER 1

THE HISTORICAL ROOTS OF THE PROBLEM OF UGANDA

(i) COLONIAL INTRUSION INTO UGANDA

The destructive nature and character of colonisation of the world in the age of imperialism calls for objective analyses. Colonisation is a socio-economic and political malaise or disease of which the colonised have long sought a cure. And an accurate cure of this disease presupposes its correct prognosis. Helpful and pertinent lessons in this regard can be drawn from the experiences of other colonised, oppressed and exploited peoples of the world.

The internationalist freedom fighter, the Canadian physician Dr. Norman Bethune[34], summarised the violent and predatory nature and character of colonisation and its forces in the following words:

> *"...Are wars of aggression, wars of conquest of colonies, then just big business?...*
>
> *"...Yes. ...It would seem however that the perpetuation of such crimes seeks to hide their true purpose under the banner of high-sounding distractions and ideals...*
>
> *"...They make wars to capture markets by murder, raw materials by rape...*
>
> *"...They find it cheaper to steal, than exchange, easier to butcher than buy...*
>
> *"...This is the secret of all imperial wars . Profit. .Blood. Money"...*

Colonialism, which is only a recent phenomenon in the millennia of human existence, is in the context of Uganda, the historical basis and root cause of the country's political problem. In this light, Uganda has to be considered as a very young country, which is shouldered with new and old problems. The advent of colonial rule, in the guise of a

---

[34] Dr Norman Bethune, Canadian international medical volunteer to the Chinese peoples liberation war] (China Today, 1946)

"protectorate" was preceded by the political preparation of the Africans for its reception by missionaries who were its ideologists and the involvement of foreign trading companies - its economic arm.

The perceptive Ethiopian Emperor Tewodros-II summed up this situation before he killed himself after the defeat of Ethiopian forces in 1868 by invading British forces thus:

"...I know their game...
"...First, the traders and missionaries...;
"...then, the ambassadors...;
"...then, the canon...
"...It is better to go straight to the canon..."

Colonisation meant war. Colonial occupation and subjection to the slavery of colonial capital was in essence the continuous waging of war on a colonised country.

The colonisation of Uganda re-shaped the existence of the people in such a way that they lost control of the major events affecting their lives. The adversities of colonial rule, opened the eyes of the colonised and moved many to identify their own friends and foes in the situation. At the time, the colonial forces, which were the first to perfect on a countrywide scale, the use of force, terror and violence in the political management of the Ugandan polity, consisted of a foreign-armed component and their local cutthroat allies. This alliance has held over time in the country in varied forms.

In the process of Uganda's colonisation and later neo-colonisation, imperialism needed to recruit local mercenaries, agents, collaborators and allies in the country. These were at first mainly recruited from the upper echelons of the then ruling circles of the former Buganda Kingdom. This caste and *"Upper Crust"* was a phenomenon developed and evolved in local circumstances. It is their recruitment and manipulation by, and collaboration with, imperialism and colonialism, which transformed them into satraps, pawns, dependants and servants of colonialism.

Colonialism shrewdly used the then fear of disturbing influences from outside Buganda borders to coax their aristocrats into an alliance with it after the defeat of the patriotic Kabaka Mwanga, the King of Buganda. The constant threat of direct domination and assimilation for instance from Bunyoro-Kitara Empire in the North West of Buganda, the appearance of white wanderers on the scene, the fear of Arab traders from the East African coast and the arrival of Islamic trading and proselytising groups from the North etc. indeed panicked the local ruling circles whose world outlook was yet largely provincial. They succumbed to the intrigues and manipulations of colonialism, which thereafter transformed them into its pawns, and instruments and tools.

At the time of colonisation the victims of armed local colonial agents in Uganda, extended their hatred perhaps on the basis of vicarious liability to whole nationalities from which these agents had been recruited. This reaction unwittingly gave colonialism a lever with which to implement the policy of *'divide and rule'*. Its cost to Uganda has remained immense.

The duty of the Ugandan people's emergent national liberation movement is to help the people overcome these distractive sentiments because their persistence leads to the fragmentation of the efforts of the common victims of imperialist domination in Uganda. Indeed, the task is also to educate the oppressed and exploited Ugandan people on the concept of limited liability of the stooges and agents of imperialism, so that the nationalities of their origin are not condemned or victimised wholesale for the collaboration of one or so of their number.

In recompense for their service and to ensure their continued loyalty, imperialism worked out socio-economic and political arrangements with leading Protestant circles in Buganda Kingdom, giving them a stake in the colonial enterprise by awarding them landed property for their personal and official use. It also ensured their preferential appointments into leading political positions in the Buganda Kingdom.

Eventually, a truncated form of the property and administrative system adopted in Buganda, was extended to a number of other Kingdom and Chieftainship areas of the country.

It is largely from the successors to this local alliance that imperialism has continued to recruit willing collaborators for its domination of Uganda. The sages of the colonised Ganda nation aptly named these mindless collaborators – the *'Omuzungu Agambye'*[35] Africans: meaning the imperial Whiteman's parrots and copycats.

---

[35] Ibid 4

The other area of recruitment of agents is the other section of the elite and false-bourgeoisie that emerged in the country under colonial rule and the period subsequent to it.

(ii) DIVIDE AND RULE

From the onset of its rule, one of the major means that imperialism used to keep the people of Uganda in a state of subjugation was the strategy of sectionalism and *'Divide and Rule'*. This strategy pervaded the economic, cultural, religious, social, and political policies of the colonial regime. It was principally directed at fragmenting any unity and common understanding for action against colonial interests. In the realm of the economy, colonial exploitation of Uganda which resulted in the uneven and unbalanced modernisation and, or development of parts of the country, gave added impetus to the policy of *'divide and rule'*.

Colonialism, as an instrument of capitalist penetration, domination and primitive accumulation thus created a framework for discriminatory socio-economic development in the country. This led to relative modernisation of only certain parts of the country. Such regions and areas were for instance, favoured with cash crop/commodity production. They were also serviced with more schools, roads and other requisite infrastructure and amenities. The non- and lesser-developed areas acted principally as labour reserves for agricultural plantations and those economic units, which were established in the other parts of the country. The strategy of uneven modernisation and development has survived well into contemporary times and continues to serve as an instrument for the perpetuation of the policy of divide and rule in Uganda by political minority regimes. This rule over the *'many'* by the *'few'* has held in the country over time with the most negative results.

The effect of this colonial strategy of divide and rule was to inculcate in the minds of Ugandans from the relatively modernised and developed regions and areas, localist and discriminative superiority mind sets and consciousness. They have thought of themselves as being more talented and competent than the rest of their countrymen and women, while the others felt cheated and embittered that they were made to feel inferior. This legacy of uneven modernisation and development, which is an inevitable phenomenon in capitalist development -and its ideologisation, continues to bedevil the politics and the question of national unity in the country. Any attempts in post-colonial Uganda to guide the country towards a national perspective have been interpreted by the elites of the formerly *'favoured'* areas as a move not only against their material and social achievements, but also as actions, which were directed against the interests of entire nationalities or ethnic groups to which, they belong.

Such sentiments have been taken advantage of by non-patriotic and pro-imperialist forces for their politics of *'Divide and Rule'*, *'Nationality/Ethnic Chauvinism'*, area- and regional-based biases, and other bigotries, etc., such as the platform of the *'North'* versus the *'South'* or those *'West'* of the Nile versus these *'East'* of the Nile, Bantu versus Nilotics, Catholics versus Protestants, Christians versus Muslims, etc.

In a country where national liberation and meaningful socio-economic transformation have yet to take place, these retrogressive political platforms prove particularly effective in mass deception, manipulation and mobilisation. These constitute a real millstone around the shoulders and neck of the people's emergent National Liberation Movement.

(iii) NATIONALITY CHAUVINISM AND, OR THE ETHNIC SUPERIORITY PROBLEM

In the context of perfecting the policy of *'Divide and Rule'* including fanning area or regional consciousness, the colonial regime also specialised in provoking ethnic chauvinism as a means and method of weakening the emergent national liberatory and popular political forces.

In Uganda, there exist nationalities and ethnic consciousness, which is characteristic of many countries where people have continued to live in nationality confines and formations. Colonialism elevated ethnic consciousness to the level of chauvinism and subsequently bequeathed it to its successors in post-colonial Uganda.

With only a few exceptions, colonialism demarcated the majority of internal administrative boundaries along nationality lines. This development influenced the structure and character of internal administration and politics of Uganda, which heavily acquired nationality or ethnic characteristics. Political leaders, who emerged from these entities, were thus largely seen as nationality representatives at the countrywide level. The demarcation of administrative boundaries on nationality lines served the convenience of colonial administration and division of colonial peoples, which facilitated mass manipulation of the African people and their exploitation. This was on the face of it contrary to the practices generalised by imperialism and its tool - colonialism - in drawing external colonial boundaries, which ignored and divided whole peoples, ethnic groups and nationalities, or even whole nations.

To imperialism, the important point was to prevent the solidarity and unity of the African people. In some cases, for instance agents from one nationality could be used to administer for colonialism a set of resisting nationalities to which colonialism was hostile. For instance, Ganda colonial agents were used to administer Bunyoro-Kitara Empire after its colonisation, and other areas of Uganda such as Busoga, Bukedi, Bugisu, Teso, etc.

In other cases, large areas, which formed part of the old Bunyoro-Kitara Kingdom/Empire, were separated from the empire and directly colonised. This was done allegedly as a punishment for Bunyoro-Kitara's dogged resistance against colonisation. In another case, for instance, in appreciation of the service that Ganda mercenary forces led by Gen. Semei Lwakilenzi Kakungulu, had made in the defeat of Bunyoro-Kitara Empire defence forces, they were rewarded with administrative positions and land parcels in Bunyoro-Kitara. In addition parts of Bunyoro-Kitara were hived off and given to Buganda Kingdom.

Nationality chauvinism has been a particularly effective instrument used to induce mass deception by social and political forces in whose interests the people have to remain divided and manipulated. This has been the principal instrument of Ugandan political collaborators and allies of imperialism, particularly those forces who have emerged from circles, which played the role of the colonial agents. The struggle for political independence which required countrywide political mobilisation, called for a necessary sustained fight against the negative platforms of all types of sectionalism and nationality chauvinism and the political interests, which used it for mass manipulation and deception.

In their attempt to build a rational basis for the defence of nationality chauvinism, the leaders of these sectionalised social and political forces deliberately propagated the position that national unity and integration would threaten the material interests, customs, values, and cultures of their entire nationalities. This negative platform continues to be one of the major obstacles against forging popular and national unity in Uganda.

A liberated Uganda of national freedom, popular self-governance and African self-becoming, will have to create the capacity to magnetise all clusters of peoples, nations and communities to a beneficially shared national community of equal peoples.

(iv) THE RELIGIOUS FACTOR

Since the advent of foreign and 'modern' religion in Uganda, religion has been the other factor made use of, as a mobilisational factor, by imperialism and its local allies to divide the ranks of oppressed and exploited Ugandans and to obstruct any processes intended to forge national unity and progress in the country. It was the context and method of introducing foreign religion into Uganda, which made religion a critical factor of division and sectionalism in the country's politics.

In the course of introducing various new religions such as Islam, Catholic and Protestant Christianity, through the ruling circles and courts of Uganda's various kingdoms and chieftainships, religion became inextricably entangled in the *'cloak and dagger'* politics of the country's kingdoms and chieftainships. Political manipulation through religion played an important role in weakening African solidarity and eventually led to the loss of the country's sovereignty.

The Role of missionaries in these intrigues was conspicuous. Indeed as one colonist said, missionaries were better than policemen and cheaper in facilitating colonisation.   This context of introducing Christianity and Islam into Uganda inevitably led to great distortion and falsification of their doctrines and indeed theological objectives. These processes shed off their fundamental humility and humanism and instead introduced the despicable elements of intrigue and sectionalism into the various religions, which were put to the service of colonialism and its vilest objectives. The said departures from genuine theological principles have mutated into the most negative forms of distortions in contemporary times. The higher religious leaderships and authorities in the country are no better than bribed and corruptible pawns and satraps who have become notable obstacles to the struggles to win national freedom in Uganda.

The earlier colonial alliance of missionaries, business, and state continues in a new form in the neo-colonial synthesis. The clergy and its leadership i.e. Christian and Muslim, continue to play a decisive role, now as part of the team of ideologists of the neo-colonial system of which the masses of the people are victims. Their role among other things is to call upon the people to bear the burdens of neo-colonialism, its tyranny, its genocide and spoliation without revolt or without reverting to necessary resistance, collective self-defence, liberation and salvation.

This religious leadership, which is a component of the country's political and ideological elite lead a fractious existence of intrigues and continuous struggles for positions, power, and wealth amongst themselves in their various religious outfits. Indeed to bring them to their original, pure, and noble religious objectives is a titanic task equal to that of self-liberation in their own context.

Today, the parameters of division that were established by the 1880's at the height of religious political contentions continue to exist in their fundamentals. Historically, religion was then misused and continues to be abused as a tool to organise and mobilise social and political forces, which are meant to manipulate and divide the people.

The Protestant forces which colonialism assisted to emerge victorious and were rewarded with, leading political positions in the administration of Buganda Kingdom and were awarded property in land, constituted the point of departure in the negative schemes which misused religion in the service of colonialism. The here of material interests took precedence over the gains to be made in the celestial and heavenly hereinafter.

The defeated and marginalised local catholic and Muslim political leadership, who had at the time allied themselves with French capital and Arab merchant interests respectively, were consoled with a token presence in the then administration of Buganda Kingdom, something to which they never reconciled themselves.

Uganda's political elite and false-bourgeoisie today, continue to misuse religion as a tool and weapon for mass manipulation and mobilisation in Uganda's politics.

The popular emergent National Liberation Movement is faced with the duty and responsibility to lead Ugandans to struggle to overcome and transcend the political divisions and sectionalism, which today is clothed in religious forms so that a common outlook for national liberation, nation formation, and national development is created. The popular emergent national liberation movement bears the responsibility to assist all to appreciate that the matter of religion and faith is fundamentally between the believers and their God.

For the believers, the time will come when they have to seize and take hold of the holy texts of religion and self-interpret them, which is the right of all believers. The leaders of their faith communities are hardly any longer the unblemished interpreters of the word of God Almighty. Apparently the bishops and higher clergy cannot resist the allure of Japanese four-wheel-drive vehicles and the largesse, which the military dictatorship gifts them!!

(v) THE CULTURAL FACTOR

The cultures of the Ugandan people constituted the other factor that colonialism had to contend with in its quest to impose its domination.

The worth of the cultures of the Ugandan people in the face of colonial rule, has to be visualized in the light of whether it proved to be a constraint to, or was conducive to the promotion, of colonialism.

The higher level of development of the British capitalist formation, which sought to subjugate the materially lesser-developed agricultural Ugandan societies proved crucial in determining the degree of their domination and integration into the uneasy colonial fostered synthesis, which was to evolve.

The imposition of colonial economic and political domination over the area which is today Uganda, was accompanied by a devastating onslaught on the cultures of the people of the area. Over time, this was variously to destroy, neutralise, disrupt, and paralyse the cultural lives and world outlook of the peoples of Uganda.

However, certain factors made the total destruction of the cultures of the Ugandan people impossible. Instead they provided a basis for the survival of some of their characteristics in their systems of languages, dances, songs, epics and what were categorised as tradition and custom. These cultural media constituted the phenomena through which the civil, political, and cultural resistance against colonial domination was sustained.

With the institution of indirect rule – colonial administration of Africans through African agents and collaborators, most negatively affected the cultures of the African peoples, which, in their interactions, made small gains but registered major losses. As a medium for dynamic expression of man's struggle for existence, the cultural mix that evolved in the womb of colonialism had the potential to become either the gravedigger of colonialism or of the local Ugandan communities. In effect, it became a handicapped animator in the freedom struggle dynamic.

The advent of colonialism unwittingly brought along with it certain gains as part of the universal heritage of mankind such as higher forms of organisation, a broader world outlook, and the possibility of learning the historical experiences and cultures of other peoples of the world. These, however, were principally to advance the interests of the local associates of the colonial system and the political elite which developed in its womb.

The local colonial collaborators were effectively integrated into the colonial processes of acculturalisation - in language, religion, world outlook, dress, mannerism, identity etc., however without destroying the shell of their Africanness.

The African cultures depicted in their dress, customs, taboos, religions or beliefs in many gods and goddesses, in the fear of the evil spirits etc., were adjudged repugnant and banished to the peripheries of colonial societies or relegated to limbo.

Yet, despite the institution of the system of exploitation, national oppression and the inhibition of 'tarnished' cultures, colonialism was not entirely assured of its local triumph over native cultures, which became more or less the salient dynamic expression of the fettered existence of African peoples.

The very same restricted cultures were to constitute the foundation of the epics, stories, dances, songs, orature, literature, poetry, and art for mass mobilisation in the struggle for national liberation. It is through these that the people's heroes and martyrs have been celebrated and immortalised.

The diversity of cultures, reflecting differences in the levels of social development and certain nationality particularities have in their specificities proved crucial in determining the possibilities for uniting all Ugandans in the struggle against colonialism and continue to influence the reaction and behaviour of various communities and peoples towards the liberation struggle. Similarly, today certain customs, traditions, taboos etc., continue to prove to be a serious handicap to the integration of certain sectors of the Ugandan people in the fight for freedom.

On the other hand, colonial indirect rule and the cultural and ideological repression of the people through acculturalised persons of higher schooling, scientific and technical knowledges, which carried an aura of authority about them, stalled moves favourable to the fullest integration of the people in the struggle against colonial rule.

The ambition of this group of acculturalised Africans to replace the colonialist in the agent governance of their peoples, their opportunism, and the processes instituted in decolonisation, all contributed to blunting the critical involvement of the people in the national liberation struggle. The despicable agent political elite saw the end of formal colonial rule merely as an opportunity to establish their own local political domination over the people. The successful replacement of the colonialist by the acculturalised Africans in the domination of the people partly explains why in post-colonial Africa including Uganda, the economy, as politics and culture have remained non-autochthonous.

Yet, there is still hope in this difficult situation. For African cultures, though repressed, banished and betrayed by the local allies and successors of colonialism did survive in the hamlets, villages and rural communities i.e. wherever the masses of people and their cultures have taken refuge. They await fertilisation from the conscious and reawakened Africans i.e. genuine people's agents of transformative change that participate with the people in the struggle for genuine national freedom and national democratic liberation.

In these processes, it is the task of the people's emergent national liberation movement to help generate, through the media of peoples' cultures, all that which is positive and necessary so as to involve all in the multiple and multifaceted struggles for national freedom taking place in Uganda.

In the national liberation struggle, the worth of the cultures of the peoples of Uganda shall be adjudged in accordance with the degree to which they facilitate, foster and help to forge community, political, national and larger unities of the entirety of the Ugandan people on the basis of equality of all.

In this glorious, but difficult odyssey to national freedom, popular self-governance and African self-becoming; whatever aspects of the peoples' cultures that can be used to effect their full participation in recreating conditions for the rise of liberated and free humanity in Uganda, shall find new promotion and development in the national liberation process, and in the defence and perpetuation of its conquests.

(vi) THE ECONOMIC FACTOR

Abdel Galil El-Emary, the pre-1952-revolt finance minister of Egypt, during his tenure of office in government, depicted the Egyptian economy as;

> *"...A cow grazing the pastures of the country; with its udders*
> *being sucked dry [of milk] from the outside..."*

This description of the Egyptian economy would be an accurate depiction of the Ugandan economy since colonisation of the country.

Colonial economic activities were initiated within the restrictions and confines of the worldwide capitalist economic system of the then British Empire. This has left a legacy, which continues to structurally determine the character of Uganda's integration into the larger world economy.

By the time of the advent of colonial rule, the area, which is now Uganda, consisted of a number of sovereign economic formations and units in which trade and exchange of commodities were being regularised. These agrarian and pastoralist economic formations ranged in variety from communal and patriarchal types to simple commodity-producing types.

At the time, Bunyoro-Kitara Empire and it's then rising offspring kingdom of Buganda, other chieftainships, and small military states, had evolved or were evolving tribute paying economies.

These economies, which remained largely self-sufficient within their collectives, were complementary, and rooted on the basic needs of their societies. It was on account of the demands arising from the economies of the Nile Valley in the North and Arab East African coastal merchant formations that new requirements were made on these local economies.

Apart from agricultural production, fishing, hunting and animal husbandry activities for the provision of food; elementary mining (of salt, copper, iron) and craft industries had been established including metal works as well as the manufacture of agricultural implements, food processing implements, fishing gear, clothing, leather products, pottery, copper and iron wares, ivory artefacts, and defence equipment like spears, shields, bows and arrows etc. These activities formed the basis of exchange amongst different Ugandan economies.

The arrival of the European commercial interests following on the footsteps of long distance trademarked the beginning of a sad set of events in Uganda's relations with the world capitalist division of labour and market. From then, this contact became the critical determinant factor in the development of the Ugandan economies.

These economies that had been organised within no less than 200 big, medium, and small political formations and units, were in time united and integrated into the world British colonial economy. This development had varied lasting consequences on these economies and corresponding social, political and cultural formations.

From then onwards, the priority in the Ugandan economies were decisively moved in favour of production and later the partial processing of commodities such as cotton, tea, cocoa, tobacco, sugar, copper, animal skins etc. for the world market. The production of anything else including food and other means of sustenance became secondary. This obviously handicapped the rise of healthy labour that would enhance the production of cash crops and other products for the world market.

Prior to this phase, however, foreign economic interests concentrated their activities within the sphere of unequal exchanges in exotic products. This was followed by a period of communication and infrastructural construction, which used forced labour. This was then, the forceful induction of the agricultural peasantry into cash crop production and other raw materials for the world market.

The need to process those products in partial form for export necessitated construction of some minor industrial plants. These grew in number with the expansion of production and the further introduction of some plantation crops such as coffee, tea and sugar. The development of Uganda within the context of the worldwide capitalist economy of the then British Empire however permitted only low and minimal capitalisation of Uganda's economy.

There was no possibility in the workings of the world economy of the British Empire to industrialise, capitalise agriculture or develop any substantial domestic market. The resources accumulated through Uganda's economic growth were siphoned for capital accumulation and formation in England and other chosen parts of the empire. On account of this, domestic market for capital or mass consumer goods remained negligible and undeveloped. The negative consequences of an economic system that generates growth without development have lived into contemporary times and continue to marginalise and destitute the African producers in the country.

In the result, the economy could consequently register some growth, but not development, there being in any case no process in place which was capable of transforming economic surpluses into capital in Uganda. Consequently, an economy has now been created which is never able to create capital from any economic surpluses that get generated in the country. This factor is key to understanding the unending socio-economic crises and backwardness in Uganda.

Ever since, this basic construct of the Ugandan economy has been thus set and has retained its basic negative anti-development orientation and structures. This has meant deeper structural integration into the broader world capitalist economy and market. From then, all local initiative was lost in the field of economy and ever since internal developments have had to be adjusted regardless of the consequences to the demands of the international capitalist division of labour. This integration has perpetuated the system of uneven modernisation and development in the internal framework of the Uganda economy.

Since then, the system of uneven economic development has bedevilled Uganda and has led to the evolution of a multi-structural and compound economic formation made up of different components such as; the patriarchal and petty commodity producing types, local private and capitalist, and monopoly capitalist types.

Such a motley collective and incomplete economic formation generates not only socio-economic backwardness, but the instability of the entire economy and very strong overall dependence relations on the world capitalist economy, which situation induces in the country negative economic, social and political consequences. These factors constitute a heavy constraint on the Ugandan people's aspirations and efforts for autonomous economic development and the constitution of a unified country.

Within such an economic formation, each group of peoples, particularly the peasantry remain isolated in their localities in the workings of the economy. They hence build only sporadic and localised, instead of common experiences with the rest of their own countrymen and women. The circulation of people in the economy is limited and thus constrains their possibilities to see and experience for themselves in commonality the basic realities of their dominated country.

This type of environment is the mother base from which evolve nationality and ethnic chauvinism/bigotry, regionalism and the divisive, sectional and manipulative political practices which plagues post-colonial Uganda. It is also the mother base that is making possible despotic rule in Uganda in the resultant climate of fragmentation and division in the ranks of the people which is further fuelled, by an extremely fractious, divided, parasitic and corrupt governing circle in the country.

Colonial and post-colonial power relations that have arisen out of this environment are autocratic and authoritarian.

The power relations in pre-colonial Ugandan states/kingdoms/chieftainships which were largely based on tribute paying relations, unlike those in non-state formations, were by their nature however less despotic. Doubtless in many of these state formations, life was cheap. These systems which saw nothing wrong with impaling kings and princes who lost power contests definitely saw nothing appalling in meting deaths to their defeated commoner subjects in bigger numbers. This foundation of human degradation in the history of the country was taken advantage of and exploited to the utmost by colonialism particularly in its early period of establishment in the country.

Today the decisive control of the country is in the hands of ravenous multinational capital and finance; in which it's natural and bio-resources are subject to open pillage, spoliation and robbery as the fruits of labour of the people get looted in broad daylight.

After liberation from fascism and its dictatorship it is imperative that the people re-assert popular, community and national permanent sovereignty over the natural and bio resources, and retain and secure – the fruits of labour and wealth of the Ugandan/Nile African people in investible forms.

Around every natural and bio resource endowment which hitherto has existed as dormant capital – related industry and vibrant productive economic activities can be initiated, built and nurtured to meet the multiple needs and necessities of the people and requisite planned, balanced and integrated sustainable development of the country and the needs of capital accumulation for endogenous and, or autochthonous development.

The key to progress is to win, the freedom to transform dormant capital into active productive capital that creates and accumulates investible capital, and to create requisite high technologically competent, imaginative and innovative quality human capital that is able to mount necessary replicable research to open up dynamic development that is embedded in society to meet its overall material, social, cultural, and the general needs and necessities of progress.

Then, society will reclaim its requisite historical initiative over the replicable processes that ensure and secure the country's powers of self-renewal.

Capital, when transformed from dormant resources and wealth created in the country by the labour of its people, is best visualized as part of the assets which can be activated to invigorate production chains and surplus producing economic activities.

Like dormant water collection in a lake, unused capital potential can be transformed into an energy producing factor (beyond its other uses for irrigation, fishing, leisure, canoeing, etc.) to power production systems of all types by which economic surpluses are able to be produced.

Thus in a treatise on Capitalism[36] Hernando de Soto Polar says:

> "...Thus an apparently placid lake water may be used to illuminate your room and power the machinery of a factory...
>
> "...What was required was an external man-made process, which allowed us, first, to identify the potential of weight of the water to do additional work; and, second, to convert the potential energy into electricity that may be used to create surplus value...
>
> "...The additional value we obtain from the lake is not surplus value (like a precious ore intrinsic to the earth), but rather a value of the man-made process extrinsic to the lake...
>
> "...It is this process that allows us to transform the lake from a fishing and canoeing kind of place into an energy producing kind of place..."

Bringing dormant capital and value into active life requires one to go beyond looking at assets as they are and calls for necessary imaginative thinking which enables one to create and generate a process for transforming the asset's economic potential into a form that may be used to initiate additional production which generates and accumulates - investible capital.

---

[36] p.41 - The Mystery of Capital: Why Capitalism Triumphs in the West and Fails Everywhere ...

Winning national freedom through political, social and national liberation is hence imperative. It is in this context that the people can take advantage of sovereign spaces that are created, to assert the fullest ownership of their ancestral lands and country, and, secure the maximal command and control of their destinies and those of their country within which they shall be able to flourish and self-become in the company of the free peoples and nations of the world.

CHAPTER 2

UGANDAN SOCIAL AND POLITICAL FORCES AND THE FORMATION OF POLITICAL PARTIES IN THE COUNTRY

Over time, since about the 1860's i.e. with the intensification of long distance trade with the outside world, but more conspicuously since the ruling and chiefly circles of Buganda and other kingdoms were manipulated to agree to socio-economic and political pacts with colonialism, several major social forces have emerged in Uganda and have ultimately organised themselves into various political formations, 'parties' and 'movements'.

The initial armed imperial forces of colonisation, which intervened into Uganda, consisted of Imperial British East African Company Limited (IBEAC) mercenaries of Indian, Swahili, Somali, Nubian groups and elements. They were officered by British and Indian elements. The other element was made up of co-opted local Ugandan cutthroats that were an essential element to provide a local face to the forces of colonisation, which were organised by the IBEAC. This infamous destructive mercenary force was a direct tool of IBEAC, which was an unabashed child of British capital.

When the project of colonisation, spread and unfolded countrywide, it was of necessity resisted by a myriad of self-defence actions under various military and political formations of African clusters of peoples, nations and communities. The fight for the control of this strategic land at the sources of the equatorial waters of the Nile River had then truly commenced.

> ➢ Seer Rembe, led the 'Mayi Mayi'[37] forces in the defence of African independence and sovereignty, at the meet point of the land that today, straddles the boundaries of the West Nile region of Uganda, the East of the Democratic Republic of Congo (DRC) and the South West of South Sudan.

---

[37] Nationalities-centred militia formed to defend their local territory against other armed groups.

➢ Omukama Kabalega and his worthy successor Omukama Kitayimbwa mobilised the entire defence forces of the Bunyoro-Kitara Empire, led by the Abarusura[38], in defence of African independence and sovereignty. At the time, the Bunyoro-Kitara Empire encompassed not only central and western Uganda and the Rwenzori Mountain territories and areas of the DRC, but also areas inclusive of north-western Tanzania.

➢ Kabaka Mwanga of Buganda Kingdom – led the Royal Buganda Kingdom forces under various formations (of the time: Christian [Protestant and Catholic] and Muslim parties, indeed under whichever cover they proved useful) in the defence of his kingdom, African independence and sovereignty.

➢ Kabaka Kalema, also of Buganda, together with Prince Mbogo and Muslim martyr Batuma, etc., led the Muslim armed forces and party in the defence of African independence.

➢ Other area and zonal forces under various community formations stood up in defence of African independence and sovereignty in Lamogi[39]/Acholi, Busoga, Bugisu, Teso, Lango, Karamoja, etc. They rose in the armed defence, to secure their ancestral lands from the ruthless armed contingents of colonial forces, as a basis to defend African independence and sovereignty.

➢ In the South West of the country, the Nyabindi[40] millenarians and the kingdoms of Kitagwenda, Buweju, Mpororo and their allies stood to stem the onslaught of the armed forces of colonisation, and in defence of African independence and sovereignty.

These forces for the defence of African independence and sovereignty went down in defeat by the stronger, better-resourced armed colonising forces, but with their honour intact.

Ever since then, the clusters of the African peoples, nations and communities have organised themselves in various forms to win national

---

[38] Infers to Royal Guards
[39] Infers to a rebellion to colonial rule
[40] Ibid 26

freedom as the basis to build a new independent and sovereign African polity and homeland.

They have had to face up to the violence of both, imperialism and its local hirelings, collaborators and pawns.

Hilaire Belloc, paid a satirical poetic tribute to the might of British imperial military muscle:-

> "...*Whatever happens we have got...*
> "...*The Maxim gun and they have not...*"

This cynical imperial outlook, which worships violence as the means of conquest and subjugation of oppressed African people, has been bequeathed to the mindless African agents and hirelings of imperialism who are its successors in the governance and political management of Africa.

Force and violence, terror and intimidation, manipulation and deception are vital tools in the imposition of the cruel rule of the African agents of imperialism in Africa.

At and during colonisation, these African agents used religious and a myriad of other symbols as forms of identify. Their continued impact into contemporary times reflects the survival of historical and political tendencies, which have been taken advantage of, to give the Ugandan false-bourgeoisie and political elite, an exaggerated prominence in the politics and leadership of Uganda.

In the specific circumstances then existing at colonisation of Uganda, in the Buganda area of the country, the originally numerous political factions which contended for power got organised into, the '*Catholic*' party, the '*Protestant*' party and the '*Muslim*' or '*Islamic*' party, based on the faiths and alliances of their leaders.

The Muslim party, which was backed by Arab merchant capital disintegrated in the face of stiff contestations with stronger, more ravenous '*European*' capitalist interests that backed the other Christian parties. Consequently, the Islamic party suffered the fate of all historic losers – social and political marginalisation.

Its original internal or local support was taken over by other social forces that were backed by stronger economic and financial interests. Indeed all the foregoing would have remained a purely local Buganda affair, had it not been for the fact that colonialism not only misused Buganda as leverage to take over most of what is today Uganda, but also used the systems of '*indirect rule*' which was instituted in Buganda and hired Ganda agent personnel as a basis of building its country-wide dominance. The structural political parameters that these experiences implanted into the soils of the country are still largely in place, and have however now mutated in form in the service of neo-colonialism.

The said parameters are bound to so remain in their basics until national democratic liberation, national construction and development, are won as the means by which Uganda shall be transformed, modernised and developed.

(i) THE LANDED AND PROPERTIED AFRICAN CHIEFLY FORCES

This force is one of the most retrogressive in Uganda. It has had at its leadership the Protestant political force which colonialism assisted to emerge victorious in the late 19th century *'Buganda Political/Religious Wars'*. They were rewarded with leading political and administrative positions in the Kingdom's government, and privatised landed property. These events transformed the character of its leadership and placed it into the hands of agent colonial administrative chiefs as opposed to clan heads who held as community leaders in pre-colonial days.

In Buganda Kingdom, they adopted His Highness Maj. Gen. Sir Edward Mutesa-II, KBE[41], the Kabaka of Buganda, as their symbol.

Mutesa-II succeeded his father, Sir Daudi Chwa, who had passed on at his mother's palace at Lusaka near Kampala. Mutesa-II had to be elected by the Buganda Lukiiko/Legislative Council by a majority vote of its members in accordance with the 1900 Buganda-British agreement.

The Lukiiko had to make a choice from two princes.

The then Buganda Katikiiro, Martin Luther Nsibirwa, supported by Serwano Kulubya (whom the Ganda chiefs who were opposed to the British restructuring of Buganda Kingdom, had named as the *"Omuzungu Agambye"*[42] for his parrot relay of the British colonial government orders and directives to them), the Anglican Bishop Stuart of Namirembe Diocese and the British Governor of Uganda backed the election of Prince Edward Mutesa.

Had an open election process been held in the Lukiiko, Prince George Kiwa Mawanda, the elder brother of Prince Mutesa, much loved

---

[41] Knight Commander, the Most Excellent Order of the British Empire
[42] Ibid 4

by Buganda chiefs and the public, would have got elected as successor to the departed Kabaka Sir Daudi Chwa.[43]

The late Kabaka Sir Daudi Chwa had in his will appointed his elder son Prince George Kiwa Mawanda as his successor. The British colonial authorities, the Anglican Church leadership and Kabaka's government under Katikiiro Martin Luther Nsibirwa ignored this royal decision.

At the election, the Katikiiro Martin Luther Nsibirwa stood up and declared to the fully convened great Lukiiko of Buganda Kingdom thus:

> "...*We have got two princes, Mawanda and Mutesa...*
> "...*The Government has chosen Mutesa...*"

This was the end of the *"selection"*[44].

Thereafter the Kingdom of Buganda got beset with severe social and political problems and uprisings which led to the assassination of the Katikiiro of Buganda, Martin Luther Nsibirwa, and setting Bulange, the king's palace, on fire in the 1949 riots.

Sir Edward Mutesa-II was later in 1963, after independence however overwhelmingly elected by the Uganda Parliament as the first native head of state of the country. He was fully supported by the Uganda Peoples Congress (UPC)/Kabaka Yekka (KY) alliance, in his election by the Uganda Parliament, but vigorously opposed by the Democratic Party and its membership in parliament.

Sir Edward Mutesa-II had earlier been deported to the United Kingdom upon his disagreement with the British colonial authorities over the then projected 1955 Buganda/British colonial-government Agreement, which was to replace the 1900 Agreement.

His opposition to the provisions that were meant to further diminish the essence of Kabaka's powers in his kingdom and its identity, won him significant popularity in Buganda and the country.

The landed and propertied African chiefly social forces blossomed under British colonial patronage and that of the *'Official British Anglican Church'* and capital interests associated with it. It later found its most eloquent expression in the founding of the "KABAKA YEKKA" or "THE KING ALONE IS SUPREME" movement in Buganda in 1961 and the

---

[43] In a paper by John C. Sekamwa, a lecturer (Faculty of Education, Makerere University), submitted to E.A. Social Science Conference in 1970, entitled *"Submission and Reaction in Buganda, 1926 - 1945"*

[44] Ibid 2. [In a paper by John C. Sekamwa, a lecturer (Faculty of Education, Makerere University), submitted to E.A. Social Science Conference in 1970, entitled *"Submission and Reaction in Buganda, 1926 - 1945"*]

HEREDITARY CHIEFTAINSHIPS PARTY elsewhere in the country. It pursued an ethnic chauvinistic policy in the attempt to preserve in post-colonial Uganda its colonial given privileges. Since then, it has been led by a section of the landed Buganda bourgeoisie and political elite which exploits the sentiment of the Kabakaship and nationality chauvinism in Buganda to push their class claims in Uganda's/Nile Africa's politics and for their own continued parasitic economic benefits.

This group constitutes one other obstacle, which militates against national equality, integration and unity in the country. Historically, their collaboration in colonial schemes to subjugate a large area of Uganda (in the East, North and West), led by the then notorious armed colonial agent, the self-styled Gen. Semei Lwakilenzi Kakungulu, has earned them the utmost hatred of the people of these areas. This armed colonial agent spread terror, extreme violence, and carnage wherever he led predatory colonial agents and forces that were under his command. This sad example has been replicated in recent times in the country and its African neighbourhoods, which have been subjected to predatory, and spoliatory armed activities.

In the absence of any thorough going social and political transformation in Uganda, many people in the country still ascribe blame for the earlier episodes of predatory and spoliatory armed activities in colonial times to the entire Ganda nationality. This negative sentiment has virtually acquired a life of its own and has been perpetuated into contemporary times. It constitutes one of the main obstacles to the processes of national liberation and integration.

A few years after independence, these landed propertied feudal social forces lost important state, and other positions of influence in the political contentions of the time. The conditions prevailing in non-popular Ugandan politics, unfortunately continues to give them presence to attempt to refurbish their political platform and fortunes in unprincipled association with any forces at all, particularly armed ones, that they hope would assist them in realising their sectional objectives.

In pursuit of this ambition, these landed propertied feudal forces sought different and multifarious organisational forms during the fascist military rule of the 1970's. They initially collaborated in the schemes of the fascist dictatorship until they were decisively set upon by its regime.

In the 1980 general elections, they used the umbrella of the Democratic Party (DP) as a vehicle for giving expression to their interests, but eventually switched their support to the National Resistance Army, when they failed to replace the traditional leadership of the DP with their own.

When after 1986, the National Resistance Army (NRA)-regime of genocide, grand spoliation and plunder gave their demands a rebuff; they yet again attempted to take over the reins of government on their own. Their defective and narrow political outlook and limited view of the problems of Uganda is a drawback to political and national progress in Uganda.

The popular emergent national liberation movement has the duty to catalyse those under its influence to free themselves from its negative ideological hold and persuade them to make their contribution in the dynamic political, social and national liberation processes where all patriots, nationalists, democrats and revolutionaries have a role to play in pursuit of the goal, to forever win National Freedom. It is also important for it to be assisted to appreciate the fact that, the support and good-will of other Ugandans is necessary to win the conditions for the dignified well-being and welfare of all as no single section of Ugandan society can alone win national freedom from imperialism, i.e. without the support of their fellow countrymen and women.

What is important is to constructively mobilise, and nationalise the mass component (peasants, tenants, the landless, rural labour, etc.) of this force, so that the sensibilities that its leadership today exploits to manipulate the masses to its negative political platform is removed to the advantage of all Ugandans.

The country cannot afford to let the mass component of this force become a prisoner of the sectional circumstance of its rise, formation and being.

(ii) BUGANDA CATHOLIC INTERESTS AND THE RISE OF THE DEMOCRATIC PARTY (DP).

In the intensity of the contentions between the Catholic and Protestant parties (later the leaders of the emergent landed/propertied feudal forces) in Buganda Kingdom politics, the Catholic political elite, whose party suffered defeat at the hands of the Protestant armed party at colonisation, vigorously fought for equality. Later these Catholic political elite in Buganda matured their struggle for equality in the politics of Buganda from a provincial into a countrywide political movement called the **Democratic Party (DP)**, which they formed in the mid-1950. The benefits of modern formal education and their partial integration into the colonial and neo-colonial structures, unlike in the case of Muslims who benefited little from either, availed the Catholic political elite, a fighting chance to assert their political claims in the countrywide arena.

The DP mentor, the Catholic Church, which had established countrywide structures and the Christian Democratic International (a child of Italian and German Capital), have continued to attempt to help market DP influence to the rest of the country as part of their global crusade against what they consider the dangers of rising communist influence in Uganda.

Part of the impetus for its formation was the fear orchestrated by leading Catholic circles and their ideologists that the **Uganda National Congress (UNC)**, the forerunner of the **Uganda Peoples Congress (UPC)**, was *"a Trojan horse"* or a camouflaged vehicle for communism.

The spread of the DP to other areas of the country was given an extra boost when through the process of decolonisation, nominal internal governance and stewardship of Uganda was to be devolved onto the local political elite. It was then that the DP was made to stake its claim with determination for countrywide political leadership rather than regional Buganda leadership.

The DP had a lacklustre performance both in government administration and as an opposition party in the Uganda Parliament. Because of the opportunism and utter careerism of its leadership, it has squandered whatever remained of its image by joining fascistic regimes that offer its leaders government positions. As a result, the **Democratic Party (DP)** now has pathological fear of any genuine political, social and national liberatory processes that would generate systems of democratic accountability to the people of Uganda. It fears the honest verdict of the people on its' mercenary character, which the DP leadership has exhibited in the past and present.

The other reason for its poor and deteriorating image is its utter subservience to the *'Christian Democratic International'*. In the age of popular struggles for genuine African political independence and national liberation, such an image is fatal to a political movement of its character. The involvement, for instance, of foreign foundations in its ideological and organisational management, constitutes a repugnant feature, which alienates all the nationalists, patriots, and revolutionary democrats from its ambit.

The patriotic elements, who for whatever reason, have come under the sway of the DP, have to stand up against these negative characteristics of their leadership as well as its sectionalist and discriminatory practices, which are meted against not only non-Catholics, but even Catholics from outside Buganda. These negative practices, which may have made sense in the original political struggles in the region of Buganda, only serve to justify and harden other sectionalist and anti-Catholic positions whose seeds British imperialism implanted into the Ugandan soil.

The most important need of the DP is to build an appreciation and understanding of the nature and character of imperialism, its interests in relationship to the Third World, the African people's cause and the need for national democratic liberation, nation formation and crystallisation, defence and enhancement of the country's national interests and the efforts to forge untrammelled processes of national economic development and progress in Uganda.

This political force has to be assisted not to remain stuck in *'yesterday'* or the past; when the people are working to win a 'tomorrow' of national freedom, equality, equity, social justice and general progress for all, without exception.

(iii) THE UGANDA (NATIONAL) PEOPLES CONGRESS (UPC): ITS RISE AND BEING

The extension of colonial rule throughout Uganda by imperialism through ruthless agent colonial military forces and the allied landed propertied feudal armed agents, inevitably provoked resistance and counter action on the part of the victim Ugandan people. The elevation of nationality consciousness to the level of chauvinism during the colonial era, and the fact that nationality and ethnic chauvinists were also the principal collaborators and local agents of colonial domination and oppression, provoked direct political action against them in large areas of Uganda. It is partly this resistance and struggles in conjunction with other anti-colonial causes which constituted the beginnings of a national movement in which the social and political forces that have organised around the *Uganda National*, later, *Peoples Congress*, have played a leading role.

Prior to the formation of the Uganda National Congress (UNC) the forerunner of the Uganda Peoples Congress (UPC), these struggles had remained largely uncoordinated and had occurred spontaneously. The UNC later the UPC, was and has remained a movement which is anti-colonial, anti-neo-colonial and anti-imperialist. It has not, in its objectives and practises, discriminated amongst Ugandans or sought membership on the basis of nationality, ethnicity, or religion and other sectional basis, but has sought to establish a basis and framework to forge national integration in a most negative structural condition in the country and in a very acrimonious political environment. The adoption by the UPC of local popular causes and struggles and its attempt to channel and co-ordinate them towards a countrywide perspective has been both its strength and weakness. Whereas co-ordination of local struggles at a countrywide level permitted it to balance things on a broader basis, the very local nature of the particularistic popular causes it adopted constituted a constraint on its political perspective.

Hence, with the advent of decolonisation, the movement garnered the predominantly Protestant and non-Catholic, Muslim, Africanist etc., support it found countrywide, while at the same time it appealed to the popular and democratic catholic support in a number of areas outside Buganda Kingdom.

It was the movement to which the authority of government was conceded by the colonial power on October 9, 1962. The anti-colonial struggle culminating in this concession, was in itself a great event which raised equally great expectations of the people in the possibilities for sustained development, prosperity, and improvement of their living conditions in the context of freedom from alien rule. These however, have to await the rise of the second and real or national liberation and freedom, which is yet to be won. For among other things, the apparently new state evolved in post-colonial Uganda was in fact only a 'doctored' parliamentarised version of the old colonial state apparatus with its inherent structural constraints. There was very little qualitative change in the state bureaucracy, education services, judicial structures, the army, police, and other security forces. The economy over which it presided and was based, remained equally unmodified in its internal workings as well as in regard to its placing in the world capitalist division of work and market. In short, neo-colonialism and its sponge-like containing effect have remained in place to fleece the Ugandan people and dissipate the expectations on the independence that colonialism had conceded to the people of Uganda. The **Uganda Peoples Congress (UPC)** had to contend within the neo-colonial context with questions of; the form of government, administrative and territorial divisions, ethnic and nationality balance in government and the army, the structure of public spending, organisation of education, official and national language, placement of development projects in the country et cetera.

It was in any case, constrained in taking any initiative towards necessary basic transformative change by the class and elite character of its leadership and the complex nature of the neo-colonial power arrangements which had been bequeathed to Uganda.

The said leadership have been and are, but simply associates of the real membership and political content of the UPC. They are, but members of a different class and societal groups, that happen to lead the producer classes that have been aligned to the Congress. This obviously constrained the level of exertion of the Congress membership in the implementation of the programmes adopted in the name of the movement. Until these producer classes burst directly into the arena of Uganda's politics as its subjects and without intermediaries, the Congress programmes will continue to suffer distortion. As the Congress vital components of youths, oppressed women, workers, poor peasants, and their allied and organic intellectuals come to truly assert themselves, a new national liberation movement may emerge on its own account, or in alliance with the producer and popular classes within the Congress.

In spite of its otherwise relatively *'good'* record of performance in the political management of the country, the UPC has yet to overcome the illusions prevalent in its thinking that national freedom, national integration and nation building, for instance, are attainable in the neo-colonial context and that balanced economic development can be achieved largely by tactical manoeuvres in the current world capitalist division of labour. It is principally these illusions that explain its past adventurism in regard to certain matters in its relations with forces and interests local and foreign that are fostered and supported by imperialism. The Ugandan socio-economic system, in which the capitalist structural imperative, of profit before all else, rules, has crippled most of its otherwise well-intentioned socio-economic programmes.

However, having once again as during the 1970's, together with the masses of the people, become the major victim of excessive violence and terror from their political opponents and the Ugandan fascist neo-colonial state, it has greater possibilities than all other political movements, organisations and parties to transform itself into an important rallying point for national democratic liberation. This however requires that it has to be able to discharge the political, ideological, organisational, and other intrinsic responsibilities and requirements of the struggle for national liberation.

The successful assumption of such responsibilities means that it must continue to popularly democratise all its basic workings, truly collectivise its decision making processes and forge a programme for national liberation that is able to assist the masses of people analyse and explain for themselves the root causes and the true nature and character of their country's problems which they have to face up to and resolve. This means that it has to be transformed from being a movement which merely enjoys the support of a large number of Ugandans, into, a democratic liberatory organisation for their fullest participation in their own liberation, political empowerment and for securing their future.

This in effect means that, the Congress has to be rebuilt from its base, including all its democratic structures such as the Congress of Workers/Labour Groups/Committees, the Congress Youth Brigade and the formerly vibrant UPC Youth and Women's Leagues which were destroyed by imperialism, its local stooges, collaborators and professional reactionaries in the UPC as an anti-colonial, anti-neo-colonial, anti-racist, anti-fascist and anti-imperialist party that stands for the Independence, Unity, Development and Prosperity of Uganda and her people. This is what would constitute a sound political platform for its transformation into a genuine national liberation movement through which the masses of people can win national freedom, people's rule and autonomous development in Uganda.

But, if like most Africanist political movements, it fails to undergo the necessary transformation into a key component of or into the required national liberation movement, it will become helplessly enmeshed in the snares and traps of the neo-colony, whose hostile political environment constrains and saps all popular potential and initiative. Indeed it is the task of its patriotic membership to seize the initiative, and take the giant step forward of leading its necessary transformation. Only such a bold move in the circumstances would enable the Congress to meet the challenges of its historic mission of organising and inspiring all Ugandans without exception to win national freedom and national democratic liberation and perpetuate these historic conquests.

The UPC political principles and party manifestos, particularly that of 1980, after the fall of the military dictatorship of the 1970's, and the Common Man's Charter of 1968/69/70 constitute a good basis, for it to have a rethink to reinvent its role in winning and sustaining political, social and national liberation in Uganda.

(iv) ILLUSORY STRATEGIES FOR OVERCOMING FACTIONALISM: THE UGANDA PATRIOTIC MOVEMENT (UPM) AND THE RISE OF THE NATIONAL RESISTANCE ARMY/MOVEMENT (NRA/M)

The evolution of the current political environment of fragmentation, division, and sectionalism has partly been due to the fact that the intervention of imperialism in the country exacerbated the earlier non-antagonistic contradictions amongst the people as to cloud the more fundamental issues that affect the wellbeing of all, and in the result generated a terrible situation of acrimony among the people.

In the contention of Uganda's social and political forces, imperialism and its local allies have used all and every means, including religious bigotry, nationality and ethnic chauvinism, to divide and manipulate the people into factions while it induce amongst them a negative framework of thought on such vital matters such as national liberation, the resolution of the outstanding national and social questions, nation formation in Uganda, et-cetera. Instead the NRA stands unashamedly promotive of the ruinous role of the iniquitous slave system the multinational capital and finance have imposed onto Uganda/Nile Africa and Africa.

Those among the political elite of Uganda, who lack a clear perspective of the situation obtaining and desperately want to rid Uganda of this negative framework, have fallen for the illusion that what Uganda/Nile Africa needs for instance, is principally *good leadership* which exists above factionalism. They have in vain worked to create elitist front organisations, which allegedly stand above sectionalism and among other things are supposed to be used to organise political and economic life in a manner that overcomes division in Uganda's politics and unfetters the system of economic production in

Uganda. Indeed, they falsely believed that an *"...integrated..."* and *"...self-sustaining..."* economy, can be achieved with the support of organs of international finance capital such as the International Monetary Fund (IMF), the World Bank and allied international financial organisations, and, with their due technical assistance and involvement, build a strong national economy. This is a strategy, which refuses to see the destructive, non-neutral and the non-mutual nature of relations that belie these said institutions and, or toxic nature of their *'aid'*! This is the slave ideology which partly inspired the formation of the defunct **Uganda Patriotic Movement (UPM)** and its successor, the **National Resistance Army/Movement (NRA/M)**. The world viewpoint adopted by the NRA/M has been used to entrap Uganda's modernisation and development efforts in the current negative international or global capitalist division of labour.

Another factor leading to this said adventurism has been their ignorance of the political and socio-economic reality of Uganda in its specific setting in the world imperialist system. The rise of camouflaged agent political movements of the NRA/M type that are the servitors of imperialism is illustrative of Africa's predicament in its struggles to resolve its outstanding problems. There can be no simplistic solution to Africa's predicament outside social, political and national liberation of its lands. Uganda's/Nile Africa's recent bitter political experiences, indicate that it is the people themselves who hold the capacity to overcome and transcend neo-colonial fascism and its tyranny in Uganda which endlessly generates ethnic chauvinism, religious bigotry and multiple negative divisions that favour the destructive and costly dominance of the country by multinational capital and finance.

The rise of organisations of the NRA type only escalates the spread of factionalism, sectionalism, and social and political fragmentation in neo-colonies such as Uganda. Factionalism as a political malaise can and will be overcome if, in the struggle for national freedom or popular national liberation, unity is promoted and nurtured from the roots of society itself rather than as hitherto vainly imposed from above society.

The other factor which has contributed as an impetus for the formation of the NRA/M is the ideology of the agent politicals and false-bourgeoisie, which deceptively represents Uganda's neo-colonial reality as being an arena in which human will and intentions, pegged on human determination, would be sufficient to overcome the terrible obtaining misery, suffering and oppression of the people in the context of the structurally constraining Ugandan neo-colonial synthesis. This deficient ideological position of the political forces that foster it is further promotive of the falsehoods, for instance, that various freedoms of the individual, human, peoples and other rights, can be actualised in Uganda/ Nile Africa in its current state as a neo-colony. Such erroneous thinking is based on the illusion that the exploitative and oppressive neo-colonial social and political systems can, given 'good leadership' be humanised and used to assert the human and peoples' rights of the oppressed Ugandan/Nile African people, who are its very victims! These old myths as continue to be propagated by the NRA and its foreign associates and, or support foundations of European and Scandinavian origin and allied ideologists, constitute no panacea to the endless sufferings and tribulations of the victims of fascist military dictatorship in Uganda. This line of thought instead creates in the people illusions, which in the end lead to cynicism and disbelief in the possibilities of winning victory over the iniquities of neo-colonialism through their own efforts. Such a situation is counterproductive to the oppressed people of Uganda and helps to protect and prolong the life of the very system from which the people only reap gross abuses, misery, and suffering.

The bitter experience of the people however, points towards the reality where the people shall on their own account and effort win human and peoples rights and freedoms, social and economic progress with the achievement of National Freedom. Then through the exercise of their sovereignty, they shall build a new and rich life for themselves in a free and independent African land in which their fundamental rights and freedoms are self-asserted and given effect. With the advantage of historical sense, it can be appreciated that the human and overall rights of the enslaved, such as was the case in the slave Egypt of the infamous biblical Pharaoh, could not be asserted or actualised, until under the leadership of the unforgettable Prophet Moses, the slaves self- emancipated and accessed the biblical land of Canaan, that was outside the control of the Pharaoh, the slave master of Egypt.

The other factor, which contributed to the formation of the NRA/M was the naked ambitions of 'the leading lights' of the NRA/M for state positions and raw power in the Ugandan neo-colony. Their determination to hold on to power today by waging permanent warfare against the people and through use of excessive force and violence;

terror, intimidation and blackmail, regardless of the consequences arising, further compounds the inherent situation of crisis and instability in the country.

In effect, this is yet another case in which gross violence and destruction such as that meted against the people in the operations of colonial agent General Semei Lwakilenzi Kakungulu seem to be repeated in contemporary times in Uganda/Nile Africa.

The NRA/M is a clear replay of the preceding colonial and neo-colonial nationality/ethnic-centred and degenerate armed political police machines, whose major function is not the defence of the interests of the people, but of their repression and the country's spoliation and plunder, despite NRA's rantings to the contrary. In Uganda's abnormal political condition today and the predominance of mercenary types in the NRA under a leadership and command that worships violence and must use it as a principal means of governance, the NRA political tenure and reign spells disaster for the country and the neighbouring African peoples to Uganda/Nile Africa.

In the mould of other militarist formations that preceded its accession to government, the NRA/M, like leeches and parasites, thrives and preys on the Ugandan/Nile African society which it is determined to hold captive, subdued and paralysed through; its regular uses of naked force and violence, terror and intimidation that it metes against the people, and its ready regular uses of its infamous weapons of political manipulation, bribery and corruption.

The NRA/M will consequently remain a mere terrorist organisation that wages permanent warfare against the people. It is folly to believe that it can support the Ugandan people to free themselves from the quagmire of neo-colonialism. By the end of its tragic mission and reign of terror in the country, history will not have little to say in the NRA's favour nor will it have ushered the country towards any "...*fundamental change...*" as it claims, which could have opened the way for society's advancement or progress.

The ever-widening gap between the NRA/M claims of achievement on the one hand, and the terrible surrounding realities in the country on the other, cannot be hidden. The simple truth is that the NRA/M is incapable of intellectually transcending its illusions, to say nothing about its quality of knowledge of the peculiar Ugandan capitalist system whose operational laws they are quite ignorant about.

Consequently what the NRA/M does in the circumstances "contradicts" all its claims, and what it ought to do cannot be done. This will remain the case until its exit from the Ugandan political scene. The NRA/M therefore finds itself irreversibly set on a historical blind alley, leading to its sure demise and perdition. Its ascendance to the governance of Uganda was only achieved through the funding and direct collusion of foreign interests and forces, which are inimical to the interests of true freedom for the peoples of the Nile River valley-lands and Africa. When its demise comes to pass, Africa will be wiser, if it can learn and put to its advantage relevant lessons from the bitter experiences of the people of Uganda/Nile Africa under the yoke of the NRA fascist regime.

(v) CHARACTERISTICS COMMON TO THE LEADERSHIP OF CONTEMPORARY UGANDAN SOCIAL AND POLITICAL FORCES

The political elite and false-bourgeoisie that constitute Uganda's governing circles, freely rotate in movement between various interdependent, but apparently contradictory tendencies within the confines of their class interests. As a result, the same set of individuals can without any shame whatsoever, come to adopt what on the face of it, are contradictory political positions.

Apart from the social and economic instabilities which are inherent in the country's neo-colonial social system; and the extreme fluidity and instabilities in the global capitalist system which find reflection amongst its agents in Uganda's governing circles; the unprincipled political about turns and sheer opportunism and careerism amongst this stratum of the Ugandan/Nile African society; is astounding.

They justify or rationalise their unprincipled, dramatic, and speculative political *"about turns"* as being necessary to accommodate the demands of changing times, different styles, political tones, and the peculiarities which are manifested within the politics and polity of Uganda. Their continuously changing political positions can however be partly explained by the endless intra-imperialist rivalry which finds reflection in the country and its politics in which they have to take sides. In any case, this class of people is equally subjected to the fragmentation and disintegration that affect all classes and groups in the tumultuous and, or turbulent systems of modernisation and economic growth without development that leads to destructive competition amongst the country's elite and false-bourgeoisie for the role of lead local political agents who serve the interests of the dominant world capitalist system.

The country's false-bourgeoisie and political elite has to viciously compete for the positions of intermediaries in the political management of the Ugandan neo-colonial social and economic system in the service of the interests of global capital concerns. This is a race in which the losers get trampled underfoot.

The majority of the Ugandan political elite and false-bourgeoisie, shall continue to be embroiled in this despicable competition until the masses of the people begin to intensify the process which will deprive them of these slave contests, i.e. actively seek a genuine and lasting resolution to the political problem of Uganda, through popular liberatory struggles. This is when some of them will begin to wake up to the rising social, popular and national demands of the times. Their class interests will however continue to constitute a serious handicap to their assimilation into the protagonist forces of the national liberation struggle. Indeed, only a minority of the members of Uganda's governing circles are likely to unite with the people in the sense of actively enjoining themselves with the people's aspirations and cause for political, social and national liberation.

The overwhelmingly subservient character of this section of society to imperialism must be taken into account and due appreciation, in the political work carried out by the people's emergent national liberation movement amongst the country's false-bourgeoisie and political elite.

In addition, the people's emergent national liberation movement will have to work hard to efface the political context which permits Imperialism and its Ugandan stooges to misuse and exploit, what were once merely local ideological, social, cultural, and political phenomena in the country, for its manipulation and division of the masses of the people of Uganda. To this end, the emergent national liberation movement has to work to accommodate all the Ugandan people in their diversity that aspire for and have to struggle to win national freedom, popular self-governance and African self-becoming in the country.

All structures constituted by man and woman, are inevitably subject to continuous change.

It is best then in this regard, when visualising the political structures obtaining in Uganda/ Nile Africa to take heed of the statement made by the Greek philosopher Aristotle, who was one of the great instructors of humankind in ancient Greece that:

*"...All things derive their essential character from their
function and their capacity; and it follows that if they are no
longer fit to discharge their function, we ought not to say
they are still the same things, but only, by an ambiguity,
they still have the same names..."*

It is evident that the time is now nigh for requisite imagination and
political innovation that can enthuse the Ugandan masses of people in
inventing and crafting viable ways and means, organisations, political
and liberatory prowess to pave the path to a new future. All victims of
fascism and its military dictatorship in the country stand duty bound to
rise to the liberatory challenges in this situation.

CHAPTER 3

THE ESSENCE OF UGANDA'S PROBLEM

In contemporary times, it is imperative that the chronic problem of Uganda be visualized in new light.

Eduardo Galeano[45], the late and lamented Latin American intellectual and poet, visualized the contexts of the situations that are similar to that of Uganda thus:

> *"...The big bankers of the world, who practice the terrorism of money, are more powerful than kings and field marshals, even more than the Pope of Rome himself...*
>
> *"...They never dirty their hands...*
>
> *"...They kill no one: they limit themselves to applauding the show...*
>
> *"...Their officials, international technocrats, rule our countries; they are neither presidents nor ministers, they have not been elected, but they decide the level of salaries and public expenditure, investments and divestments, prices, taxes, interest rates, subsidies, when the sun rises and how frequently it rains...*
>
> *"...However, they don't concern themselves with the prisons or torture chambers or concentration camps or extermination centres, although these house the inevitable consequences of their acts...*
>
> *"...The technocrats claim the privilege of irresponsibility...;*
>
> *" '...we are neutral...'*
>
> *"...they say..."*

The struggle for national freedom and political, social and national liberation in Uganda is now as complex as the obtaining global and national situation demands.

Ever since the last quarter of the 19th century, imperialism has been confronted with the problem of building internal power relations that

---

[45] Galeano - Collection of Poems, 1991, p.108

would ensure or sustain Uganda's slave placing in the world capitalist division of labour and market.

This placing in the world's capitalist economy is a central aspect of the problem of Uganda. In the final analysis, this is what principally continues to determine the nature and character of the power relations and state administrative structures, which have evolved in the country. These structures have to be aligned to meet the capitalist structural imperative of ensuring economic surpluses and profit for capital in the Ugandan economy.

It was in the vain search for suitable power relations and state administrative structures that would uphold the basic demands of imperialism that *'indirect rule'*, the harbinger of today's neo-colonialism in Uganda, took root not only in the kingdom and chieftainship areas, but throughout Uganda. The exigiencies, and difficulties of maintaining political power in the face of the stiff opposition and resistance of the people determines and defines the necessity for the 'hidden' and, or indirect and masked character of alien supported rule and power relations in Uganda. The Federal Constitution and power arrangements bequeathed to Uganda at political independence (1962), the unitary Republican State Constitution (since 1967) and the subsequent Fascist State Constitution (of 1996); were mechanisms forged to superintend Uganda in a way, which would preserve Uganda's placing in the world capitalist division of work and market, and, secure often by force or engineered consent, the survival of the system of plunder and spoliation of the natural and bio resources of the country and robbery of the fruits of labour of the Ugandan people.

The latter constitution provides for Uganda to be run on the basis of hegemonic allied bloc of local agents and *'nyampalas'*[46] from the political classes in the country. It has been the most suitable instrument for the control, administration, and management of the Uganda, which serves the fundamental interests of imperialism. Indeed any attempts at popular and national democratic actions and necessary constitutional formation while Uganda remains a neo-colony are only likely to be cosmetic additions to power arrangements which marginalise and practically disenfranchise the common people in the politics of Uganda and enhances the careerist role of the country's false-bourgeoisie and the Ugandan political elite. It obstacles and makes impossible the direct participation of the majority of her people,

---

[46] Ibid 2

(youths, peasant, pastoralists, Indigenous Peoples, labourers, workers, poor women, artisans, the self-employed and indeed all the producers of the country's sustenance and wealth, and the unemployed), in the governance of Uganda. It is a falsehood that such constitutions can be made into instruments of popular, social and national democracy!! Peoples' rule in its genuine sense, can only mature in conditions where the people and their social and political organisations have overcome the structural political and social constraints of the neo-colony and have initiated irreversible processes that confer upon themselves the subjectivity of their own history.

The real issue of major concern to Ugandans in contemporary times is that of winning national freedom, which is a necessary condition to create national peoples power and modalities for its judicious exercise, and not merely that of superficial constitutional reform that is meant to sanctify neo-colonial despotism. The claims that constitutions and even a neo-colonial constitution at that, with humanistic preambles, bills of rights and similar articles can provide a legal framework which may be successfully used to fight for the freedom and rights of the people, ignore the critical absence and non-existence of suitable conditions of their realisation in neo-colonies. In Uganda's situation, where civil society, suffers gross constraints and the producer classes and their allies have yet to assert their presence in political society and where militarism has made the state, its courts and other civil structures its direct dependencies; it is only a new, qualitatively more suitable and accountable democratic political power which will contain and neutralise the neo-colonial and militarist power (and not merely a constitution); that can create conditions where all can successfully fight to assert their democratic rights and freedoms. The latter demands that neo-colonialism, its militarism and tyranny must first of necessity be politically overcome and transcended so that suitable conditions for the emergence of sovereign power makes it possible for the people to assert their democratic rights and freedoms.

No mere agenda-driven Constitution will ever bestow upon the common Ugandan peoples, the power they have not won themselves in reality or in practise. No constitution will guarantee for the common people of Uganda the rights and freedoms they cannot directly assert or which they do not practically maintain through their own power which is supported by a political and an economic system which is truly their own. A Constitution merely provides for and recognises a specific system of power relations and its parameters, but cannot bestow power or transfer power from one class to another. For human freedoms, which are largely dependent on the reality, nature and character of the political power in place, like power itself, are won and not merely granted.

The peoples struggles in Uganda cannot hence merely revolve around the question of constitution or new power arrangements in the neo-colony, but are meant to create a political foundation which will permit the rise of a new, sovereign, democratic, and just Uganda. When national freedom and national democratic liberation are won and a new, just and democratic Uganda rises, a popular national democratic constitution will be designed reflecting the people's interests and rights in the context of popular national democracy. This truly popular and home grown and autochthonous constitution shall provide the necessary political/legal framework for the further fostering of national and popular democratic processes and power. The false democracy which starts and ends with the election of the country's rulers from the idle classes has, until now, permitted the parasitic careerist elite and false-bourgeoisie to paralyse the masses after the day of their election into positions of governance, through wide-scale political deception and manipulation, while these same tricksters get empowered to share with imperialism in the ruthless plunder of the country's biodiversity and natural resources endowments, and at the same time benefiting from the game of open day robbery of the fruits of labour of the people.

Historically, the misuse by imperialism of Buganda Kingdom Protestant forces or the armed forces allied to the governing circles of Buganda, in combination with the Indian and British commanded Swahili and Nubian colonial mercenary forces, to subjugate large areas of Uganda for colonialism constituted the rise of the military machine requisite to open up the country to the build-up of local allied governance formations loyal to the imperialist system that has with new configurations continued to dominate Uganda. The entire gamut of colonial politics, which followed thereafter revolved around the questions of preserving, modifying or reforming the legacy of indirect agent rule such as the 1900 British-Buganda agreement and other similar pacts. The politics of neo-colonial Uganda has continued to be tainted with the ideological positions and sentiments propagated around these political arrangements. The Kabaka Yekka (KY) movement [and its successor Conservative Party (CP)] for instance, bases all its political programmes on the need to revive the essence of these said socio-political arrangements. The social force organising for it in this context, remembers with nostalgia that the impoverished land tenants, the landless, the poor peasants, and the farm hands in Buganda who constitute the majority in that area, were placed in a situation where they have had to support the beneficiaries of the 1900 British-Buganda arrangements because of the sheer economic and political prowess that the said landed and propertied circles wielded over them in Buganda. The said economic and political power which was instituted throughout the systems of family, nationality, ethnic and pseudo-feudal ties, which generate nationality discrimination and ethnic chauvinism meted against migrant labour in rural Buganda, broke the possible solidarity of the impoverished masses with other Ugandans. They had little option but to side with their masters.

Their situation is characteristic of the down trodden who live in a socio-economic system of servitude and are deprived of the vision of prospects of their own liberation. Until Uganda begins to undergo the necessary processes pertaining to national liberation, which would restore the confidence of its people in the prospects of their freedom and collective strength, the negative ideology of these landed and propertied circles will continue to be used to justify the dominance of the local lords of plunder in the lives of the masses of people in Buganda region. In a compound formation such as the multi-structural, multi-nationality, multi-class, and multi-faith dependent society that has emerged in Uganda, it is understandable how the 1900/1955 agreement and similar arrangements of indirect rule and sentiment associated with them have remained crucial as ideological and mobilisational tools in the country's political life.

The process of decolonisation preserved the principal interests of imperialism in Uganda and sustained its concerns and that of her allies as underpinned by the 1900/1955, and such other similar, arrangements. These interests were fundamental in defining the nature and character of power relations, which were established at colonisation and, configured immediately before and after independence, as well as the state structures, which were adopted for the exercise of political power.

As a result, there has not emerged any complete, sovereign or independent, national governance formation or state created by a truly independent and autonomous national political power, but merely an administration and its structure in the service of the interests of neo-colonialism and its parasitic local agent alliance.

What became conspicuous in a situation such as this is the burden of negative traditions, the ideology imposed on the people by the pseudo-feudal, colonial and neo-colonial power systems of domination, political isolation of communities in nationality formations etc. These have combined to insulate the people from practical experiences of other struggling peoples of the world who find themselves in a similar predicament as Ugandans.

It is this said legacy, that all those forces that are interested in freeing the political, economic, cultural and social development of Uganda from the dominance of imperialism are working to overcome so that, national freedom/national liberation and nation formation/constitution, national development are inaugurated and achieved, and a new, just, sovereign and democratic Uganda can be born.

In the final analysis, it is the country's negative integration into the workings of the world capitalist division of labour and market that gives life to the anti-democratic system which constrains any possibilities for creating popular sovereignty in the country.

This subservient link with the world capitalist system has constrained all the possibilities of, autonomous economic development and overcoming economic backwardness in Uganda. It makes it impossible to initiate a process of overcoming under-development, economic backwardness and the institution of new systems and processes for national economic development.

Whereas in the past, the country registered economic growth and surpluses, these could not be transformed into a capital base for development, due to the constraints inhibiting the country's progress in the world capitalist division of work and market, which makes it impossible to transform surpluses into national developmental capital.

Uganda's economic experience ever since political independence shows that no possibilities for genuine national economic development exist for it in the current world capitalist division of labour and market. Every conceivable economic policy has been tried for the development of the country in the context of the world capitalist division of work and market including active regional economic co-operation in which Uganda and Tanzania constituted the largest markets for the products of foreign investments that were based in Kenya. This latter regional economic reality has so remained in fundamentals, though European, Asian and other forms of foreign capital have made direct inroads into the Ugandan market. Uganda to date remains in basics, an agricultural commodity producing economy, rooted in the household producing units.

Economic independence calls for the necessity to re-embed the economy into the needs and imperatives of providing the social, material, developmental and cultural requirements of the people of Uganda. Hitherto the country has been driven by the world capitalist economy and its needs, instead of those of the people and the developmental needs of the country.

A summary of Uganda's recent experiences in the world capitalist economy will illustrate the extent to which the country is without a future of genuine development within the current negative world capitalist division of work and market.

a) Between 1962 and 1967 the country's economic policies favoured balanced budgets, tight control of money supply, free global movement of capital and an open door to foreign investments. This was the phase of liberal economic policies and the era of the famous 3 'Cs' (Coffee, Cotton and Copper) and 3 'Ts' (Tea, Tobacco and Tourism). Each raw material was meant to provide a base for planned construction of related industries in the country's then projected development processes. The driver points of these developmental processes were the Uganda Development Corporation (UDC), the (central) Bank of Uganda (BOU) and local and national institutions of Co-operatives.

b) Between 1967 and 1969 the same policies were basically continued, but with a greater stress on selective investments in a national development perspective. This involved combining private capital and state or state-backed investments and activating co-operative capital in the economy.

c) The third phase, which ran from late 1969 to early 1971, was a period of re-evaluation. It recognised the inherently exploitative nature of the global capitalist economy, the inequalities imposed on under-developed countries in global trade, finance, and in the capital accumulation and investment systems of the world capitalist economy, and the impossibility of fostering an autonomous development process within its confines.

It was recognised definitively by 1970 that winning autonomy from this exploitative global socio-economic system, which constrained the possibilities of Uganda's economic progress, could become possible if and when the necessary transformation of the society upon which the system was imposed in Uganda was realised and catalysed to forward drive overall transformative change in the country.

Resistance and sabotage from imperialism and its local vested interests though foreseen, managed to assert itself vigorously enough to smother by 1971 any strategies that were intended to win freedom from this system. A malnourished and weak child of imperialism, which Uganda still is, obviously could not win a frontal war against a physically fit and robust rogue father. It was a frontal confrontation of unequals. Except for some indigenisation or localisation of the service economy i.e. acquisition of ownership of local trade and economic services, there was an inevitable wholesale return to the policies of classical neo-colonial economic system in 1971. Then, the Ugandan false-bourgeoisie expelled its Indian/Asian counterpart in order to seize for itself the role of sole intermediary in the economic exploitation of Uganda by imperialism. Ever since, the economic policies and programmes of the country have continued to be tossed back and forth between competing variants of the same policy positions, which favour the interests of global capital in Uganda.

In the context of the country's economy of obsolete agricultural methods and non-organic indigenous light industry, the only rational strategy for salvation appears to lie in working out a popular development strategy aimed at initiating locally rooted industrialisation processes that will bring about an agricultural revolution in a new democratic Uganda. The sad reality today is that all Uganda's attempts to achieve real national economic progress have been constrained by the workings of the global capitalist economic framework where without external capital and technical assistance, it is difficult to see through even the smallest development project. 'Development' projects of any kind at all have been initiated only with the grace of foreign godfathers who profit from them. Today, not even the dimmest light is in sight for the genuine economic development of Uganda. Indeed, economic decay and stagnation that faces Uganda has now compounded the escalating indebtedness of the country and the corresponding social calamities, which these generate and continue to buffet the unprotected Ugandan masses of people.

The full impact of these worsening conditions have yet to be felt as they get steadily compounded by the monetarist *'Structural Adjustment Programs' (SAP)* imposed through the International Monetary Fund (IMF) and its associated agencies. These measures have resulted in the steady erosion of the common people's production capacities, regular production activities and purchasing power in Uganda's multi-market economy. This economy negates all possibilities of reviving production with which to create necessary or requisite surplus levels that would be used to generate autonomous development in the foreseeable future.

With this perilous experience, it should be clear even to the most short-sighted or myopic that Uganda's economic problems are not merely transient or even of a monetarist nature. But alas!

The demeaning role of management of Uganda's crisis-ridden socio-economic system is principally left by imperialism to its surrogate, local social and political groups whose job it is to preserve and promote its interests in return for crumbs from the masters' tables. This servant-like linkage to the system of imperialism and the zero-sum contentions among the country's social and political forces for local power hegemony in the country is central in defining the directions in which the Uganda crisis is headed.

Uganda's socio-economic system, which evolved and matured as a dependent formation of imperialism, has from its inception constituted an obstacle to the autonomous socio-economic, political and cultural progress of the country. Through its linkages with imperialism, this system pillages the country and viciously exploits its people while relaying to Uganda the traumatic eruptions and convulsions occurring in the centres of the world capitalist system to the overall detriment of this unprotected African country and her people.

The net effect of the contradictions, antagonisms, and conflicts there arising, explains why Ugandan political institutions are in permanent crisis and why political instability and turbulence is typical of the Ugandan situation. The country's inherent problems stem first and foremost from the truncated and perverse neo-colonial capitalist socio-economic system, which is now in deep crisis. The problems of disunity are therefore, not as have been alleged, that they emanate principally from the inherent incompatibility and divisions of the country's nationalities, ethnic groups or political party sectionalism. Visualised in this perspective, it can then be appreciated that these are not the type of problems, which are to be overcome simply by creating new constitutions or merely effecting regime change or its political leadership in administering the Ugandan neo-colony.

It is therefore clear that without Uganda winning an existence of its own, independent of imperialism, the Ugandan crisis will continue to deepen and get compounded by the inevitable and inherent political conflict and conflagrations of violence and bloodshed that get generated in place in this African country.

The people's continuing struggles to defend themselves from the vagaries of the crisis of this system, will therefore not end until the impediments that the system has erected, blocking the country's forward movement to National Freedom and unhampered political, economic, social, and cultural progress, are overcome and transcended.

This fight for genuine National Independence calls for the total mobilisation of the country's fundamental political forces, i.e. the entire ordinary people. These are the only forces capable of being constituted into a conscious, organised, productive people's fighting organisation which has the strength to stand its ground, overcome alien pressures of all forms while creating the material forces; economic, political, military, technical, scientific and cultural for the unencumbered, untrammelled or autonomous development of the country.

The common Ugandan people have nothing to lose from the neo-colonial system of which they are victims and which treats them as mere objects, but their perilous slave existence of endless suffering and extreme distress.

CHAPTER 4

THE POLITICS OF NEW FASCISM, MILITARISM, AND MASS MANIPULATION: THE CRUEL 'NYAMPALA'[47] AND AGENT RULE OF "THE OMUZUNGU AGAMBYE"[48] AFRICANS IN UGANDA

> "...Our system is one of detachment: to keep silenced people from asking questions, to keep the judged from judging, to keep solitary people from joining together, and the soul from putting together its pieces..."

Eduardo Galeano

The African fascist dictatorships such as that which has reduced Uganda to the slave conditions of plunder and open spoliation by ravenous interests of alien capital and finance, and their forces of utter greed have had to evolve its own destructive type of fascist leadership and system of fascist rule. Fascism was depicted as follows:

> "...Fascism denies that the majority, through the mere fact of being a majority, can rule human societies ...
>
> "...By democratic regimes we mean those which from time to time the people is given the illusion of being sovereign while true sovereignty lies in other perhaps irresponsible and secret forces ...
>
> "...Fascism rejects in democracy, the absurd conventional lie of political equalitarianism ..."

[Il Duce (The chief) Benito Mussolini/ Founder of Italian fascist movement; The butcher and genocider of the Ethiopian people]

One great mind, a renowned Italian writer and intellectual, Ignazio Silone, in his effort to shed light on the character, tragic political role and erratic behaviour of the self-styled, Il Duce (The chief), Benito Mussolini – the Italian fascist leader, advised the following to a friend who sought to write Mussolini's biography:

---

[47] Ibid 2
[48] Ibid 4

*"...The key to understanding Mussolini is his inconsistency;
both of character and ideas, combined with the extra-ordinary
intuitive capacity for improvisation...*
*"...In every crisis of his career, he swung over completely from
his previous attitude, and always successfully...*
"...The only constant was his desire for power...
"...You should always bear this in mind...
*"...The suddenness of Mussolini's emergence as a leader was a
result of dramatic political events that unfolded at the
beginning of his career...*
*"...He was sprung into a sudden prominence, for which he was
completely unprepared...*
"...Mussolini had very few and very confused ideas...
*"...Even in his early socialist days, he did not adhere to
orthodox socialist doctrines...*
*"...You must resist the temptation of creating a consistent
figure. It would always be a falsification..."*

Another poet and Greek revolutionary, the late Alexandros (Alekos)
Panagoulis, had this to say on the character of Benito Mussolini, the
fascist self-styled Il Duce (The chief) of the Italians:

*"...When I was in Rome, I saw a film with Mussolini speaking to
the crowd from Palazzo Venezia...*
*"...I was astonished and wondered how Italians had managed to
put up for so many years with such a ridiculous man who spoke
in such a ridiculous way...*
*"...And yet Mussolini was a powerful dictator and in this way
capable..."*

Panagoulis[49] on another occasion could not, but exclaim:

*"...God damn it! You cannot let a whole nation be transformed
into a herd of sheep...*
"...And listen, I am not dreaming of utopia...
*"...I know very well that absolute justice doesn't exist; that it
will never exist...*
*"...But I know there are countries where a process of justice
gets applied...*

---

[49] Alexandros (Alekos) Panagoulis, Poet and Greek political prisoner September 1973] - in Oriana Fallaci: Interview with History, 1973

"...So what I am dreaming of is a country where those who get attacked, insulted, deprived of their rights can demand justice in a court...

"...Is that too much to ask?...

"...Bah! It seems to me, the least a man can ask...

"...That's why I get so angry with cowards who don't rebel when their fundamental rights are violated...

"...I wrote on their walls while in the Greek fascist prisons that:

"...I hate tyrants and cowards disgust me...

"...It is an honour for Italians that, Benito Mussolini, came to the end he did..."

After the fascist dictatorship was defeated by Italian partisans and allies, Benito Mussolini was apprehended, timely tried and punished.

Mussolini and his fellow European fascists, who included Adolf Hitler of Germany, Gen. Francisco Franco of Spain, Antonio Salazar of Portugal, etc. shared many common characteristics as political personages that have played tragic roles in the histories of their countries and the world.

These were degenerate political personages who had to face up to the impossible situations of vainly attempting to contain and estop the direct intervention into history by the oppressed and mass of exploited and marginalised European humanity. Their attempts to contain and bring to an end the social and political turbulence and volatility inherent in the systems, over which they presided, proved futile.

In Asia, in Indonesia, in Haiti, in the Caribbean, in Central and Southern America etc. fascist social and political systems were created especially after the end of the Second World War, to contain and bring 'order' to the instabilities that the ruthless neo-colonial socio-economic systems; generated into place in those countries.

Africa, itself a long standing victim of capital driven spoliation, has suffered tribulations that are comparable to those of the peoples who have fallen victim to impossible iniquities in older non-African fascist social, economic and political systems.

The abnormal political conditions that have prevailed in Uganda for the past decades, pose a major problem for all those who are placed in a position of responsibility for running this system, faced as they are with the great opposition and resistance of the Ugandan people and the general turbulence which is inherent in the Ugandan social system.

The lead supervisory role over this increasingly shaky system is often the prize that the Ugandan false-bourgeoisie and other pro-imperialist political forces fight and compete for. From time to time when this task proves too difficult, all their democratic pretences are tossed aside, and imperialism and its local allies resort to authoritarian or unadulterated violent and despotic management of the system under armed force and military formation.

The overt encouragement and support that imperialism has given to coup d'états or military intervention in power relations in Uganda, and the opposition it has exhibited against a popular resolution of the country's political crisis, betrays the magnitude of the crisis, which can only be temporarily contained by such overt interference in the country's internal affairs. Because the local allies of imperialism and the guardians of their interests in Uganda, are unable to control the central factors that determine the major events in the country, the proper management of Uganda's continuously fluid and disruptive if not turbulent socio-economic system, becomes an impossible task, even under a military formation. The vain attempts, which have been or are made through the use of force and violence to govern Uganda have plunged the country into an almost permanent crisis, political turbulence and instability. The magnitude and seriousness of the crisis is also reflected in the chronic factional struggles that continuously divide and split the ranks of the local allies of imperialism in Uganda.

These factional struggles wreak havoc on the much-needed unity of the neo-colonial leadership of the country and weaken its ability to handle popular political eruptions and rebellions for freedom, which inherently emerge in the country. It is an impossibility to maintain even a semblance of unity among the local agent politicals who manage the country's neo-colonial system. Yet, for imperialism, this is the litmus test for all regimes that run neo-colonial Uganda.

Persistent failure to fulfil the requirements of unity amongst the governing political elite, partly explains the quick rotation of regimes in Uganda in which the influence of imperialism stands dominant. This situation has placed the Ugandan allies of imperialism in a serious predicament and without a way out.

Consequently, illusions now have to be propagated yet again, to the effect that political factionalism and instability inherent in the country's political and socio-economic system can be overcome if an elitist organisation with allegedly *'messianic'* leadership is created for the country. This idea was central in the formation of the **Uganda Patriotic Movement (UPM)**, forerunner of the National Resistance Army (NRA). The NRA/M however proved to be only yet another of the militarist organisations created from above society in the vain attempt to stem the problems of political factionalism, division and instability in Uganda. Today, it finds itself as a political minority in the predicament of trying fruitlessly to root itself into the reality of Uganda against the overall mass opposition from and resistance of the people.

The idea of overcoming political factionalism amongst the elite and Ugandan false-bourgeoisie may be an attractive idealist sentiment, which is however unachievable in the neo-colonial reality. The lure of such simplistic solutions for overcoming factionalism have led many, including some of the intellectuals who are imbued with good will for the people, to set up political organisations and movements in the name of the people which however are not rooted in them. Unwittingly, these misguided intellectuals only help to fuel the very factionalism that they wish to overcome!! In this regard, they are a large part of the malaise or disease, not the cure of factionalism.

This is the experience in the anti-fascist struggles of the 1970s, and from the mid-1980s up to now in the struggle against fascism, its militarism, genocide, spoliation and plunder in the country. This social category often unwittingly pretends to be a cure to the country's chronic political malaise. Yet, in effect, they are the significant part of the political problem of Uganda.

In the current situation of incomplete, and perverse capitalist development of Uganda, the Ugandan false-bourgeoisie and the political elite cannot be welded into a stratum or class which would resolve contradictions amongst and within itself by consensus and hence promote its requisite class unity. The environment, in which it is rooted, i.e. of speculative agent economic activity and intra-imperialist rivalry over Africa's strategic and mineral resources, only makes the unity of this group more problematic and its continued central role in governance unsuited.

The glaring failure to build a sustainable alliance of the **Uganda Peoples Congress (UPC)/Kabaka Yekka (KY)** leaderships in the 1960's and the disintegration of the **Uganda Nation Liberation Front (UNLF)** within only eighteen months from its formation, are an eloquent testimony, of the inability of the political elite and false-bourgeoisie to unite in a neo-colonial Uganda. The latter front, the UNLF, was a child of political convenience of the leadership of nineteen elitist and exile organisations on the one hand, and the UPC, KY and Democratic Party (DP) exile leaderships on the other. A similar fate has met the NRA/M militarist alliances, which have been formed with their fellow political opportunists and warlords leading or claiming to lead tribally or ethnic based armed outfits. The threat of fragmentation facing the country's political elite and false-bourgeoisie, and the deficiency in their political cultures undermine the efforts made to unite them as a governing class. Their lack of command of the economic power of the country debilitates them and undermines their efforts for class unity.

Moreover, the processes of decolonisation, which gave them undue prominence, did not help matters. They thrust upon the country, borrowed forms of political organisation at independence and an alien state organisation, which was superimposed on a very complex reality. This reality contains multi-layered, multiple ideological-political tendencies and extremely fragmented political groups. Many of the political organisations led by the Ugandan political elite and false-bourgeoisie, for instance, while claiming to be national; merely reflect the reality of political fragmentation amongst the elite and false-bourgeoisie, and diverse non-national, political and ideological tendencies.

Only a popular national democratic liberation movement can serve as the starting point from which Ugandans can begin to overcome factionalism, and the unprincipled schemery among the country's false-bourgeoisie and political elite. For, winning national freedom from imperialism through forging a national democratic liberation movement means working to build a uniting and magnetising political and socio-economic environment, where divisive politics of the elite and false bourgeoisie is negated and the unity of the people and national organisation is made principal and fulcrumic.

Indeed, it is only the success of the process of popular national democratic liberation that will also save the country from the false line and adventure of vainly trying to create messianic leadership as a means for solving the country's problems.

Ugandan revolutionary democrats must not fall for the illusions propagated by the discredited agent political elite. Their historical role is not to unite the Ugandan elite or pseudo-bourgeoisie who are not representative of the people, nor to act in place of the people, but rather to enjoin and help actualise the aspirations of the people. Their role is to stimulate and co-ordinate the people's initiative, to encourage them to further dare act to win national freedom, to dare think for themselves, and even to dare make mistakes in winning national freedom and to learn valuable lessons in the process by correcting them so as to gradually gain control over their own destiny. This is what will assist the people to learn to acquire a deeper understanding of their common liberatory struggles, and enable them to progress toward the collective and conscious transformation of their world. Otherwise, Ugandan revolutionary democrats will become mere accomplices in the neo-colonial processes, which are meant to dissipate and disorient and paralyse the liberatory mass movement.

Revolutionary democrats will therefore have to learn from the masses of exploited and oppressed African people, and with them, be able to collectively defeat the schemes for perpetuating those myths, which serve the interests of imperialism.

Ugandans must not continue to battle in vain to create the imaginary 'good leadership' of the NRA type or 'nyampala'[50]-run elitist political movements, which are allegedly endowed with the unique capacity to overcome and transcend factionalism in the country. Genuine popular and democratic leadership which the people command and stands accountable to them shall only arise in the context of national liberation which is to lead to the resolution of Uganda's historical and political problems.

It is imperative for Ugandans to appreciate the fact that, it is only in this process of popular and mass struggle for national liberation that a united popular national democratic leadership of the country, which is at one with the cause of the people shall evolve and rise.

The real mission of the National Resistance Army/Movement (NRA/M)-regime of genocide, spoliation and plunder and its underlying motive for its accession to government, is to impose the much needed mafia order amongst Uganda's neo-colonial 'nyampala'[51] and agent politicals under a 'new-look' fascist authoritarian military formation for 'the organised spoliation and management' of the country on behalf of imperialism. The accession of the NRA to government has been intended to eliminate what are considered obstacles to this imagined order and 'unity' amongst, and of the country's agent politicals. In this regard, the 'game plan' of the NRA regime differs in no way whatsoever

---

[50] Ibid 2
[51] Ibid 2

from the militarist regimes that preceded it. But neither imperialism nor the NRA regime of genocide, spoliation and plunder, have the power or ability to better manage the ever haemorrhaging socio-economic system and political upheavals which are inherent in Uganda's neo-colonial system particularly when it hits peak crisis.

The NRA regime of genocide, spoliation and plunder is simply yet another militarist caste created at the new critical phase of primitive accumulation of capital by dispossession to impose order and govern Uganda on behalf of ravenous imperialism.

This caste of local agents, *'nyampalas'*[52] and the *'Omuzungu Agambye'*[53] Africans, which inherited, carried over and exacerbated all the faults of the old agent governing classes, or the country's political classes, took undue advantage of its placing and exploited the urge of the people to win for themselves necessary dignity to get to government.

Yet, it can hardly fulfil the tasks of maintaining 'order' which imperialism demands of it, because, like its predecessors, it is powerless to resolve the social crisis that on end buffets Uganda, which is a product of the endless crisis of economic structures within the worldwide capitalist system. It has neither national nor trans-national power to overcome this endless and destructive crisis. Moreover, the hegemony it attempts to build has no solid national class foundation to back it. It neither enjoys unqualified political support from the country's producer classes nor from any single rural, let alone a solid urban class stratum. The country's public servants and employees and other service personnel are held at ransom as its pawns and satraps.

In the circumstances, as the masses of people rise to confront the crisis in which they are engulfed, the regime of genocide, spoliation and plunder is forced to ensure its survival in government by violence, terror and intimidation, subterfuges, open lies and manipulation of the people. It is in this perspective that the aggression that the regime of genocide, spoliation and plunder metes against the people has to be understood; for the NRA from its very inception has been fighting the people who have refused to fall for its illusions.

The regime's hold on the Ugandan political situation is therefore ever precarious. The NRA regime merely fulfils the function of military occupation of the country as is required by imperialism during profound

---

[52] Ibid 2
[53] Ibid 4

all-round crises such as those, which engulf Uganda today. This regime of genocide, spoliation and plunder seeks in vain to build a countrywide alliance of political schemers, careerists and speculators (who are either harmless to or are in direct service of imperialism) behind a '*...strongman...*', or a type of '*...helmsman...*' or '*...bully-boy...*' to whom all authority and power of direction is supposed to be reposed. In the circumstances, the deepening political quandary of the regime and its lack of positive popular achievements leads it into tactics of mass deception where it has to falsely laud non-existent achievements such as '*national unity*', equality, prosperity and progress, and to constantly propagate falsehoods that are intended to deceive the peoples of the world and to distract the masses of people of Uganda from the need to overcome on their own account and steam the crisis engulfing them in conditions of deep misery and great distress. The fascist military regime therefore has to continue to attempt to falsify reality and seek to distract the people from the imperative need and duty to face up to and work to resolve the real problem of Uganda. This charade cannot continue forever. It is political fraud.

The issues at hand in the Uganda of fascist military dictatorship, spoliation, plunder and gross mass economic distress cannot for instance be, the rule of '*Southerners*'[54] as against that of '*Northerners*'[55], or the rule of those political elite '*East*' or '*West*' of the Nile, or that of creating the allegedly good leadership of the NRA type. The regime's project of a political minority ruling a dissenting political majority, by force and violence, terror and intimidation, political manipulation and deception now stands naked before all.

These falsehoods only reflect the continuing dishonesty and hypocrisy of the parasitic Ugandan political elite and false-bourgeoisie who wish to perpetuate their degenerate intermediary role in the governance of the country under marauding imperialism.

The NRA-regime knows that it hears only its voice while it hangs on the illusion that what it hears is the voice of oppressed Ugandan people! As a result, it refuses to understand why the people do not act or behave as it expects of them, i.e. why they are in continuous agitation and revolt.

---

[54] Infers to the 'Ntu' (Bantu) nationalities. A platform on which the National Resistance Army was constructed that the Ntu (Bantu) were marginalised in the governance of Uganda. Ibid 1.

[55] Infers to the non-Ntu (Bantu) largely associated with 'Nilotes' (People of Nile River) said to have dominated / monopolised the instruments of power and political governance of Uganda. Ibid 1 & 39.

The NRA-regime of genocide, spoliation and plunder is making a serious mistake if it believes for one minute that the hostility and opposition of the people to its rule of terror, violence, and spoliation is temporary, transient or is merely a passing phenomenon. Such illusions result from its refusal to appreciate the very grave political and socio-economic situation of deep crisis that it has triggered, and catapulted the country into. The only possible resolution of this all-encompassing and destructive crisis is through winning at last, for Uganda/Nile Africa, national freedom and democratic liberation from imperialism, and the power of independent being and self-renewal.

At such a point as Uganda has now reached, no amount of demagoguery or manipulation can erase the political urge for National Liberation, for these are the moments when the fascist military regime's political deception and trickery become transparent to the country's millions of oppressed and exploited, and indeed exhaust themselves. At the same time, the country has now reached a historical junction, which demands that society's problems be resolved by those forces with the capacity to move it forward, i.e. outside and far beyond the contemporary overall socio-economic and political quagmire. The debilitating lack of popular support in the continuously deteriorating socio-economic and political situation, where the regime has to attempt nevertheless to manage the endless crisis, induces it into desperation; to effect more callous spoliation and pillage, and to fight for its life by unleashing greater terror and repression against all those who continue to rise against the terrible misery that they suffer.

These disparate and repressive acts are aimed at permanently cowing down the people so that they can continue to be taken undue advantage of by the parasitic political elite and false-bourgeoisie. These notorious practices shall have to be effaced in the emergent processes of national democratic liberation. To achieve this, it is necessary to nourish a democratic alliance of the producer classes and toiling masses of the people of Uganda, who are the only people who can constitute a permanent bulwark against the cruel and destructive rule and dominance of imperialism and its local allies. This liberatory alliance cries to be built amongst and from toilers and labourers, workers and impoverished peasants, small producers and farmers, native and indigenous peoples, urban and rural impoverished, slum dwellers, artisans, artists, impoverished intellectuals, students and youths, Uganda's multiply oppressed women, and all victims of marginalisation in the country.

The issue of principal import in the country now is winning national freedom and establishing popular and national democratic power and, not the enactment of fictitious constitutions or the holding of sham elections, which are intended to trick the masses into assisting the regime overcome its chronic predicament of political illegitimacy. A neo-colonial system, which inherently exploits, marginalises and oppresses the masses can never be democratised nor transformed to the service of its victims.

The people, who are the first victims of imperialist oppression and exploitation, are able to see through the regime's political deceptions, when it falsely claims that, with discipline, hard work, leadership codes, etc. in a situation in which corruption is endemic; general poverty shall be overcome and prosperity achieved.

Over time, as the level of general and mass revolt heightens, the NRA-regime will be forced to try to present any fleeting bad and unjust political arrangement which it may make with political careerists, opportunists and job seekers, and speculative warlords etc. as political solutions to the political crisis of the country and falsely present itself as a saviour of the terrorised populace. But beasts are not known for making peace with their prey. Peace, at this juncture of crisis in the country, can only be achieved through the total popular political effacement of fascism and its military dictatorship in the country and the uprooting of the basis of the rise of possible similar dictatorships in the future.

Meanwhile, in its external relations, the regime uses the obtaining international environment in which opportunism is dominant, to attempt to ingratiate itself without principle with whichever powers, countries or international connections it believes can be used to extend its tragic tenure and hence continue repressing the people of Uganda. In pursuit of this goal, no level of opportunism or financial cost is a constraint to the regime, because its international connections now become its major preoccupation and lifeline in its vain struggle for survival.

Fascist military dictatorship and its regime in Uganda hence, continues to exist due to a constellation of internal and external factors. Internally it runs a system of political, ideological, and military repression and overall marginalisation of the mass of the people. This repression stems from the regime's secret operational political programme which is based on the premise that, political and national affairs, are not the concern of the masses, nor of the regime's political opponents or critics or those who do not belong to it, but are 'the' concern of only the regime's despotic commandist leadership and the organs of its allied servant armed formations, i.e. their High Commands and Army Councils or sometimes marginally the fascist regime's pawn political organs.

The latter, are permitted idle deliberation when the regime has from time to time to diffuse rising political pressure or seek some kind of lame political legitimacy. On this basis, all mounted political activity is meant to deceptively appear to involve the masses. Further, it is the position of the fascist military dictatorship that if they, the masses of the people, are to be involved to any degree in decision making over their local affairs, the regime's leadership must exercise political and ideological tutelage over them. Hence, in its view the masses of people should not be permitted to develop and hold self-initiative in matters that concern them and their country, or organise on their own steam or even use other fora such as the political parties with which they have been acquainted or are associated to assert their legitimate rights. The fear that the people may in the process become impossible to be brought under necessary control, is a *Sword of Damocles*[56] that hangs over the head of the fascist military dictatorship.

The fascist military dictatorship is thus set for a political take-over of mass organisations of workers, youths, women, co-operative unions of peasants/farmers, and where necessary even professional organisations. Where this is not possible, it must destroy them and create new surrogates in their place so as to defuse the threat of being politically and organisationally outflanked by the evolving mass and national liberation movement.

The major thrust of fascist military dictatorship is to divide, weaken, and paralyse all political initiatives outside its confines so that it controls all political life throughout the country unchallenged. Simultaneously, it endeavours to terrorise Ugandans into submission

---

[56] Here it infers to an allusion of imminent and ever-present peril faced by those in positions of power.

The famed "sword of **Damocles**" dates back to an ancient moral parable popularized by the Roman philosopher Cicero in his 45 BC.

Became an idiom - from a story about one **Damocles** who had to eat his food with a **sword** hanging over him, which was tied up by a single hair.

through the might of its military machine in order to demonstrate that it is invincible.

Any revolts erupting in the country have to be suppressed violently. In the case where it is not successful in smothering any particular revolt, it has to coerce the people to respond to its ideological and political system through further naked shows of force and co-optation by bribery. These revolts are then channelled into directions suiting the regime while giving a false impression that, the regime is free with respect to the constraints set by imperialism and could therefore progressively realise the popular democratic and national aspirations in Uganda.

On the other hand, the reality of Uganda's/Nile Africa's neo-colonial quagmire objectively places the suffering masses, socially and ideologically beyond the reach of the regime's populist demagoguery. This is why the masses of Uganda's popular classes are able to see through sham elections and other political charades induced by and managed by fascist military dictatorship and its regime as manipulative schemes for their co-option. Unable as it is, to depend on any solid class support in Uganda, or on any other political movement with substantial mass following, the regime works to gain the support of a fraction of the country's intelligentsia, whose apparent still largely credible and positive societal standing it exploits to its own ends, thanks to some residual respect which the masses still have for Uganda's intelligentsia. This intellectual segment of the false-bourgeoisie is thus transformed into hirelings and mercenary functionaries of the regime. Because of the economic straits in which they find themselves, they are easy to compromise, with privileges that permit them to improve their standards of living, acquire luxuries, foreign currency, facilitation to travel abroad etc., which are denied or put beyond by cost to the rest of the Ugandan population at large. Their bourgeois aspirations to individual economic and social promotion and, the delight they take in assuming positions of authority without accountability to the masses, makes such sector of the country's intelligentsia easy prey to the snares of the agent fascist regime of genocide, spoliation and plunder.

They are, however, not totally blind to the precarious situation of the fascist regime they come to serve. For, upon acceding to positions in the state apparatus or in its ideological or economic units, each of them tries to make a quick financial kill for self while in office through corrupt practices, private appropriation and accumulation, and commercial speculation. Hence, they concentrate their work effort principally on those projects, which generate personal rewards and benefits for themselves.

Those who think and take a contrary position to that of the fascist military regime are quietly muzzled or ostracised and publicly humiliated. Thus, cut off and insulated from productive labour processes and real involvement in the general struggles of the masses, the regime is able to transform this corrupted segment of the intelligentsia into a set of *'tamed'* minds, pawns and mercenary professionals at its service.

Held virtually at ransom by the largesse of the dictatorship, many become integrated into its system and are misused to propagate the ideological themes of the fascist military regime. Principally, they are assigned the demeaning task of the ideological repression of the masses of the people of Uganda, through being seconded to; mass media organs, educational and ideological institutions, commissions of inquiry, select expert committees, advisory organs/consultancies, even to the spying units of the fascist dictatorship etc., which are used to attempt to destroy the emergent national liberatory process. Their most important function is however to help present to the world a picture that covers up the genocide, spoliation and plunder, occurring in Uganda. Their duty is to serve up to world public opinion a false picture of political normality and tranquillity, so as to isolate the struggles of the Ugandan masses of people for national freedom from the deserved solidarity of the peoples of the world, and consequently, sanitise and absolve the fascist military regime from accusations of crimes against humanity which it perpetuates in Uganda

The truth however, is bound to come out as the tempo to the people's struggles rises and honest intellectuals begin to work in earnest in the teeth of oppression and repression, torture and death to expose and resist the regime which is the tool of fascist military dictatorship.

On the other hand, at the local parochial level to which it belongs, the regime of genocide, spoliation and plunder, becomes a definite liability to the pro-imperialist internal and regional alliance that helped it to ascend to government. Its efforts; to enslave the people of Uganda/Nile Africa as it vainly attempts to build its political hegemony in the country, make it increasingly high-handed. In tandem with its vain attempt to suppress the people and subjugate them to its cruel rule, the regime stands compelled into escalating the use of excessive force to hold in place and ends up intensifying the occupation of the country, principally by naked military force. In its frustration, the regime has similarly little or no recourse, but to resort to naked fascistic measures against its own deserting service personnel, minions, former allies and friends.

The oppression that the regime of genocide, spoliation and plunder unleashes, to defend its fantasies or what it erroneously considers a genuine *'people's revolution'*, i.e. the terror it directs against the peoples emergent national liberation process, has earned it the undying hatred of the Ugandan people.

In this kind of desperate situation, the regime becomes increasingly susceptible to the strategies and tactics of the other more experienced social and political forces, which are in contention in Uganda. The social and political forces which are organised around the Democratic Party (DP) and the 'Kabaka Yekka' (KY) movement/Conservative Party (CP) (hitherto the junior political partners of the regime) for instance, may continue to use the regime's *'cover'* to physically settle accounts with their Uganda Peoples Congress (UPC) opponents and members of other liberatory and patriotic forces. The regime of genocide, spoliation and plunder will then be made to consequently harvest the corresponding wrath and hatred of the people in such cases. The hitherto collaborating political forces will at the time of their desertion of the regime solely ascribe the crimes they have committed under the umbrella of the fascist military dictatorship to its regime and its leadership. The National Resistance Army's (NRA) ascendance to government in Uganda has hence created circumstances which permit a free hand for the Ugandan reactionary forces to terrorise, and massacre their political opponents and those who do not support these forces of death.

Consequently, a countrywide political climate has been created where there can arise no acceptable pretences whatsoever which can be used to justify the regime's continued governance of Uganda. Its management of Uganda through the use of excessive force, terror, deceit and terrible corruption, cripples economic production and disrupts the reproductive process of the system whose further development they, as agents and *'nyampalas'*[57] of foreign and, or

---

[57] Ibid 2

multinational capital and finance interests, are supposed to foster as an imperative. The regime therefore fails even in this most basic and elementary demand which imperialism makes on it. In such predicament, it resorts to tactics meant to divert the minds of the people from its unresolvable dilemma, by subverting neighbouring countries, or even waging war on or within them. Such adventures shall however be to no avail to the further sustenance of its tragic tenure in Uganda.

In this kind of situation, the objective laws that govern the demise of non-popular regimes and governments in neo-colonial Uganda will come to apply to the regime of genocide, spoliation and plunder. As these laws take effect, the people's emergent national liberation movement has to brace itself to take advantage of the opportunities it offers, to galvanise the entire people to achieve at last genuine national freedom and liberation. It is imperative that not only the current military regime of genocide, spoliation and plunder gets finally politically defeated, overcome and truly transcended, but that conditions which give birth to such fascist dictatorial and despotic regimes are never allowed to rise again in the country.

In short, it is not merely the current fascist military regime that has to be effaced, but the socio-economic and political system upon which regimes of its nature and character are created. This is the principal point of difference between on the one hand the aspirations of the people, and on the other hand, that of the country's political and parasitic elite and false-bourgeoisie, who may be aiming to merely replace and, or substitute themselves in place of the fascist military regime. The latter merely wish to replace the militarist regime of genocide, spoliation and plunder in the governance of the neo-colony by a masked civil-military alliance. On the other hand the people who are victims of the fascist dictatorship shall be compelled to assert their democratic sovereignty by any other means necessary which will ensure and guarantee the sustenance of the conquests of national liberation.

The contemporary demands of the people are not about 'change without change' but transformative change, which they themselves command and control, which change in its course, is able to revolutionise even its own starting presuppositions.

To win and guarantee this political triumph, it is necessary that the mass support for national liberation in the country be transformed in the liberation into genuine focused mass participation and the fullest ownership of the liberatory processes. Only such strategy can hence forth ensure that the entire people themselves intervene en masse in their country's history, so that they face up to and come to master the real problems facing the country, and therefore hold their own destiny in hand, i.e. assert the fullest ownership of their country and, maximally, the command and control of its destinies.

The liberatory processes, which the contemporary situation and political problem of the country calls for, are about breaking the mould of the iniquitous caste and class politics of post-colonial Uganda by which the parasites that prey on the oppressed and exploited, thrive.

The Latin American catholic intellectual Leonardo Boff[58], commenting about situations similar to those that entrap Uganda aptly noted:

> "...The process of liberation brings with it a profound conflict...
> "...Having the project be clear, is not enough...
> "...What is necessary is a spirituality of resistance and renewed
> hope to turn ever back to struggle in the face of defeats of the
> oppressed..."

The liberatory struggles are hence continuous processes that have to always fall back to the valid aspirations and efforts of forward march to national freedom, popular self-governance and African self-becoming as their central points of reference. Despite the ups and downs of these processes, the fundamental remains; that Ugandans must on their own account win that cardinal right to establish sufficient autonomy to shape the political, social, economic and cultural systems of their country, and to assert for themselves, the rights to live fruitful, happy and prosperous truly human lives, without the subhuman conditions of exploitation, destitution, marginalisation, hunger, disease and non-knowledge.

---

58   The Origin of Liberation Theology/ Boff, 198, p.20

CHAPTER 5

UGANDA THE ROAD TO A NEW, JUST AND NATIONAL DEMOCRATIC UGANDA

(i) THE TASK OF NATIONAL LIBERATION IN UGANDA

It is important to understand that, the masses of the people who have risen for social, political and national liberation stood up to confront not merely the genocide, spoliation and plunder meted out by the fascist military regime, but to put to permanent end its militarism, dictatorship and tyranny. The regime's attempts to contain the neo-colonial political and socio-economic crisis engulfing the country will remain futile. Instead, the fight for national democratic liberation from the dominance of imperialism, which shall in its maturity come to assume a popular revolutionary character, shall further unfold.

The attainment of popular national democratic liberation is a necessary revolutionary stage for the people of Uganda/Nile Africa to win for their country, a truly sovereign existence and a personality of its own, independent of imperialism. This is what shall enable them to pave the road for the independent and autonomous beneficial development of their country. Indeed in the process of national democratic liberation the people shall have to assume the responsibility of resolving the national question, through winning national freedom, and asserting social justice which are necessary conditions for nation formation in the country.

(ii) THE NATIONAL QUESTION

The resolution of the national question is one of the major tasks of popular national democratic liberation. It has two interrelated aspects; national liberation and nation formation. The reality of the country, and the Ugandan people's history of struggle mean that both tasks have to be executed concurrently, thereby giving rise to a situation where the realisation of one aids that of the other. The clusters of peoples, nationalities and communities of the country once in a state of freedom, can become the power and the magic wand with which to create in the country a nation, which shall be the common body of equal peoples, nationalities and communities.

(iii) NATION FORMATION

At political independence, i.e. the transition from colonialism to neo-colonialism, a number of features that constitute a nation had evolved, but the task of forging the Ugandan nation could not realistically have been advanced, for Uganda had not yet won the conditions and autonomous political power necessary for nation formation.

Colonial development constituted an environment where loyalty to the nationality or ethnic or religious groups and area of origin rather than to Uganda was dominant. On the other hand, the reality of unequal (colonial) development of Uganda provided no suitable socio-economic and material base for nation formation; rather it encouraged a climate of division and fragmentation. These negative legacies of colonial rule have lived into contemporary times and continue to exert their malign influence, including suffocating the rise of sufficiently deep-rooted and lasting, common experience amongst the people, and other vital unifying factors such as development of a common language. The new societal ties (economic, social, political, cultural and spiritual) which emerged and developed in the colonial and neo-colonial synthesis were limited in effect because they are of an external orientation and have occurred within the frame-work of old structures of society which have not lost their influence.

In the absence of a liberatory political process to overcome the divisive rule of neo-colonialism, whatever amount of work is put into nation formation is squandered. The forces pulling the people away from the task still hold the initiative in the situation. In Uganda, a new political elite has recently joined those forces and other opportunistic groups imbued with an erroneous interpretation of the national question.

Many of these people, who have themselves set up numerous elitist political movements, believe that the Ugandan nation is already formed and constituted. To them existing Ugandan political movements and parties who have matured in the womb of the truncated Ugandan socio-economic system and society are the principal causes of division of the nation. To them, the strategy of forging the nation through the development of a people's national liberation movement, which must win national freedom from neo-colonialism, constitutes an unjustified and disruptive action against the imagined nation of Uganda already in existence. The misguided line is unable to appreciate that it is the socio-economic realities of neo-colonialism, which principally foster sectional and unbalanced development and hence destroy all possibilities of national cohesion and nation formation.

Basing themselves upon their erroneous theoretical premises, and supported by forces seeking to sustain the neo-colonial political and economic system that imperialism bequeathed to Uganda at independence, they vainly attempt to obstruct the current struggles for the national democratic liberation being waged by the people. This political line must therefore be rejected not only because it is wrong, but also because it serves to derail the process of winning national freedom from imperialism and neo-colonialism. Indeed, it is only upon this new foundation of national freedom that the people shall build the Ugandan nation for the first time in history, on an autochthonous political, ideological, cultural, economic, and material base from the communities upwards, which foster the cohesion and integration of the people.

The practices adopted in post-colonial Africa on nation formation and, or building have proven to be wanting.

The opposed tendencies of, on the one hand, external integration of post-colonial Africa, i.e. into the global capitalist system and, on the other, of internal disintegration – paralyses Africa's efforts to achieve nation formation in its various polities and win conditions for African self-renewal.

In post-colonial Africa, political power systems have created conditions, which have permitted a concentration of wealth generated in Africa and the means of production and exchange into the hands of a few ravenous intermediate Mafia or a few rascals or groups of perennially greedy fortune hunters. This is a most harmful situation to Africa.

It inherently generates a festering situation of conflict between on the one hand, the few and on the other, the often-marginalised millions of oppressed and exploited humanity.

This conflict is often also reflected in the simmering contentions between enclosed nationalities and enclosing state formations and systems.

These states have been held in place by the use of force and violence, terror and intimidation, political manipulation and deception. Under this process – clusters of peoples, nationalities and communities have had to be held together, even without their consent.

The All African Peoples Conference (AAPC) held in Ghana in 1958, made a resolution to reformulate the colonially set African political geographies and boundaries. This resolution was unfortunately over turned across board by the year of African independence -1960.

The new African governing classes believed in the theory and practices of unity by *"coagulation"* of various nationalities, ethnic and demographic - specific expressions. Africa has since been forced to run on the same spot in the matter of nation rebuilding.

To the new governors of African lands, this was taken to be a most appropriate and solid basis for Africa's forward movement and progress. The old structural and political order of colonial capitalism offered a familiar statal and geographical framework for the then new ventures of primitive accumulation which globalising capital instituted in Africa.

The African governing classes worked in tune with globalising capital, with which they organised collaboration.

The result was – that the birth and nurture of new African nations, became abortive.

The other path of nation building and, or formation that was never favoured by the African political elite and classes was that of reformulation by which disparate clusters of peoples, nationalities and communities etc., could be united on the basis of their common social, economic and cultural interests. The idea is to build the nation from the bottom or society's base upwards, as opposed to that of forcing the amalgamation of various disparate elements downwards from the top.

The path of nation building via processes of reformulation means working to harmonise in a country specific social interests that are either identical or similar. The resolution of such common social questions on collective bases can hence become the basis of resolving the national question and building necessary commonalities in this endeavour.

The idea is hence to start laying a foundation for nation building and formation by working to meet the real and immediate needs of the people at the bottom or base of society and showing by practice the import of this autochthonous method of forging unity.

In this regard, the people have to face up to the need to assert the command and control of their own communities, enhance the need for understanding how to maximally use this command and control in the effort to improve their overall lives and assert the need to forge necessary suitable means to make such improvements possible.

Outstanding social needs and endemic poverty, destitution and want entrap African people en mass. This situation which cuts across every ethnic/nationality groups, and area and geographical space in Uganda and Africa are best addressed by instituting focused autochthonous development processes, which benefit the majority of the African people.

Africa's problems of general and intra fragmentation are best tackled by larger focused popular, democratic, co-operative and collective actions to overcome common problems – by all the clusters of peoples, nationalities and communities affected.

The involvement of each community in the resolution of the problems within their localities and beyond – creates a basis to cooperate with others who face similar or the same problems. Each community in this regard is helped to appreciate the relevance of common and wider effort across – localities, areas, regions and indeed the country.

This reality of common concern, if given life – would help to redefine or reformulate the attitudes of isolation within which communities have become entrapped – giving birth to new realities that show that the wellbeing and welfare of each cluster of peoples, nationalities and communities is the wellbeing and welfare of all.

The key in this process is mass participation to create mass agreement, for united and common action to resolve common problems across areas of concern.

The imperative is to struggle to create necessary sustainable popular consensus to lift all from given deleterious situations that affect the well-being and welfare of all.

The African diversities and multiplicities in this regard can become Africa's source of necessary strength to animate the masses to collectively face up to their existential and developmental problems.

(iv) NATIONAL LIBERATION AND THE FORCES IN CONTENTION

The achievement of political independence through the process of decolonisation has only been a stage in the struggle for national liberation. In this phase, the host of negative legacies of colonial rule have been compounded by the system of neo-colonialism through which in contemporary times various stronger powers seek to dominate non-developed countries like Uganda.

To dominate these countries, imperialism normally falls back on the forces, which were relatively favoured and used in the administration of the colony. The best weapon of the oppressed for countering these machinations is the creation of a strong national democratic liberation movement which must initiate a political process to unite the ranks of all who seek deliverance from their debilitating slave existence in the neo-colonial framework that engulfs the country.

In this era, where the struggle against imperialism is global in scope, the Ugandan peoples emergent national liberation movement has to co-ordinate its action with other national liberation movements in Africa and other parts of the world in the common effort to achieve national freedom and liberation of all.

In the context of Uganda, building meaningful solidarity with other oppressed people demands that the Ugandan people take advantage of the general crisis facing the country to win national liberation, which is a prerequisite for permanently overcoming that crisis. This means, in the first instance, creating untrammelled political sovereignty of the people through their own full participation in and ownership of the process of winning national liberation and thereby weakening the malign designs of imperialism on the country.

Consequently, the national liberation must be a process that emancipates and humanises both the mindless agents in the service of imperialism and the oppressed in the country. Above all, it must lead to the liberation of the multiply and most oppressed section of the Ugandan society, namely, the Ugandan women. Without this, the Ugandan people as a whole will always remain enslaved, for true emancipation means the liberation and humanisation of all.

(v) THE FORCES OF FASCISM AND MILITARY DICTATORSHIP

As is typical of all Nile River riparian lands, Uganda was essentially colonised by military conquest, and is, today, as a neo-colony, still under military dictatorship. The alliance and collaboration of the local Ugandan agent bloc and imperialism which holds the country and her peoples in subjection to foreign domination, and sustains and defends the slave relations now therein instituted, is constitutive of the bloc against which, the masses of the people of the country must struggle in order to win national freedom and liberation.

In the situation of Uganda, the interests and forces, which continue to aggress, wage relentless warfare against the people of the country and hold them in servitude, include:-

a) The system of imperialism itself, and the leadership of those political forces fostered by imperialism to govern Uganda on its behalf – the ones the sages of the Ganda Nation aptly named: the *'Omuzungu Agambye'*[59] Africans or the imperial white man's African parrots and copy cats.

b) Those individuals who continue out of their own choosing to be in the service of the fascist regime of genocide, spoliation and plunder and its repressive machine, i.e. members of its armed security, intelligence, police and state administrative organs, and its other repressive apparatus.

c) Intellectual, media and propaganda mercenaries and members of organisations which seek to legitimise, or justify the continued existence of the fascist regime of genocide, spoliation and plunder, or in the case of its demise, the rise of a similar successor regime in its place in Uganda.

d) All careerists and opportunists who have formed the habit of welcoming any regime of oppression and dictatorship, or despotism, and often prostrate themselves before the master of the moment to gain favours, positions, and offices.

e) All foreign interests and forces, and those ruthless fortune hunters, often non-Ugandan, who directly or indirectly assist in repression, spoliation and domination of the country, in particular, those who due to their interests in the geo-strategic setting of Uganda, or in her wealth, stand in the way of the National Democratic Liberation process of the people of Uganda.

These are the forces, which today, obstruct the progress of the oppressed and exploited masses of people of Uganda towards the achievement of national freedom and liberation from imperialism.

---

[59] Ibid 4

(vi) THE PEOPLE AS THE BASIS FOR NATIONAL LIBERATION

Since its inception fascism and its dictatorship has waged general warfare against the people of Uganda. The war-destroyed areas across Uganda are the eloquent evidence of this destructive warfare.

Definite opposed groups fight wars, which are political contentions of bloodshed. Since the advent of foreign rule in Uganda, the people have had to rise to fight against these forces of aggression. This is a struggle, which shall continue in various forms until the country is sovereign again. The people who are today the victims of exploitation and social marginalisation, oppression and repression hold as the principal foundation for winning national freedom. In this regard, national democratic liberation cannot be achieved without the understanding, support and empathy of the oppressed and marginalised majority of the Ugandan masses.

All those persons in the country who are oppressed and repressed, exploited and impoverished, and marginalised into subhuman existence by imperialism, neo-colonialism, and the fascist regime of genocide, spoliation and plunder and consequently, desire to rid themselves of this oppression and dehumanisation, constitute the category of the people who are the subject of liberation.

Historical experience has shown that what constitutes the people is a dynamic category of society. Hence, as realignment of forces continuously takes place in history and society, what constitutes the category of the people and their forces often also change. In Uganda today, these forces include all those who seek liberation from, the oppressive slave reality that imperialism has fostered and helped to nurture in Uganda for its control and exploitation.

They are those who, today, are fighting the system, which the regime of genocide, spoliation and plunder presides over; of uneven development, nationality and ethnic chauvinism, religious bigotry and discrimination, poverty, social inequality and marginalisation, state violence and terrorism, endless tortures and overall dehumanisation.

They also include all those who see the path to national freedom as passing through the process of national democratic liberation and all who yearn for a new, just and democratic Uganda, which is dignified, prosperous and progressive and is the mother of all its equal clusters of peoples, nationalities and communities.

(vii) POLITICAL STRATEGY AND FORMS OF STRUGGLE TO WIN NATIONAL FREEDOM

In concrete terms, the needs of national liberation now demand the crystallisation of mass political activity that will ensure the achievement of national democratic liberation, i.e. mass activity which is suitable to the successful discharge of the political tasks that today face the Ugandan people.

Indeed, in the history of the struggle of the people of Uganda to win national freedom ever since the last quarter of the 19th century to date, several forms of struggle, ranging from war to open mass liberatory activities, have emerged. Combined mass civil, political, and cultural struggles of the people may be the necessary, yet unorganised means with which to defeat the fascist dictatorship that has waged general warfare against the people of Uganda.

After the last anti-colonial wars which ended in 1913, the Ugandan people depended predominantly on political mobilisation of the masses for reformist 'political' action through demonstrations, strikes, boycotts, civil disobedience, participation in qualified elections and limited insurrections. These in themselves have proved quite inadequate in the face of persistent militarism and regular use of excessive force in Uganda's colonial and post-colonial politics. The point is to generate mass struggles across the length and breadth of the country to paralyse and politically defeat military dictatorship in Uganda.

In the late 1970's, armed warfare, i.e. the contention of armed formations as distinct from a people's war, was initiated. The limitations of this line are there for all to see. It does not centrally involve the popular masses that largely remain spectators in the struggle. In the Ugandan experience, the wars of the late 1970's and the 1980's may have been used to defeat governments, but they did not lead to processes for winning national freedom or national liberation from imperialism.

The strategy yet to be appreciated which the people have increasingly worked to set into motion is that of revolutionary mass action which is instituted through the process of *popular participatory struggles*. This is meant to enable the masses to take advantage of the free spaces that arise in the struggle to mature their political aims, and objectives through their own effort and full participation by involvement of thousands or millions of individuals in the various tasks that are required in the liberation effort. Through this method, the people get mobilised, politicised, organised, inspired and coalesce all effort necessary to win national liberation, nation formation and constitution, and the emergence of sovereign national democratic power, in place of the authority of the fascist dictatorship. Thus, as the popular struggle progresses, democratic power is built in place, and liberated zones are created, and fascist military dictatorship gets politically paralysed or contained countrywide, thereby enabling the people to initiate, establish, and exercise their fullest sovereignty.

It is this process, which makes it possible for all the people to confront the dictatorship, unite their ranks, and overcome their varied and diverse attitudes including problems of cultural particularities. This then enables the building of a disciplined, responsible and accountable people's national force, which is endowed with the all-important organic connection and strength to protect and enhance the sovereignty of the people. The people organised, together with popular political mass formations, can easily and effectively paralyse, contain and defeat the standing power of the fascist neo-colonial state and military dictatorship.

All factors considered, this strategy is emerging as the most viable route in Uganda's national liberation struggle. Its importance lies principally in the fact that it ensures that the gains of the people's liberation struggle is secured and perpetuated by their own initiative and democratic power, and that 'warlords' in and outside government do not emerge to squander the gains of the people's liberation struggle.

Popular focused countrywide actions for national liberation makes it possible for the people to transform themselves into full and equal citizens of the emergent, new, just, and democratic Uganda. It combines into powerful civil, political and generalised struggles – which create conditions for the masses to build their own sovereignty in place of the power of the fascist military dictatorship, which promotes the interests of imperialism, neo-colonialism and division in the country.

In this type of struggle – there can be no distinction between liberators and the liberated. All become liberators and winners of national freedom and protagonists of a new Africa that measures and is able to rise to the challenges of a future of multiple developmental possibilities.

(viii)   TASKS OF THE PEOPLE'S EMERGENT NATIONAL LIBERATION MOVEMENT

The tasks and challenges faced by the Ugandan people in the quest for national liberation, calls for the development and consolidation of a democratic political force that galvanises a countrywide effort for the political defeat of the fascist military dictatorship and ensures the winning of national freedom and the institution of popular self-governance in the country.

The people's emergent national liberation movement will therefore have to work to unite all popular, nationality, community and mass democratic and patriotic forces in order to mount concerted political and focused multiple-faceted offensives for the purposes of realising the noble historical and liberatory aspirations of the masses of people of Uganda.

After years of fragmented action against the fascist military dictatorship, it is now imperative for popular national liberation efforts to be co-ordinated in a way, which was previously lacking. One of the major tasks at hand is to transform popular resistance from mere specific rebellions, uprisings, insurrections and revolts into larger mass formations with the strategy and capacities to win national democratic liberation.

Thus, with the people having engaged the fascist regime and its military dictatorship spontaneously and on their own initiative, the task for the people's emergent national liberation movement is to help co-ordinate and unite these separate, but strategically common efforts, improve upon their all-round liberation skills, and channel these efforts to overcome the dictatorship's temporary superiority in technical and material resources. It is only in the process of focused mass action that the people will through their own effort and participation; successfully paralyse and dismantle the political, economic, and overall strength of the agent fascist military regime of genocide, spoliation and plunder.

The pursuit of these objectives means that, the people's emergent national liberation movement must create and establish diverse programmes and projects to impart the necessary political awareness and practical skills to prosecute the struggle for liberation to the end.

The self-defence and protection units of the people in various parts of the country have of necessity to be integrated into a nationally co-ordinated mass instrument for national liberation. This calls for political and field personnel and cadres from the nuclei of the people's mass liberation struggles to be deployed into various units to help them channel their efforts in the direction of winning national liberation and freedom.

To ensure the success of the people's mass struggle for liberation, it will be necessary to ignite public opinion in favour of the processes that the emergent national liberation movement triggers in place. In this regard, the popular mass movement must disseminate necessary information to arouse national awareness about the real nature and character of the struggles on-going and developing in Uganda.

The emergent national liberation movement must equally assume its responsibilities to galvanise the efforts of all other patriots who have been stranded and stuck in the camp of the fascist dictatorship and its warfare formations for one reason or another. It must not crudely consider all such patriots, simply to be a willing part of the fascist dictatorship. This is also the case with those who belonged to former state armed and security forces. The most important consideration in this regard, is that they should be ready to demonstrate in practice that they are faithful servants of the people and must not have committed acts of oppression, dehumanisation or atrocities against them. It is the responsibility of this group of patriots caught up within the ranks of the fascist dictatorship, to fight against it from within, in coordination with the people's liberation strategy and programme.

The people's emergent liberation movement is thus presented with the principal task to mature authentic mass popular and, or people's liberation formations that base themselves on strict political and liberatory discipline.

In this process, priority has to be given to mobilising impoverished peasant groups that are being disinherited of their patrimonies and lands, and have to self-defend and self-emancipate. This condition places them in insurrectionary situations as all others who have the genuine urge to win national freedom, and owe their allegiance to the people, Uganda and emergent democratic Africa.

In addition to such groups, patriotic youths and students have to be assisted to rise to the occasion so that they struggle for their own future and open for themselves, and all in Uganda and Africa, the doors of beneficial developmental possibilities.

In liberated areas, where the authority of the people is democratically established, it will be imperative to help the masses of people form or create their own mass self-defence and protection from possible aggression by the fascist military dictatorship.

The people's emergent national liberation movement bears the responsibility and has the duty to enhance the development, internally and externally, of the necessary political and diplomatic linkages for the advancement of the national liberation struggle and winning, at last, national freedom.

It shall seek to obtain the necessary intellectual, technical and material assistance from other people's organisations, movements or countries that are appreciative of and sympathetic to the national liberation struggle and revolutionary aspirations of the Ugandan/Nile African people.

Yet all such assistance must only be supplementary to the locally mobilised and secured resources, for there are plenty of necessary national liberatory resources, in the country itself. Indeed, the resources, which the fascist dictatorship holds custody of and claims ownership over, and are being used to repress the people, belong to the Ugandan people, their communities and nationalities.

This struggle cannot be confined to one nationality or ethnic group or to one area, region, religion or any particular political movement, organisation or party. This courageous struggle for a new, just, and democratic Uganda of necessity must hence unite the efforts of her entire people and their national democratic and patriotic movements, and mass and community organisations.

The popular emergent national liberation movement has to be conscious of the fact that the fascist dictatorship continues to create a situation which generates sectional quarrels and divisions, and endlessly fuels disunity and conflicts that helps create the opportunities for the fascist dictatorship to continue to pillage and loot the country, while the people's efforts get harmfully diverted into fratricidal and secondary struggles.

It is the duty of the people's emergent national liberation movement to initiate processes that neutralise and transcend these negative distractions.

The evolving unity fostered by practical action for national liberation and freedom which will result in the adoption of a common strategy against fascist military dictatorship will continue to make possible the forging of the democratic political liberatory unity that is necessary to politically defeat and overcome the dictatorship and win victory.

(ix) BUILDING THE FUNDAMENTAL STRENGTH OF THE MASSES

The process of people's struggles for liberation evolves practical forms of action that weaken the political, economic, and overall strength of the dictatorship and undermine its control over the country, and secure space for the exercise of the people's sovereignty. The combination of countrywide mass actions and the political strength this generates constitutes the foundation for the people's forward movement to national freedom.

The experiences of the Ugandan people hitherto, however, show that this road to national freedom is long, full of trials and tribulations.

From the initial steps that have been taken, until final popular victory over the fascist dictatorship, the struggle for liberation shall continue to go through many more difficult and complex stages; and may, at times, even suffer significant reverses.

The point, however, is for the people's emergent national liberation movement to help create in the masses of the people the necessary endurance and perseverance to enable them overcome one obstacle after the other and win popular victory step by step.

Where mistakes are made, a way to correct them has to be sought and found.

Where successes are achieved ways to further advance, improve, and consolidate, such victories have to be forged.

What is of paramount importance is for the people's emergent national liberation movement to be steadfast in the vision of winning a new, just, national democratic and prosperous Uganda. It will be necessary then, to clearly understand the daily changing realities of the people's struggle so as to be able to motivate and inspire them to overcome all difficulties and hardships and finally to ensure popular political victory over the fascist military dictatorship in the country.

The strategy of people's mass struggle for national democratic liberation must be to exhaust and paralyse the dictatorship and practically sap its will to occupy a hostile population. In other words, the people must continue to utilise the strategy of *'The War of the Flea'*[60], which aims at wearing down the occupying dictatorship and

---

[60] The War of the Flea: A Study of Guerrilla Warfare Theory and Practise 'Book by Robert Taber.

power while at the same time gaining strength so as to help intensify the political fever which debilitates and finally overcomes the fascist military dictatorship. In this process the people have to maintain their initiatives and freedom of action – as to where and when to act for liberation, while at the same time building and solidifying their own strength, as popular power, and thereby asserting their democratic sovereignty.

The personalised war machine of the fascist military dictatorship is a Goliath. For, though it has vicious repressive manpower and is strong in technical means, it suffers from lack of necessary political legitimacy and a myriad of basic and structural ailments within itself and its forces. The weak socio-economic system, over which it presides and is racked by inherent permanent instability and endless crises, weakens its overall capacity in its hopeless fight against the liberatory forces.

The military dictatorship has inherited and exacerbated the problems of the neo-colonial state of Uganda, which has to preside over a continuously fluid alliance of Uganda's fractious agent political classes within the complexes of a multi-national, multi-faith, multi-structural, and multi-class society. Its control over the decisive points of the system it presides over on behalf of its alien masters and interests can only be largely superficial and ephemeral.

Consequently, when faced with a superior popular, mass, countrywide political liberatory process for winning national democratic liberation, the dictatorship cannot, but be wholesomely defeated.

The experiences of Uganda hitherto, has demonstrated beyond any doubt that, the political, socio-economic and power relations fabric of a neo-colonial Uganda already in deep and irreversible crisis, is totally unable to withstand any type of sustained focused mass struggles and actions against the fascist military dictatorship. It equally has no capacity to contain significant power struggles within its ranks or between the different sectors of and factions in its state apparatus. This structural malaise is partly what explains the demise of several past governments and regimes in Uganda. Indeed the law governing the demise of neo-colonial regimes in Uganda is not about to change.

The fascist regime's demagoguery and its many divisive methods of political manipulation, are bound to exhaust themselves in the face of the ever-worsening overall socio-economic situation that it helps to create by its ineffective, wasteful and repressive rule.

In strategic terms, the people's struggle for national freedom, popular self-governance and African self-becoming has had to be protracted, because this has been their first real experience of people's struggles for political, social and national liberation since colonisation and the loss of native African communities' sovereignty. The liberatory forces have had therefore to proceed in their struggles almost from scratch, in all aspects of people's liberatory struggles whose processes are both an art and a science.

In this long march, the people are however already acquiring the necessary skills and expertise for mastering many relevant forms of struggle. They have already begun to show by their competence in multifarious practical actions that, they are learning their liberatory lessons well and becoming equal to the problems that confront them.

The long drawn out nature of this struggle is however a dynamic process that depends on the evolving relations of struggle and power between the fascist military dictatorship, its war machine, governance apparatus and alien backers and masters on the one hand, and the ever-rising, fundamental strength of the masses of oppressed people and their allies on the other hand. Critical in defining these relations of power, is the mounting overall crisis that the military dictatorship faces, which include:-

(a) **Political.** The failure of the fascist regime of genocide, spoliation and plunder to impose its political hegemony in Uganda and over real popular political forces in the face of mass challenge and generalised resistance to its misrule.

(b) **Economic.** Severe countrywide economic distress, the failure to move the economy to definitive surplus production levels, the dominance of irregular trade and speculation in the economy, and the impossible endless uncontrollable levels of mass poverty, huge deficits and gross national and international indebtedness in an economy which is ever more dependent on conditional hand-outs from the centres of the world capitalists' economy and its financial agencies. The system of production and its reproduction suffers endless emasculation and gets crippled by unparalleled corruption and the regime's permanent aggression against the people of Uganda and those in its African neighbourhood. Intensified and continuous haemorrhage and flight of potential capital from the country and the uncontrollable flight of professional and skilled national human resource and manpower from the country compound this situation.

(c) **Social.** The inability of the majority, (whether workers, public servants, general employees, professionals, farmers or poor peasants) ever to make ends meet and the failure to be defended and protected from the perilous hazards of the situation.

(d) **Military/Security forces.** The permeating of society's ills into the ranks of the armed and security forces of the fascist dictatorship e.g. poverty, and other deprivations that the ordinary soldiers or members of the regime's war machine, police and security forces suffer and face. These negative conditions dehumanise the common soldiery, their families and dependants and undermine their moral standing in society and before all.

Further:

** The transformation of the dictatorship's armed forces into a police force for internal political repression presents a classic dilemma of fascist dictatorships, which the military regime cannot overcome.

** The transformation of the police installations and facilities, prisons, jails, and civil courts into military dependencies and their overt use by the military to maintain political control of the dictatorship over the country, comes out as part of the regime's programme of deinstitutionalisation in the country.

** Monopolisation of all important political decision making in the state by the Commander-In-Chief, his family and the clique leadership of the fascist regime leaves it in splendid isolation from both the regime's military base and society.

** Alienation of increasing numbers of patriots in the regime's military machine and army, police and security forces, and of those who cannot stomach the extreme repression, spoliation and plunder perpetrated by the regime in Uganda, is liable to increase.

In this situation of crisis, the struggles of the people, the common victims of oppression and repression and the country's devastating socio-economic and general adversity, become more co-ordinated, united and mobilised by the hardness of their lot. They come to gain greater self-confidence in their increased ability to decide to challenge the military dictatorship as and when they choose. They acquire the ability not to be deceived by the demagoguery of the military dictatorship and its false promises, and are able to see through its schemes of manipulation and its pretensions, and its activities to contain their collective discontent by continuing to mete against them endless warfare, intimidation, terror, violence, and acts of war. Indeed, it is in this situation that the people's emergent liberation movement can be able to tighten, through every successful mass political activity the encirclements of the fascist dictatorship and thereby effect its political defeat.

With these opposed positions built to maturity in the country, it will then be clear that the critical moment, i.e. for winning liberation and instituting popular power by the masses, will have arrived.

This is the moment when even the most intimidated and docile of the people who are oppressed by imperialism, neo-colonialism, and their agent fascist regime of genocide, spoliation and plunder, will loudly dare revolt and be able to hit at the targets of their accumulated anger.

And, as the striking power of the people builds in strength, even the external friends of the dictatorship will begin to desert it and leave it to face the music alone. It is then that the people will launch the final onslaught against the control points and apparatus of the regime of genocide, spoliation and plunder leading to its political defeat and disintegration.

As these final contentions for national liberation and freedom are won, the common reality of the people's experience countrywide will open new possibilities for resolving the contradiction of a country, which is not yet a nation. These include the rise of a new national consciousness and a democratic people's culture whose roots are set and grow in the people's sustained struggle for freedom, popular self-governance and African self-becoming.

A people's nation state can then be built by processes of democratic reformulation rather than forceful coagulation of its various elements on the strength of national people's democratic power, the increasing common experiences of the people and an evolving equality of all of the country's clusters of peoples, communities and nationalities.

The people will then have laid a firm foundation for the consolidation of their sovereign democratic power, replacing the power of neo-colonialism and its agent military dictatorship, which now subjugates, represses, and exploits their majority on end.

From the ranks of participants in the national liberation process, there will emerge a category of persons with sound political, technical, organisational, scientific, and other necessary capacities whose job will be to lead the construction of a new sovereign, just and prosperous Uganda. From these and other popular categories of the people, a foundation for constructing self-reliant and non-parasitic people's defence and security systems will be laid. The key personnel to man this system shall be made up of the most meritorious sons and daughters of the country.

However, a cautious democratic approach in their selection must be followed, on account of the country's previous sorry experience in the formation of *'state armies'*. This negative legacy must be transcended in the new Uganda that emerges with the winning of national liberation.

The people's armed security forces in a new, just, democratic Uganda must be an element of the people in uniform, politically disciplined, technically efficient, creative and productive. They must be self-reliant in their basic needs, so that they do not as in neo-colonial Uganda, degenerate into tormentors, torturers, and terrorisers of the people. In the long run, the entire people themselves shall have to be armed to defend their own interests, for they alone are the surest guarantors and defenders of their interests.

The people's long march to Ugandan national freedom, popular self-governance and African self-becoming shall triumph, for political possibilities now exist for creating new forms of popular power, and of social, economic and military organisation that are capable of permanently superseding the power of imperialism, neo-colonialism and its local stooges and agent guardians of its interests in Uganda.

(x) DEFEATING THE UNRESTRICTED FASCIST AGGRESSION AND RELENTLESS WARFARE METED AGAINST THE PEOPLE

Fascist dictatorship has continuously generated and executed unrestricted multifaceted aggression and warfare against the people of Uganda/Nile Africa, over the decades.

This relentless onslaught must be brought to an end.

Fascism has meted against the people, political, ideological, psychological and physical aggression, which has ruined and traumatised millions of people in the country and its African neighbourhoods.

History and the liberatory experiences and examples, should provide the basis to create the best assets to forge, requisite political weapons to terminate the ugly warfare, which the dictatorship imposes upon the people.

In this regard it becomes necessary to fall back to history and its pertinent lessons. Accurate knowledges of history can provide a foundation from which to draw relevant examples to forestall and defeat the continuous fascist aggression and warfare meted against the Ugandan and Nile African people.

Geoffrey Till[61], a maritime historian, aptly contexts how history can be utilized as an asset in this regard:-

> *"...The chief utility of history for the analysis of the present and future lies in the ability of not to point out lessons, but to isolate things that need thinking about ...*
>
> *"...History provides insights and questions, never answers...*
>
> *"...A good grasp of history will tell us what the future could bring, but there is no denying that history warns, rather unsportingly that major surprises occur...*
>
> *"...Furthermore, because humans are active historical players, their beliefs about the future, can function either as self-fulfilling or self-negating prophesies...*
>
> *"...The future is not 'out there', fixed, just waiting for the passage of time to see it unfold...*
>
> *"...Instead the future remains to be made, to be constructed by people, including by people in conflict, who strive to make a future that they prefer..."*

The armed conquest of Uganda/Nile Africa by imperialism has had to be perpetuated into contemporary times by means of overt and covert warfare mounted against the people, who have been subjected to the rule of force and violence, terror and intimidation, political manipulation and deception. Over the past decades the fascist regime has perpetuated its cruel rule over the country and people through the strategies and processes of infiltration and destruction, and encirclement and suppression of community, social and popular forces. It has thus mounted and waged permanent warfare against the resisting, oppressed and exploited people of the country. In this, the

---

[61] Geoffrey Till: Maritime Strategy and the Nuclear Age (London 1982) pp.224-5

fascist military dictatorship harvests counter actions that the people mount against its impositions.

The many facets of the resultant contentions between, on the one hand, the forces of the fascist dictatorship and, on the other, the counter, self-protective, forces of the people, have been manifest in political, ideological, psychological, spiritual, military, trans-military and other non-military forms.

Although war is a core means of warfare, it is not its only form. In general, warfare is about politics and political contentions; contestations for dominance and power, and is an instrument of policy regardless of the character of the particular issues over which there is contention or that feed the conflict or light its flames. Warfare involves the totality of political contentions and is also about contestations of world viewpoints, cultures, socio-economic interests, particular personalities and personages etc., who are, of course, of various characteristics, ambitions, vanities and peculiarities. It is folly for the victims of fascist dictatorship in Uganda/Nile Africa not to come to understand that they have been subject since colonization to a state of endless warfare, which those who prey on their fruits of labour and the natural resource bounties of their country have continuously imposed upon them.

The fascist dictatorship, as a front agent of multinational capital and finance in Nile Africa, runs a system which is predicated on the strategy that the economic warfare it wages against the Nile African people which generates for them *"an accumulation of misery"* is a necessary condition corresponding to the *"accumulation of wealth"* for the dictatorship and its masters.

Continuous waging of warfare against the politically dissenting majority of the people of a country is hence a condition precedent for the continued existence of the slave or political minority system in the imperialist dominated countries.

The rule of fascism in Uganda has stood on its head, the age-old wisdom of kings and queens that;

> *"...the resort to war as a core instrument of warfare is the final argument..."*

Indeed, warfare, is best visualized as a holistic destructive process in which war holds as a core instrument. In the processes of warfare, many factors in its context such as origins, meaning, character and consequences unfold to give character to its complexities.

The military dictatorship has for decades and years continued to wage an unrestricted warfare against the African clusters of peoples, nationalities and communities in the country.

It is evident, that this warfare which has exhibited many facets or elements of aggression against the people – political, ideological, psychological, military, trans-military and non-military has continued to cost the Ugandan and Nile African people, most dearly.

Hitherto – the victims of the destructive fascist warfare that continues to be meted against the masses of people of Uganda/Nile Africa, their intelligentsia and the otherwise fraternal African peoples in countries that neighbour Uganda/Nile Africa have concentrated principally on excoriating the tool(s) that fascism and its military dictatorship use to repress them. This shortcoming leaves the matter of necessary effacement of fascism, which is the major malaise, unaddressed.

These tools of repression would hence be best visualized not only in their specificities, but also as the inbuilt destructive apparatus and instruments that are the vital weapons and tools of fascist dictatorship with which it has continued to wage relentless warfare in the country.

This connectivity and structural synthesis is what has to be duly analysed, interrogated and problematised. For in the end, in the after of fascist dictatorship in Uganda/Nile Africa, when responsibilities for many sad and inhuman happenings come to be apportioned, then, it will only be fair that each responsible person or persons, or elements in the destructive dictatorship bears his or her own cross - no more, no less.

Indeed, Justice to the victims of fascist dictatorship, which shall constitute the basis of national reconciliation in the after of the dictatorship, and in the processes of the humanization of society and the Nile African youth, woman and man in the after of fascist dictatorship – calls for, or demands no less.

Having taken over Uganda/Nile Africa by military conquest and, or armed force, contemporary imperialism and its local tools, agents and allies have sought by all and every means to prevent any popular liberatory initiatives to bring their evil occupation of the country to an end.

For well over three decades, they have sought to militarise every political, social, and national liberatory contention in the country; so that they can utilize overwhelming military force to subdue all incipient, emergent and rising political opposition activities against its cruel rule.

They seek to distort the essences of the political contentions that have arisen in the country which are only partially military. In holistic terms these contentions are first political before they are military.

The strategy of the dictatorship is meant not only to transform, but also redefine these contentions as being wholly or solely military in nature and character. The truth however, is that these political contentions in contemporary times are political, social, military, trans-military and non-military. There are many elements that reflect the totality of the warfare, which the dictatorship wages on the people of Nile Africa.

The obsession of the fascist military regime in Uganda/Nile Africa with the utility of massive military hardware and equipment or the prevalent threat of its use, to settle political accounts with its foes, is in effect not a measure of its avowed strength and invincibility, but its greatest weakness.

It blinds the dictatorship's policy makers and strategists to the wider picture of requisite social, political and military strategy, which in their proper proportion include the facets not only of a military kind but of trans-military and non-military ones as well. Fascism however blinds the regime to which force is the principal means of political contention. The fascist regime - its military command and political leadership - in Uganda/Nile Africa is in the like of the one-eyed Cyclop of Greek mythology who when he was blinded by Odysseus with a burning stake faced total defeat and destruction. The military command of the fascist regime is hence unable to see and perceive the obtaining reality in the social political contentions that are ongoing in the country.

This inherent blindness of the fascist dictatorship, is a boon to the social and political liberatory forces that is an asset to be taken due advantage of in the liberatory struggles.

For the liberatory forces, the primary challenge is to seek an accurate perception of the extant reality of things in the country and its' neighbouring African environs from which to build a winning strategy.

The French historian, Ferdinand Braudel likened visualization of the unfolding of African history to the observing of a river in full flow – i.e. which parts belong merely to the confused and often chaotic river of events, and which to the shaping of the river bed? Where does the bed of the river decide the flow of history, and where does the flow itself, weaving and eroding by its sheer unceasing power, shift the bed into a new direction? For these are two histories, the contingent and the structural.

And the essential problem is to take these histories in the same grasp:

> *"...the history that moves from one moment to the next, riveting to the eye of the beholder by the mere fact of its shifts and dramas, and the underlying history; saying little, almost unsuspected by its actors or observers, but a history which nonetheless persists, no matter what may happen, against all wear and tear of time..."*

It is possible, as has happened in Uganda/Nile Africa, for ephemeral and contingent history and its furious unfolding to be misread and misinterpreted as the fundamental and not contingent form of the historical flow; with the result that the decisive and structural history is given a perverted visualization, or that the real history is instead ascribed a contingent character.

When this happens, an inaccurate appreciation of reality becomes primary and instead the resultant distortions and misrepresentation of reality become principal.

In Uganda/Nile Africa, the fascist military dictatorship has concentrated on generating distortions and widely disseminating the mis-readings and distortions of the said realities in the country.

It has also sought to stress the depictions of its means and tools of dictatorship, which it presents as an inevitability that has to be borne and accepted by all, rather than provide the examination of its roots, nature and character as intertwined means that are rooted in the systems of mass oppression, repression and exploitation under fascism and its dictatorship.

The Ugandan neocolonial state and its current military dictatorship, cannot, but be visualized in the context of their real utility to fascism and the interests of its wicked masters in the country. They are not as presented, the real epicenter of power in Uganda/Nile Africa, but are merely agents of their masters who are the criminal global capitalist interests that they serve.

The analysis of their nature and character, however, is a necessity arising out of their presence as the *"agents and means"* used by multinational capital and finance interests in the realisation and sustenance of the fascist system and dictatorship in the country.

The neo-colonial state and its military/security forces which are the fulcrumic means to fascist governance need to be interrogated and theorized as vital parts of the matrix of fascism and despotic governance in Nile Africa.

Johann Wolfgang Von Goethe[62], the German writer (Faust), philosopher and Scientist once wrote:

> *"...Everything factual is already theory..."*

Frederick von Hayek, the Austrian economic market theologian and, or theorist, and the economic guru of Prime Minister Margaret Thatcher[63] of the UK, on his part noted that:

> *"...facts without theory are silent..."*

Interrogating the sad reality of Uganda/Nile Africa, a country which has virtually been placed under military rule since colonisation, with the exception of short periods of civil democratic governance after independence, calls for and necessitates an overarching explanation of the long standing political tragedy of military misrule.

On January 25, 1986, the 15th anniversary of the Israeli-British backed coup d'état of the Gen. Idi Amin-Dada, the current military dictatorship in Uganda was hoisted into governance, via the assistance of alien imperial interests and the then political leaderships of two East African neighboring countries, to succeed another military regime, which had earlier overthrown the then elected government of the State of Uganda on July 27, 1985.

These military regimes, have presented a distinct problematic of military intervention into political governance as armed organizations, led by their leaderships, who have notoriously displayed often, specific, eccentric and peculiar character. This intervention by army formations pose one of the biggest question marks in both the political history,

---

[62] Theory of Colours - Johann Wolfgang von Goethe; Translated from German by Charles Lock Eastlake; published 1840 by John Murray Albermale Street, London.

[63] Leader of the Conservative Party from 1975 to 1990 and Prime Minister of the United Kingdom from 1979 to 1990.

contemporary and continued being of Uganda/Nile Africa as a viable polity.

These armed formations, imposed themselves as the local points of gravity in the political power relations in the country, with each seeking to visualize the long standing political problem Uganda as a simple fixable matter, in the like of a nail that is out of synchrony - which they being the hammer, can easily be forced into place.

This is a catastrophic visualization and indeed a terrible misreading and misunderstanding of the political problem of the country.

The projection of this simplistic viewpoint or perception of things has been and is a most poor reading of the complex political question of Uganda/Nile Africa. This is a country, which like the other riparian lands of the Nile River, is of critical geostrategic interest to imperial concerns and powers, which hold dominant influence in the politics, economics and power relations systems that have been evolved in the Nile River valley lands.

Indeed from the time of the imperialist colonisation of these lands, the armed formations that have been used to occupy them, have overtly, saliently and, or covertly been used as instruments to hold centre-stage in the political power relations that have arisen or emerged in these riparian lands of the Nile valleys and Basin.

The commonalities between these military governance systems have remained most telling.

They have possessed no real roots of relevance in the needs of the local or domestic producer classes despite their claims to the contrary.

These armed formations have been designed, redesigned and, or re-sculptured as personalised power instruments of their Commanders-in-Chief and leaders who have had also to act their country's heads of state and, or government.

Their venal behavior as personalised military machines for predatory and spoliatory activities in the country or in the country's African neighbourhoods have deeply alienated these military machines from the oppressed and exploited masses of the people in Uganda.

The grossly dictatorial and corrupt character and practices of the Commanders-in-Chief of these armies have become legendary.

The majority of the country's schooled persons, no less, whom the army victimises, the millions of the schooled unemployeds or under-employeds and professionals, traders/entrepreneurs, commissioned agents of multinational corporations and associated interests, the country's hard put intelligentsia, and many persons of this social categories, etc., do not regard or take the neo-colonial state, or its military and security forces, as a positive instrument for meeting their class interests. The military dictatorship constitutes a significant part of the structural obstacles that have closed the path to the realization of their otherwise dignified wellbeing and the expected contributions that they can make to the uplifting of their lives and of giving selfless service to their country and people.

Following upon the corrupt example of their Commander-in-Chief; serving army and security officials have as well become deeply corrupted and occupied in the mad race of amassing huge private fortunes for themselves. They have, without any iota of shame lived well beyond their means, in utter profligacy and untold ill-gotten wealth amidst impossible accumulation of moneys, of all things, in a country where the great mass of people are marginalised to exist in untold poverty, indigence and want.

These military officers, like the civilians whose relatives walk the corridors of power in the country are prone to get involved in every murky money making racket and scheme, in smuggling, in drug, narcotic and human trafficking, gambling and money laundering, and all manner of imaginable corrupt activities for self-gain.

Having risen to their positions often by chance, luck and even treachery, their loyalty to their command and leadership, and, or to each other is ephemeral.

The very possession of huge personal money holdings in accounts in foreign banks undermine their will to make sacrifices for projects and programmes that do not elicit for them self-gain or profit.

The leaderships of such states that have run regimes of spoliation, terror and repression serve and have served as commission agents of the interests of multinational capital and finance, with which they have made and continue to make incredibly huge lucrative deals in arms and software deals and purchases.

Being accountable largely unto themselves alone, rather than to the people who pay taxes to fund them for their upkeep and development; and to facilitate their operations, including even their repressive, spoliatory and predatory activities in and outside the country in neighbouring African environs; they enjoy autonomy which they take maximal advantage of. Such a neo-colonial state squanders in broad daylight and with impunity resources that would otherwise be utilized to open up developmental possibilities that could benefit the country and its peoples. The abuses to which the autonomy of the military state, its bureaucracy and governance systems, have been and is put can no longer be hidden.

Their relative autonomy, for one, places before or at the disposal of the Commander-in-Chief and his associates, unprecedented opportunities for self-gain and profit.

They have a free hand in the purchases of armaments and military equipment of all types, often old and not so new or refurbished ones from which they massively profit and self-gain.

They rent the country's spaces out at high fees to foreign army formations like the US Africom[64] or the US Africa Command.

They freely deploy the state army and security forces for hire to foreign interests and countries in blatant disregard to the country's state constitution and laws.

The military state deploys in the name of the country's development, vast economic and financial resources, much of which is drawn from a large proportion of the economic surpluses generated in the country and from other funds that are borrowed in the name of the country from external sources, without any oversight by and/or accountability to the people.

The vast scale of public expenditures establishes an independent economic base and vested interest for those in command of the state.

These expenditures and programmes which should be utilized as resources otherwise necessary to meet national modernization and development needs, are hardly ever questioned or interrogated by anybody else let alone those outside the parameters of state power.

The army Commander-in-Chief and the country's Head of State cannot in this system of military rule, be questioned by any other authority. He exists above the law, and is both the law and the in charge of the country's treasury.

Despite the Constitution of the country and the Army Act, conditionalities and requirements in the management of the military - the Commander-in-Chief, is and holds as the exception to the set management systems, and rules. Indeed he organizes the army and its

---

[64] AFRICOM is responsible for U.S. military operations, including fighting regional conflicts and military relations with 53 African nations. Its area of responsibility covers all of Africa except Egypt, which is within the area of responsibility of the UNITED STATES CENTRAL COMMAND.

operations by martial law under the cover of public and national security.

The demands made for state expenditures and the manner of their disbursement are logically influenced by the motivations for and the interests of private benefit of those who are in charge of each given transaction, project or program.

They also get partly influenced by the collective demands of the state's security system, e.g. the military itself and mercenary politicals, that have vested interests in channeling public funds into projects and programmes that serve their given interests of self-gain, which often stand in contravention of other outstanding needs in the country's economy that get deprived of necessary resources and funding. Often other vital interests of producers in the economy etc., are just overlooked or ignored while multiple obstacles get placed on their way to seek necessary alternative sources, however deserving and justified these may be in the national or public interest terms.

Corruption and bribery thereby become generalized as the ordinary or normal order of things because of the proliferation of administrative and petty paper controls that the state everywhere imposes in place. Bribing state officials at all levels is a channel by which those in command of the state machinery siphon off huge amounts of resources, and the country's surplus for their own private gain.

The enrichment of public officials - politicals, bureaucrats, military and security officers - thereby becomes an uncontrollable epidemic.

The corrupt in positions of power do everything possible to multiply their ill-gotten gains. They take over banks and financial houses which they derelict while they also pilfer from state and national corporations till these get collapsed.

So long as the fascist socio-economic and political power system guarantees the commitment of the guardians of the neo-colonial state to maintain the social order over which the military dictatorship presides, the sacrifice of a portion or part of the country's economic surplus is considered by the fascist system as a legitimate price for its ultimate survival.

The political management of the economy over which this state presides is, however, subject to the capitalist structural imperative which in the final analysis compels the state and indeed all capital and profit run enterprises in the country to follow or attune their activities, projects and plans to the demands for the realisation of economic surpluses and profit or else face unresolvable crises, bankruptcy or even economic collapse.

In the structurally bleeding economy, such as that hosted by the neo-colonial state and fascist dictatorship in Uganda, the creation of effective representative political institutions through which political pressure and public scrutiny could be imposed on the state and its administration; is wholly negated.

Where these or such institutions may be allowed for one reason or other to nominally exist - even in their shadow forms - parliamentary institutions and political parties often get atrophied, while effective power gravitates or gets moved into the hands of those who constitute the command of the military and security forces, and those who run the bureaucracy, etc., – i.e. those who hold at the real center(s) of power of the dictatorship.

In this situation, civilian governance and the parliamentary facades in the country does in no way prevent the full deployment of the military against popular struggles for freedom, political autonomy, peoples and human rights etc. These popular and democratic struggles have been and are subject to severe repression.

Beyond these political facades – the military becomes or comes to act as a law unto itself in the repressive, spoliatory and predatory offensives it carries out within the country and in its African neighbourhoods. The military here, led by its Commander-in-Chief, becomes a power that is subject to no other authority, except in the formal terms, that which is set by its own Command.

The Commander-In-Chief of the fascist army and military stands as a vain braggart and showman who to quote George Eliot, is,

"...like a cock who thought the sun rises to hear him crow..."

In effect, the army of fascist dictatorship gets deployed and is made to operate under unproclaimed martial law, which in reality supersedes all constitutional and legal constraints.

Martial law makes possible, extreme arbitrary rule not only in regard to offensive and repressive actions, but also even in regard to administrative actions.

The ruthlessness of the processes of capital accumulation in Nile Africa and the overall destructive and, or negative impact which they generate against the exploited and oppressed masses of people is both gross and grave. Primitive accumulation that is mounted by capital and finance interests in Africa is based on robber processes which negate all law and regulatory processes. These processes by their very nature negate all law and the fundamentals of legality and the observance of the Rule of Law. They even violate the capitalist calculus, which is operative elsewhere in non-banana republic capitalist formations.

These outlaw systems of governance and political management create arena or fields of general destruction.

To its politicals, as the historian Sir John Harold Plumb aptly noted of a similar earlier capitalist formation;

> *"...the aim of politics was not directed to liberties ...*
> *"...to Justice, but to pursuit of office, because office meant*
> *power, privilege, or perquisite and was a vital key to success in*
> *a race that trampled losers underfoot..."*

These robber systems of governance are in effect, products of systems of ruthless primitive accumulation, which inherently on end generate arbitrariness in governance. They constitute a basis for negating democratic governance, the rule of law and legality in alien capital dominated Africa.

It is philosophical folly to believe that these robber systems can ever be democratised or humanised. As elsewhere, they can neither legitimise themselves nor their cruel and destructive rule.

The fascist dictatorship in Uganda is a typical example of the foregoing.

It has, despite the said unresolvable dilemma, however, still to try to fashion ideological justifications of its dictatorship, particularly since its gross repression of the civil population is continuous and difficult to hide. Co-optable political parties, civil society formations and parliamentary assembly, intelligentsia, gullible media, clergy etc. are often, with small monetary fee and other bribes, made to pitch in to attempt to provide if ever possible, political legitimacy to fascist dictatorship within the framework it sets in place.

Yet even in a fascist dictatorship, the neo-colonial state, though a tool or instrument of oppression and repression is never monolithic. Its victim peoples can with due wisdom and perspicacity have generated in place a stream of mass political contentions within its spaces, such as during the military regime's often much orchestrated general and presidential elections. The challenge is to utilize these opportunities to raise genuine popular and national democratic forces against fascism.

Contending interests which seek various forms of political representation in the fascist system and the neo-colonial state and vie with each other for positions of influence; and often in non-fundamental ways, crave to be co-opted into the processes for the formulation and implementation of public policy along the lines that serve their co-optable interests, are from time to time accommodated to attempt to fool the people and the democratic world and lend the neo-colonial state and its military dictatorship legitimacy.

Concessions made by the fascist dictatorship to such co-optable interests, such as granting permission for their involvement in electoral contestations - i.e. for low or middle grade elective seats and positions in the state; permission to hold rallies of political opposition parties, student, labour and other civil society demonstrations etc. - are largely meant to blunt and forestall the drive to their oppositional objectives.

The fascist dictatorship therefore stands amenable to permitting superficial modifications and reforms of its governance system, which lend it the lie of political accommodation. The obtaining reality of fascist dictatorship is that its political system is discriminatory and exclusive of all others who are not of its ilk. Experience and political practices have shown that no real democratisation of political power is possible within the fascist system of Uganda/Nile Africa.

The only way out of, forward and upwards from the fascist dictatorship is to impose a rupture and, or a break and open up possibilities for a popular democratic alternative to rise in its ashes and ruins.

The fascist social order and its dictatorship have to be overcome, transcended and left behind as a superseded formation which makes possible the opening of a new door to a new history of positive possibilities and the rise of a liberated and free African humanity which will bear the responsibility to democratically self-govern, under their newly rediscovered collective self-initiatives; seize the wheel of history and forever turn it in favour of liberated African humanity.

Today, it is as if, in these times, the liberatory example of Prophet Moses, the liberator of slaves in Nile Egypt, has come to hover over Uganda/Nile Africa. Such situations are pregnant with many liberatory possibilities. In this regard, Leon Trotsky, one of the prominent leaders of the Russian revolution, with great perception noted that;

> *"...Revolution is impossible until it's inevitable..."*

Ugandans/Nile Africans now stand before a history of complex possibilities.

After decades and years of protracted political, ideological, spiritual, psychological etc. contestations with the evil Pharaoh, the slave master of Nile Egypt, his state bureaucracy and armed/security formations, the slaves seized the ripe moment of liberation and Passover, which had got matured through focused mass rupture with the old slave social and political formation.

That focused mass political action for social, political and national liberation was, multifaceted and multi-frontal. The offensive mounted to disarm the armed forces of the evil Pharaoh and his system, was only one facet or element in the frontal effort to paralyse and politically defeat the evil Pharaohnic slave polity. The inclement weather, which arose during the height of the liberatory actions was of course duly taken advantage of by the liberatory forces.

This liberatory strategy remains legitimate and holds its potency in modern times. It is a political project, which unfolds in the like of an earthquake or wind. Its movement is felt, but not seen by the eye.

The political project involved at the liberatory process led by Prophet Moses in Nile Egypt, of focused mass action for liberation, is not only replicable in modern times, but is imbued with similar liberatory spirit.

The liberatory political project in the then slave Nile Egypt, is in fundamental ways and many essences akin to that which is underway in fascist occupied Nile Africa.

Like then, at the time of the Pharaoh, the slave master of Nile Egypt; the liberatory process in Nile Africa never seeks to take over and inherit the old social order of human enslavement, but to politically defeat the fascist dictatorship at the watershed point at which to effect a rupture with its evil order and work to build in its place a new humane and just social order of equity and equality of all Nile African peoples, nationalities and communities.

The high objective of the liberatory process is to generate the rise of sovereign networked spaces that enable the exploited and oppressed people to coalesce into firm self-protection formations, to which due liberatory support is provided so that they can by their self-initiative, self-motivation and focused actions permanently defeat the dictatorship by their concerted actions.

The leadership of the multi-frontal liberatory struggles in the country will have to be moulded from the various elements - in the general political, social and national liberatory struggles and in the military, trans-military and other non-military contestations in the country that inherently rise in the liberatory struggles.

The great Chinese sage Lao Tzu made propositions on the essential characteristics of such leadership. These propositions remain valid even in the contemporary times:-

> *"...As for the best, the People do not notice their essence...*
>
> *"...The next best, the People honour and praise,...*
>
> *"...The next, the People fear and the next the People hate...*
>
> *"...When the best leader's work is done, the People say:...*
>
> *"...We did it ourselves..."*

The Chinese philosopher Confucius held the opinion that:

> *"...He who exercises government by means of his virtue may be compared to the North polar star, which keeps its place and all stars turn towards it..."*

The foregoing point, to some of the principal characteristics to be considered in developing and evolving the type of responsible and accountable popular and community servant, developmental and progressive moral leadership which African peoples, nationalities and communities have long sought to nurture from within their ranks.

What is however critical is that after the tragic tenure of fascist dictatorship in Nile Africa, a democratic, accountable and responsible leadership is evolved that is not only imbued with historical sense, or holds a historical perspective, and the attitude of courage, to face up to the facts of this difficult and complex world that is saturated with toxic anti-African prejudices; but still has faith in the historical possibilities of humankind and the future.

Such leadership will recognise the moral obligations incumbent upon it to enjoin all sectors of mankind to fight against the evil and destructive imperial system which traumatizes, maims, oppresses, and dishonours those who live under it, and today struggle to protect and further nurture just and humane societies and environments which would be fit to sustain God's humanity on earth and in this turbulent universe.

Consequently, after fascism and fascist dictatorship is defeated, overcome and transcended,

"...the Africans whose hands..."

the poet noted,

"...have laid the foundation stones of the world...",

shall self-secure for themselves the freedom, the independence and capacities requisite to create, accumulate and deploy for their own development –

"...capital..."

as that indestructible accelerator of the processes of development of the productive forces, for truly autonomous, equitably shared and beneficial African development.

It is evident that after over three decades of destructive fascist dictatorship – its regime has closed all possibilities and avenues of political dialogue, discussion and engagement for the genuine resolution of the political problem of Uganda/Nile Africa.

In this situation the people of right stand justified to seek all and any means requisite to assert to free themselves from the destructive misrule of the fascist regime.

In contemporary times, the right to freedom and self-determination of peoples and nations stand indefeasible. Indeed given the experiences of freedom achievements in contemporary times, the way forward to freedom cannot forever be denied or closed to the people.

Throughout human history, peoples struggling for freedom, have had to seek and device novel ways and means to win freedom. For nowhere has non-popular power of the oppressors ever accepted without resistance the freedom demands of the oppressed.

The well-remembered African American, Frederick Douglass, who fought and won freedom from US slavery – famously noted that;

"...Power concedes nothing without demand. It never did, and it never will...

"...Find out first what people will submit to, and you have found the exact amount of injustice and wrong which will be imposed upon them, and these will continue till they are resisted with either words or blows, or with both...

"...The limits of tyrants are prescribed by the endurance of those whom they oppress..."

In such situation – resistance against oppression, exploitation and overall dehumanisation becomes an imperative duty.

Frederick Douglass[65] noted that oppressed man and woman;

> *"...may not get all they pray for in this world; but they must certainly pay for all they get...*
>
> *"...If we ever get free from all the oppression and wrongs heaped upon us, we must pay for their removal...*
>
> *"...We must do this by labour, by suffering and if needs be, by our lives, and the lives of others..."*

The Irish people and nation, who were for long subjected to brutal British colonial rule, occupation and land dispossession – and processes and programmes of primitive capital accumulation for British capital – struggled for long for Irish freedom and independence; using political and armed actions. For a long time – Europe held deaf until the twentieth century to the Irish demands of independence and self-determination.

In 1907, a young, then only 18 years old, Indian student at Eton, one Jawaharlal Nehru[66], later the first Prime Minister of independent India, excitedly wrote a letter to his father Motilal Nehru (a barrister), who was in India about the then new liberation organization that had arisen in the Irish freedom and independence struggle in 1905:

> *"...Have you heard of Sinn Fein?*

[He enquired from his Barrister father]

> *"...It is a most interesting movement and resembles very closely the so called extremists of India...*
>
> *"...Their policy is not to beg for favours, but wrest them..."*

Nehru's letter was a note depicting great foresight.

In the Northern part of America – in the then British colony, the independence movement of its people – was formed and, or crystallised in the thick of political and armed struggle of the colonized people for independence, towards the end of which the American freedom fighters issued, the now world famous, *"...Declaration of Independence...,"* which Thomas Jefferson, later US Secretary of State and President of

---

[65] An Autobiography: The Life and Times of Frederick Douglass published 1881 Boston: De Wolfe and Fiske Co.
[66] Jawaharlal Nehru, 12th September 1907, in D. Norman ed.; Nehru – The First Years, New York (1965) p.12.

the Republic was tasked to draft for adoption by various US state's elected Congresses.

The 1916 daring proclamation of Irish independence and an independent republic was a most profound and an earth shaking act.

The two instances of freedom struggles in Ireland and North America – later the United States of America – against Imperial British occupation and rule, are renowned and have earned their distinct places in history.

These are demonstrative examples of the many liberatory experiences whose demands and challenges have gone to define what strategies, methods, ways and means, or activities may be adopted in the effort to win national freedom and independence of a people.

CHAPTER 6

AFTER FASCIST DICTATORSHIP: QUESTIONS AND THEORIES ON TRANSITION TO POPULAR SELF GOVERNANCE

The complexity of transition – to new social orders, from the old cannot be underrated. The poet T.S. Eliot[67] sums this situation best:

> "...Time present and time past...
> "...Are both perhaps present in time future...
> "...And time future contained in time past..."

The longing to move and, or gear the present into a new better and more humane future, though often derided – is a regular feature of the human condition that never ceases to aspire for new beginnings that are yet to be realised.

The challenge in Africa is to pave paths to the aspired for new social orders – within which free African humanity can live and self-govern, flower and flourish in prosperity and due dignity, and self-become in shared happiness.

This path of transition commences or begins from the African villages – in the African village communities – as formations with and within which firmly grounded genuine new beginnings can be constructed and nurtured.

The obtaining citadels of modernity, now built in towns and political capitals from which multinational capital and finance interests and its African agents and allied political classes issue and impose their costly and ruinous commands to the African villages – will have of necessity to be substituted and replaced by systems of equity and justice that are tempered by the genuine needs and developmental necessities of the African villages.

Today every African political capital is, but an *'imperium in imperio'*, 'a republic within a republic', or 'a state within a state' and are in their fundamentals alien and in effect not organic to the texture

---

[67] T.S. Eliot, 'Burnt Norton' Four Quarters (1936)

of the African countries which host them at tremendous undeserved sacrifices and costs to the oppressed and exploited African peoples, their nations and communities.

The African peoples imaginative genius, that gets crystallised, developed and demonstratively unfolds in the dynamic of political, social and national liberatory struggles, that is to the benefit of popular self-governance in secured independent and sovereign African geographical spaces; will guide the invention of and transition to the glorious and dignified future that the African people have long aspired for and deserved as the humanity made in the image of God Almighty.

The experiences of other free peoples of the world who have successfully transitioned from the old dehumanising social orders to the new – liberatory ones have to be examined and interrogated as exemplary human efforts from which pertinent lessons can be learnt and taken due advantage of.

Indeed, it is in the invention of a new future and humanist social order that the real history of free humanity will once again begin - to unfold in Uganda/ Nile Africa, as the poet T.S. Eliot postulated:

> *"...Here the impossible union...*
> *"...Of spheres of existence is actual...,*
> *"...Here the past and the future...*
> *"...Are conquered, and reconciled,...*
> *"...Where action were otherwise movement...*
> *"...Of that which is only moved...*
> *"...And, has in it no source of movement..."*

When the evil social order of fascism and its dictatorship are defeated, the new world of open historical possibilities that arises – has to be taken advantage of to effect organised transition to a new social order based on the aspirations and hopes, needs and necessities of the communities and society of the free in Uganda/Nile Africa.

African political independence has hitherto not effected, a rupture or a break with the old social order, which has been overtime moulded and dominated by alien capital.

This old order has metamorphosed, but has retained its structural fundamentals.

The African political terrain stands bereft of examples of successful transition to systems of peoples democratic self-governance, largely because the African revolts have been contained before their maturity into full-fledged revolutions. The old colonial social order, which has been the offspring and servitor of alien capital and finance interests, has in socio-economic terms not yet been dismantled. This continuity still burdens Africa.

The situation of definitive structural continuities is not accidental.

Their harmful impact on Africa is profound.

Africa is held up in a situation of *"change without change"* and is forced to run on the same spot, in terms of historical progress and forward march in history.

In this historical paralysis and socio-economic stagnation – Africa stands faced with the responsibility of reclaiming self-initiative over its own life as the means with which to break out of the captivity imposed upon it by multinational capital and finance interests, and its hegemons.

The African agent governing classes, have not only succumbed to this slave situation, but have together with the interests of multinational capital and finance which dominate Africa actively promoted the continuity of this malign condition.

The end result is the total marginalisation from political power and disenfranchisement of the masses of the African people. Everywhere in Africa – the political, social and national liberatory efforts that sought to win new, free, independent and sovereign spaces within which the African people could establish systems of autochthonous popular democratic power and democratic self-governance – have either been stymied or aborted.

African agent political classes and elite, victims of cultural and ideological domination and westernisation today unashamedly revel in and, or celebrate their tragic slave roles of collaborators of alien socio-economic interests – a position which they continuously justify with the ideologies of alien capital driven modernisation.

It could not in the circumstances be otherwise.

It is folly to imagine that these slave systems can become fountains of human and peoples rights in Africa. It is best to recall the time proven statement of Rudolf Rocker, an Austrian anarchist activist – made in 1938 that;

> *"...political rights do not originate in Parliaments; they are
> rather thrust upon them from without...*

*"...And, even their enactment into law has for a long time been
no guarantee of their security...*
*"...They do not exist because they have been set down on a
piece of paper, but only when they have become the ingrown
habit of a people, and when any attempt to impair them will
meet with violent resistance of the populace..."*

The African agent political classes and elite are products of the successful projects of decolonisation, and new colonisation of Africa by multinational capital and finance. This slave relationship largely holds to their benefit and that of their bounden African agents and *'nyampalas'*[68] who are their collaborators in the haemorrhaging of the continent.

Decolonisation and new colonisation are hence processes that have largely ensured the survival of the requisite *"continuities"* from the colonial past in the contemporary dominance of Africa by alien economic interests.

The otherwise necessary rupture or break with the malign and terrible realities of the history of African enslavement and domination by multinational capital and finance has hence not happened in Africa.

In terms of historical progress and forward march, Africa is held up in the malign conditions of implosive paralyses and stagnation, internal disintegration and even regress.

Without effecting a rupture or a break with the continuities of the past or a break with the realities or a history of slavery and a dominated Africa under alien capital interests – there can be only superficial and no meaningful transition to new systems of democratic popular self-governance.

Decolonisation led largely to the Africanisation of the political management of African polities by the African political elite. These successors of colonial managers of Africa – run particularly discriminative caste and, or class systems, which have totally excluded by law and political practices the oppressed and exploited masses of African people, from the exercise of political power of self-governance.

The obtaining emasculation of the masses within the socio-economic framework of deep adversity further ensures that the exploited and oppressed African masses – firmly remain outside the framework of political governance.

---

[68] Ibid 2

Even in African countries that have undergone armed struggles and revolutionary action for liberation – such as Algeria, Mozambique, Angola, Guinea Bissau/Cape Verde, South Africa, Zimbabwe, Namibia, etc. the systems of exclusion of the masses of people from political power exercise has been significant. Their various attempts to found popular political systems foundered and were aborted. Decolonisation and governance by the political elite instead triumphed.

Leaders of revolutionary liberation movements – have either been assassinated, violently overthrown, or in one way or another disabled from supporting the oppressed and exploited Africa masses in their popular struggles to win national freedom and build necessary capacities with which to establish systems of – peoples democratic self-governance.

There have existed beyond this situation, many other drawbacks of – social, organisational, cultural and ideological handicaps imposed on the people that have disabled the oppressed and exploited African masses from asserting, on their own account, their right of democratic self-governance.

The African political classes together with the global system of imperialism – have done and continue to do everything possible to blind the oppressed in Africa to the possibilities of winning the struggles for political self-emancipation and creation of the capacities that are necessary to institute – democratic self-governance by the African masses of people.

The learning and knowledge acquisition processes that are generated in the freedom and liberation struggles can be utilised to open up new vistas within which to acquire the multiple knowledges and capacities necessary to create the conditions for building and moulding systems of popular democratic self-governance of the masses of African people.

Education for liberation has to be made into the means with which to help invent a path to the future of popular democratic self-governance – whose power would be used to activate the masses to leap into the condition of real command and control of their destinies and those of their countries.

The African masses of people, despite being victims of relentless oppression and exploitation, repression and humiliation, can be assisted to rise to the condition where they are enabled to acquire necessary knowledges for self-governance.

History has shown that illiteracy, or being unlettered, is no bar to political consciousness; that is a pivotal factor with which many disadvantages can be overcome by appropriate knowledge acquisition and organised intelligent action. In effect, popular struggles equally, do constitute vital means to raise levels of consciousness.

Through appropriate knowledge acquisition efforts, progress can be made through struggles whereby new talents come to emerge while requisite knowledge advances in leaps.

The path to acquire appropriate knowledges and awareness of obtaining, but ever changing realities is never smooth. Many obstacles stand on the way to accurate knowledge acquisition, including those contrived to blind the enslaved by those others who are beneficiaries of given slave systems.

The fundamental of the African peoples struggles for freedom, popular self-governance and African self-becoming is at the core of these struggles. The battle of conceptualisation on the nature and character of the realities over which African struggles take place is fierce.

The African writer and intellectual, Ngũgĩ wa Thiong'o, writing on the theme of *"Education for National Culture"* – perhaps better couched as *'Education for National Liberation Culture'*, noted the dilemma faced by both oppressor and oppressed in conceptualising the inhuman condition where the oppressor dehumanises the oppressed and attempts to justify and explain away this tragic condition as 'natural' – hence something to be simply borne out by the oppressed without much ado. The effort requisite – to draw out with the oppressed, the opposite of what the oppressor presents as "rational", has to be made.

Ngũgĩ wa Thiong'o[69], depicts the obtaining slave situation and said dilemma thus:-

> *"...A is sitting on B...*
>
> *"...A is carried, fed and clothed by B...*
>
> *"...what kinds of education [analysis and explanation of things] will A want B to get?...*
>
> *"...In other words, education for what kind of culture and consciousness?...*
>
> *"...A will want to educate B to obscure the fact that it is B who is carrying, feeding and clothing A...*

---

[69] [Ngũgĩ wa Thiong'o: Education for National Culture, Paper presented at the seminar: Education in Zimbabwe, Past, Present and Future - 1981, 7/8

"...A will want B to learn the philosophy which says the world does not change...

"...A will want to teach B the religion which tells him that the present situation is divinely willed and nothing can be done about it, or that B is in the present position because he has sinned, or that B should endure his lot because in heaven he will be in plenty...

"...Religion, any religion is very useful to A for it teaches that the situation in which A is sitting on B is not brought about by man, it is not historical; on the contrary, it's a natural law of the universe, sanctioned by God...

"...A will want B to believe that he, B has no culture or his culture is inferior...

"...A will then want B to imbibe a culture that inculcates in him values of self-doubt, self-denigration, in a word slave consciousness...

"...He will now look up to A's superior culture. In short, A will want B to have the education which on the one hand will deny him real knowledge about the status quo of A sitting on B; and on the other, impart a culture embodying the values of slavery, a slave consciousness or world outlook...

"...This will make B subservient...

"...For A wants B not only to be a slave but also accept that his fate or destiny is to be a slave..."

This type of education, is what in essence imperialism and its African agents, 'nyampalas'[70], pawns and collaborators (the 'Omuzungu Agambye'[71] Africans, the imperial white man's African parrots and copy cats) have been socialising the African youths, men and women into, which embodies values, consciousness and a world outlook that is in harmony with the ruinous projects of imperialism in Africa.

Professor Yash Tandon[72] notes that:

"...It produces an African who has internalised the distorted consciousness that blinds him into not seeing and insensitivities him to the violence, the oppression and exploitation that is going on all around him, or into not seeing and minding, but resigning himself to it...

---

[70] Ibid 2
[71] Ibid 4
[72] Militarism and Peace Education/p.72,

> *"...The other purpose is to produce an elite which has imbibed the culture of imperialism and which then becomes the medium of neo-colonial oppression and exploitation..."*

The essence of education for liberation or liberation education which would seek to realise the very opposite of the slave colonial and neo-colonial education, has again been aptly summed by Prof Ngũgĩ wa Thiong'o[73] thus:-

> *"...B on the other hand will want that philosophy which teaches that everything changes, that change is inherent in nature and human society...*
>
> *"...He will embrace that religion which teaches that the system of some people sitting on others is against the law of God...*
>
> *"...B may want to re-evaluate his past and he will discover that he was not always a slave, carrying, feeding and clothing A...*
>
> *"...Thus he will embrace that education which shows him quite clearly that his present plight is historical not natural, that it was brought by man and can also be changed by man...*
>
> *"...B will embrace that culture which inculcates in him values of self-confidence and pride in self, values which give him courage and faith that he can do something about his present plight...*
>
> *"...In short B will want that education which not only gives him knowledge about his plight, but a liberated consciousness, a consciousness urging him to fight for freedom...*
>
> *"...Now it is possible that A and B are not necessarily conscious of the education and culture and world outlook they want...*
>
> *"...But the fact remains that there is an education system which imparts a culture embodying a consciousness corresponding to the objective position of B...*
>
> *"...The two types of education, culture and world outlook, are in mortal struggle for A is trying to make B embrace a slave consciousness so that he, can rest in peace...*
>
> *"...But B is also struggling to evolve an education that imparts a culture that frees him from intended slave consciousness so that he can with confidence overturn A and be free to now carry, feed and clothe himself..."*

It is hence necessary not only to draw distinction between, on the one hand, slave education and, on the other, liberation education, but

---

[73] Ibid 68 - p8/8

to appreciate that the two world outlooks or viewpoints held are not only distinct and different, but are in a state of antagonism with each other.

The late Brazilian revolutionary educationist, Paulo Freire, friend of the unlettered oppressed of the world and author of the *'Pedagogy of the Oppressed'* and many related scientific works, publications and books on pedagogy, argued that the ignorance and lethargy that the poor suffered were the result of their victimisation under conditions of economic, social and political domination. This was a situation that could be overcome via struggles of political, social and national liberation, Paulo Freire proffered.

The poor have been held in subhuman conditions in which it has been most difficult if not practically impossible, to achieve the critical awareness and knowledges requisite to mount combative responses to free themselves from the extant malign condition within which they stand trapped.

Throughout Africa – oppressors have also abused systems of education to generate *'cultures of silence'* in the face of terrible systemic mass oppression and degradation amidst adversities in which the masses of the African people stand entrapped.

With dialogical processes and incisive collective interrogations of reality, every human being, no matter how disadvantaged, impoverished and illiterate, and no matter how deep he or she is wallowing within the state of non-knowledge, can be activated to develop due awareness of the ruinous oppression and degradation to which one is subjected, and be persuaded to work to free self and get motivated into actions for self/collective salvation or self/collective emancipation and for effecting necessary positive change in his or her conditions of being.

The person or human being, hitherto enslaved and dehumanised by social adversities, including relentless oppression and repression, degradation and humiliation, can be assisted to win back the right to say his or her word, and thereby boldly set forth and express his or her actual opinion as to what the world that is, should become, and work to realise that world.

With rising awareness of the sad socio-economic realities within which they stand trapped, the profoundly harmful and deep adversities that get thereby imposed on them, the poor can draw out and work to assert and actualise their aspirations to self-emancipation and live as free people, with definitive due entitlements and rights.

They are then able to cultivate their minds and free themselves and their thinking from the constraining complexes of enslavement and domination while developing and strengthening their own capacities to face up to overcoming and transcending the challenges that stand before them in this most difficult world.

Everything and all challenges they come to face - is best placed or put against a question mark, while the constraining impossibles that the oppressors inculcate in them, can begin to be redefined as possibles.

The late lamented Amilcar Cabral, the revolutionary liberation leader and theoretician of the African liberation struggle in Guinea Bissau and Cape Verde, summed up this experience thus;-

In the national liberation struggle:

> *"...The mass of workers and, in particular, the peasants who are illiterate and have never moved beyond the confines of the village or region, in the contact with other categories shed the complexes which constrained them in their relations with other ethnic and social groups...*
>
> *"...They understand their situation as determining elements of the struggle, they break the fetters of the village universe to integrate gradually into the country and the world; they acquire an infinite amount of new knowledge of use to their immediate and future activity within the framework of struggle; and they strengthen their political wareness, by absorbing the principles of national and social revolution postulated by the struggle...*
>
> *"...They thus become fitter to play the decisive role as the principal face of the liberation movement..."*

In the struggle for national liberation, new humanity can be moulded on the basis of the inculcation and internalisation of positive practices of democracy, of criticism and self-criticism, of education for national liberation, of the practices of collective self-reliance and overall collective and best management of assets of the struggle, and informed operation of leadership from the moral high ground within the liberatory processes which bestow honour to selfless efforts and sacrifices which the national liberation struggles exact, and have exacted in the past and over time. Building positive practices in the national liberation struggles that give due value to human integrity, social and gender equality, nationality equality, and to the necessity of realising due all-round development of African humanity, upon whose shoulders the development of Africa and the responsibility to acquire the capacities requisite for Africa's full resurrection, renaissance and self-renewal will much depend; hold as imperative.

In addition, the context of national liberation struggle can be taken due advantage of to make the positive idea and practices of social, political, economic overall solidarity with the oppressed, exploited and the needy, in the country, into a common humanist habit – that defines the distinct essence of Africanity and gives due worth to progressive African cultures and their humane practices.

With successful inculcation of the foregoing, the fundamental elements of the dynamic for national liberation and the awakening of the oppressed and exploited – the masses of the people of Uganda/Nile Africa – should be able to animate themselves to work to sculpture and mould a glorious future for themselves as free self-becoming humanity, after the political defeat of the fascist dictatorship in the country is successfully effected.

The task of crafting a basis of popular transition to and invention of a new future in Nile Africa – remains to be discharged. In the contemporary times, the question of popular transition after the demise and perdition of the fascist dictatorship can no longer be visualized merely in the national perspectives, but with the benefit of the understanding and appreciation of similar efforts in the global terrain.

It is then necessary to seek to imagine, for instance, what autochthonous forms and structures of democratic participation can best serve to skill, capacitate and train the oppressed and exploited knowledge-deficited masses of people of the country to successfully mount and sustain their systems of self-governance, which would rekindle on a continuous basis their desire and imagination to institute systems of popular self-governance in the country.

Appreciation of the knowledges and experiences of how other struggling peoples of the world have sought to institute for themselves systems of autochthonous democratic participatory governance, would fall in handy in the effort of Nile Africans to create their own systems of popular democratic self-governance.

When old minority based dictatorial political systems and social orders have been brought to an end and doors to another history have got opened, a number of critical political questions come to the fore.

What is the future to be?

How, given the end of the old order, should a new beginning be made?

How is the transition to the future to be organised and realised, given the often inherent difficulties of low governance capacity levels and inadequate skills requisite to directly engage the masses of the people in the processes of popular self-governance?

Great thinkers and theoreticians of liberatory struggles and processes, have taken various positions in interrogating, analysing and conceptualising – vexed and critical matters of transition from, the old social political orders that are run by political minorities and dictatorships, to novel autochthonous democratic self-governance of the formerly impoverished, exploited and oppressed masses of people.

Among these, have been historical political personages – such as Thomas Jefferson of the USA *(who was envoy to the leadership of the French revolution, became US Secretary of State and the 4th President of the USA)*, Vladimir Ilyich Lenin of Russia, Antonio Gramsci of Italy, etc.

The revolutionary events that constitute a rupture and, or break with the past, and mark the political defeat of the old social order, are in effect only a new beginning in terms of instituting requisite political transition.

These events, open up periods of transition which aim at attaining the goals of successful liberatory and, or revolutionary processes.

The idea and concepts of transition in liberatory processes have remained matters of serious, vigorous and critical debate.

The transition to new political power relations and realities, have been complex processes.

Often the means used at effecting requisite transitions – have conflicted with and the often proven contradictory aspired for and, or desired popular democratic ends and objectives of liberatory processes.

Thomas Jefferson, like other revolutionaries, understood that liberatory events that overcome old social and political orders not only create ruptures or definitive historical breaks with the past, upon the defeat of their old regimes, but also create independent and sovereign spaces within which to unfold the many possibilities of the future.

Indeed Thomas Jefferson conceived the course of liberatory processes and revolutions in the like of, or as a flowing river, in which each stage reached in the river flow, is only a beginning of the next.

And so, to Thomas Jefferson, the liberatory events become continuous processes and transitions that never seem to come to an end.

His novel conception of transitions generated in and within liberatory processes – set transitions as a critical factor in the tumultuous processes of continuous or endless rebellions for popular democratic self-governance.

To Thomas Jefferson – liberatory processes and revolutions must be continued endlessly, while the people who have to hold the responsibilities of democratic self-governance, get skilled, capacitated and trained not only to manage the varied often tumultuous transitions arising in the situation, but also in the arts and techniques that perpetuate systems of democratic self-governance.

The Russian Vladimir Lenin – himself an active revolutionary of his time – presented a most comprehensive analysis of *"transition"* which has influenced the interrogation of this critical political question, since.

Lenin not only interrogated the possible role of state power and democratic governance or rule after the success of the liberatory events, but ideologically and politically won the political contestations that he and his colleagues had engaged in with their opponents – the Social Democrats and Anarchists who held other views on the critical matter of transition.

To Lenin, the state is always an instrument of class oppression that stands in the way of the high goals to create new, fuller democracies which would no longer be or hold as

> *"...a democracy for the minority, not only for the possessing classes, or only for the rich...",*

but instead –

> *"...a democracy of the poor, democracy for the people..."*

In this new democracy the people would be able to actively and collectively self-rule or self-govern - managing the economy, organising political exchange and communication, and resolving social conflicts, with no other power such as that of a hegemon, standing over them.

To flower this new and popular democracy - the old minority interest state, and any state of such nature and character, must be abolished.

Lenin, on the other hand actively opposed the Anarchists, who proposed the abolition of the state in a single stroke or decisive act, the moment the liberatory and revolutionary events lead to the defeat of the old power and regime.

To Lenin, the Anarchists fail to take into stock or recognise the deleterious effect that defeated oppressive powers have had on dehumanising the masses of people and the real conditions of multiple adversities within which the *"people"* and, or masses of people have been forced to exist, and the resultant condition of their factual lack of capacities necessary to successfully mount, on the basis of necessary knowledges, systems of self-governance and popular democracy.

It was hence imperative, argued Lenin, to understand that the liberatory process has to work,

> *"...with human nature as it is now, with human nature that cannot do without subordination, control and managers..."*

Politics have to be thought and due actions made in terms of the real circumstances that obtain - at the time of the defeat of the political power of the old social order; not otherwise.

Capacitated and skilled people who can govern have to be developed.

They cannot emerge on their own, spontaneously or immediately, upon the defeat of the old political power system.

The social democrats of Lenin's time, had postulated that the old state apparatus had to be maintained and kept in place, as the means with which to manage and run a country after revolution, and as an organ to reconcile social classes!

To Lenin, the social democrats belonged to a category of people who sought to realise *'change without change'* and were averse to revolutionary and transformative change. They sought succession to the old power rather than transition to a new democratic power of popular self-governance and self-rule.

Lenin, finding himself side by side with, or as if standing between the two positions - of the Social Democrats who sought *'change without change'* and would hence preserve the state of the old social order, and the Anarchist position of immediate abolition of the state of the old order; proposed the adoption of the process of revolutionary transition to a new power. The obtaining reality however was that the aims and objectives of the revolution would only be realised over time.

The state apparatus that existed after the triumph of the political liberatory process and defeat of its old regime could only be *"withered"* away as its obnoxious sections were progressively loped off. In addition, the dictatorship of the poor that replaces bourgeois dictatorship, defers democracy that would be achieved or attained when *"transition'* is complete.

For Lenin, the liberatory or revolutionary event causes a historical break that opens a new historical process. The Social Democrats see no revolutionary events, only continuous happenings of reforms in governance, and hence processes that do not break with the old order or occur without rupture with the old order.

The Anarchists on their side see the revolutionary events and their profound nature and character and believe that everything can be changed overnight.

After the political triumph of the liberatory events, Anarchists proceed on the assumption that, the masses of people are already capable of popular democratic self-rule, and will be ready to assume their due democratic responsibilities of self-governance once the repressive apparatus of class rule is collapsed and, or is out of the way.

For the Social Democrats, the masses of people can never be capable of leading and operating democracy and democratic governance. These matters are best left to given knowledgeable and capacitated rulers, who alone can dispense power in a country and "on behalf or in the name of the masses".

For Jefferson and Lenin, at the political triumph of liberatory and revolutionary forces, and the political defeat of the political power of the old order, there is need to train and capacitate the people to self-govern.

'Human nature' of the masses of people, which Lenin notes, has been formed and moulded by and in subordination to the oppressors of man, has to be made anew.

The knowledges, capacities and skills necessary for democracy and self-rule, must be learned and acquired through democratic education, capacity development and training.

According to Lenin, over time;

> *"...observing the simple fundamental rules of every day social*
> *life in common will have become a habit..."*

The period of *'transition'* is hence a time of necessary democratic education and training in which the masses of people learn how to rule themselves, and in which democracy becomes an ingrained characteristic.

In transition – Lenin draws a sharp division between 'means and ends' and between the form of transitional rule and revolutionary goals.

Jefferson's notion of transition recognises the dynamic relations, which arise between revolution and constituted governance, which is subject to periodic rebellions and revolts. He held the opinion that processes of constituent power must continuously disrupt and force open the established constituted power and its governance systems.

To Jefferson, rebellion is not just a matter of correcting wrongs by the government and only valuable if its *'cause'* is just, but that rebellion has an intrinsic value, regardless of the justness of its specific grievances and goals. Periodic rebellion is necessary to guarantee the health of a society and preserve public freedom.

Jefferson was of the view that rebellion should not just become the constant condition, but rather that it should eternally return.

Jefferson was quite or perfectly aware of the destructive cost of rebellion. He held the view that the sacrifice of a few lives was understandable when freedom was at stake; as written in a letter to one of his friends and correspondents:

> *"...The tree of liberty must be refreshed from time to time*
> *with the blood of patriots and tyrants...*
>
> *"...It is its natural manure..."*

Jefferson promoted rebellion against what he adjudged as injustice – whether in revolutionary Jacobin France to which he was an envoy, in America against tyranny of the British King in colonial and pre-independence times, in independent USA: when American farmers, many of whom were veterans of the revolutionary war of independence *(including Daniel Shays, their leader),* organised armed resistance to block the courts and state authorities from sequestering or seizing their farms and properties, and to free their imprisoned comrades from jail. Even when these rebels were defeated and hunted down, and their leaders executed, Jefferson still supported their right to rebel against what he considered the injustice meted against them.

The court of the state of Massachusetts had ruled to imprison farmers who could not pay their debts, seizing their land and property.

Jefferson saw the virtue of a continual return to rebellion as the necessary means for a periodic re-opening of constituent processes. It was his view that, a people and society cannot be allowed to get stranded by a constituted power, but must periodically be opened up to new constituent processes.

No matter what the cost, freedom won had to be sustained if necessary by continuous rebellions.

Jefferson's notion of revolutionary transition is akin to the idea of permanent revolution. He supported periodic re-inventions or renovation of revolutions.

The transition of rebellion/revolution to democracy and back to rebellion is hence endless or has no end point, but only temporary and dynamic periods of stability.

Jefferson's contribution to revolutionary theory is that the *'means'* and *'ends'* of transition are, unlike Lenin's position, never entirely separated; living democracy is both the goal of liberatory/revolutionary process, and also the 'means' of its achievement.

In Jefferson's political canon – the term *"republicanism"*, meant democracy.

His central concept of *"republicanism"* meaning democracy was set thus, he wrote in the US journal;

> *"…Were I to assign to this term a precise and definite idea…*
>
> *"…'Republic' I would say purely and simply…*
>
> *"…It means a government by its citizens in mass acting directly and personally, according to rules established by the majority; and that every other government is more or less of this ingredient of direct action of the citizens…"*

Jefferson's postulated method of democratic governance was direct participatory action of the people in governance – not via representatives who get chosen at, or during electoral processes.

How then can such popular democratic government that is constituted by the direct and active participation of the people or citizens, be both the goal of revolutionary transition and the means of achieving it?

Here, we are faced with the dilemma that Lenin noted, of proceeding in the implementation of transition, after the triumph of the liberatory and revolutionary event and the political defeat of the political regime of the old social order; by making use of *"human nature"* or obtaining humanity – that had been trained by its oppressors to be subservient and passive, and indeed not yet capable of self-governance.

This humanity that exists at the triumph of the liberatory process and the political defeat of the political power of the old social order – may hold negative habits and may be ignorant or wallowing in or immersed in a state of extreme ignorance and non-knowledge. The oppressed and exploited knowledge-deficited masses of people cannot instantly be transformed by the liberatory processes to become the fountains of knowledge or indeed hold necessary capacities for effective and efficient democratic self-governance.

Transition therefore remains as the necessary means with and within which to raise by education and training the masses of people to become the responsible and capable participatory operators of democracy and capacitate them with skills and knowledges requisite to rule themselves or self-govern.

Transition to popular self-governance, hence holds as the condition precedent to meeting the goals and objectives of liberatory processes.

There is the notable innovative example of the element of participatory governance system of the North Eastern Brazilian city of Porto Alegre which boldly adopted a popular budgetary process for itself – based on a radical budgetary reform of the relationship between the public, the government and business in Porto Alegre.

The objective of such radical reform – has been to prevent *"corporate business"* domination of the democratic process, and, thereby, make it possible to enable or give the city authorities and popular civil and democratic forces leverage against corporate power in the decision making process.

To appreciate the innovative participatory budgetary process adopted in the city of Porto Alegre – it is best that its phases be set out in extenso:

The annual participatory budget process of Porto Alegre is structured by a number of phases.

The process begins every year in the month of March with citizens' forums or fora being set up across Porto Alegre's sixteen geographic and sectoral areas of the city.

Forums of five hundred to seven hundred people elect two delegates/representatives and two alternates to serve for one year on the budget council.

In the months of April and May of the same year, the forum of elected delegates/representatives organise smaller assemblies to propose the budget priorities of the public for the following years. Between May and mid-July, the proposed budget priorities are forwarded to the current municipal council (*33 councillors elected by traditional democratic means*). Simultaneously the forum representatives attend training sessions on municipal finance.

The budget council and municipal bureaucrats construct a draft budget, which is sent to the mayor and municipal council for consultation.

Between October and December, the participatory budget council amends the budget for final approval from the municipal council and for eventual implementation in January of the following year.

Altogether the four phases aim at maximising public involvement in setting the city's social and economic development priorities.

The success of the innovative participatory budget process in Porto Alegre, despite the constraints it is subjected to in the Brazilian capitalist formation, found echo around the world that aspires for and seeks liberation, the self-becoming and the self determination of peoples, justice, social equity, peace and equality of peoples.

The participatory budgetary processes adopted in the city of Porto Alegre in Brazil stands as a pointer to what should be possible in effecting transition from the old to the new order when free spaces are liberated for the self-becoming and self-determination of the oppressed humanity in the world.

There have been other innovative and imaginative intellectuals who have theorised the question of revolutionary transition to new democratic power systems after liberation from the old social orders of dictatorship.

One theoretician, Slavoj Zizek, has postulated on the need for revolutionary transition that can transform the people into a popular self-governing category – under the provocative political proposition that is set out as a call; *"...to return to Lenin..."* According to Slavoj Zizek;

> *"...We should bravely admit that it is in fact a duty - even 'the' duty - of a revolutionary party to...*
> *"...dissolve the people and elect another...*
> *"...perhaps as mockingly postulated by the poet Bertolt Bretch, that is to bring about transubstantiation of the old opportunistic people into a revolutionary body that is aware of its historical task to transform the body of the empirical people into a body of Truth..."*

Zizek stressed the need for this transformation as imperative. He has been relentless in the criticism of those who should, but fail to face up to the challenge of organised and educated transformation, while wittingly or unwittingly counting on the spontaneous virtue, wisdom and goodness of the people.

This transformation is understood not only to come from above, i.e. from outside the people, but as the means with which to induce and effect a radical leap. Yet the processes of transformation as presented still remain significantly opaque.

The form of political authority that is to lead this operation is radically different from the new democracy that Lenin saw as the goal.

Zizek proposes no mechanism for achieving transformation.

His reference to the notion of transformation is an attempt to emphasise how drastically the social body has to be transformed.

This formulation encapsulates the idea of a radical leap rather than the idea of a continuous becoming.

Another notable theoretician was the late Ernesto Laclau. Laclau considered democratic politics as, the end point of an extended logical sequence, beginning with his assertion that the social field is radically heterogeneous, and has no spontaneous or pre-given order.

To Laclau, the logical process leading to politics and ultimately to democracy begins with the myriad of social demands that arise in society - such as the demands for bread or food, basic rights, entitlements to social, human rights, or freedom, etc.

The common nature of these demands, he suggests, are best recognised and appreciated, so that they can be articulated together and arranged as;

> *"...a chain of equivalents..."*

This

'...chain of equivalents...'

should be given coherence so that out of the plurality of demands a popular common identity is constructed to produce

"...the category of people..."

- i.e., that of the humanity which objectively holds similar interests.

This construction of the human category of the people is the necessary and essential condition for democracy.

The identity of this human motor, which holds the potential to drive the movement of things, is critical; for the creation of the category of the *'people'* is never spontaneous. Indeed, nothing in those demands individually considered generates a commonality such as *'a manifest destiny'* by which these popular demand elements should tend to coalesce into some unity. In effect, nothing in them anticipates that they should constitute *'a chain'*.

Moreover, a chain of equivalents does not immediately or spontaneously create that critical category of the people.

What is necessary in this regard, insists Laclau, is the rise of a hegemonic figure that stands above the social field who from that transcendent position, is then able to guide this process, articulating the individual elements, posing the need for and actualising requisite unity for creating that pivotal critical political category of a people.

This not yet fully-fledged *'transcendence'* is, but *'a failed transcendence'* that nonetheless is able to fulfil the critical role of generating dynamic hegemony that will keep the emergent political and social bloc in continuous formation.

The hegemonic figure here arising may not necessarily be a political party or organisation. What is important, is that it nonetheless fulfils the critical function of a hegemonic figure that holds and actualises necessary organisational prowess.

The fact that the occurrence of the revolutionary event creates a new situation which calls for transition at a time when the people have as yet not built the capacities requisite to self-govern or self-rule, raises the question of what is to be done in such a situation?

According to Slavoj Zizek and Ernesto Laclau the population has to be transformed by a figure of authority or a hegemon, a political party or organisation which stands above the people who are to be enabled by democratic education, capacitation and training to rise to assume their role of self=governance after the revolutionary event.

This undemocratic intervention of a hegemon in the process of transition is supposedly meant in the end, to result in the realisation of democracy and popular self-governance.

The common recognition by Jefferson, Lenin, Zizek, Laclau, etc., that the time of liberation or the success of the revolutionary event in overthrowing the old order; finds the oppressed and exploited masses of people still handicapped, amidst historically imposed multiple disabilities that bar them from immediately assuming their due roles of instituting self-rule or self-governance, raises the necessity for the people to get transformed through processes of democratic training and education to enable the people to get capacitated for democratic self-governance or self-rule.

Jefferson like other revolutionary theorists, e.g. Mao Tse Tung, Antonio Gramsci, Lenin, etc., saw popular education as a condition precedent to enable the people accede to democratic self-governance or democratic self-rule. Jefferson devoted considerable attention to popular and democratic education and training. He championed the right of access to schools and libraries (knowledge and data banks), which were essential for the creation of new habits, skills and knowledges with which to nurture, mature and sustain popular democratic self-governance.

In the second decade of the 19th century, Jefferson proposed for the establishment of systems of *"wards or little republics"* in the USA as an experiment in popular local autonomy. This was the time Jefferson boldly critiqued that lack of democracy in USA political life and its constitution.

Jefferson sought to get established systems of active and direct political participation of citizens, and their control organs of power. He felt that forty years after independence – the USA revolutionary process had stalled, fallen back on itself and become closed in a constituted power.

Jefferson's idea to re-open the revolutionary process sought to divide each 'county' into wards of such a size that every citizen could participate in political deliberations actively and in person. These little republics would have full autonomy to decide on all local issues, controlling matters of public interest, justice, police, planning, public welfare, etc. He further proposed that the wards send delegates to compose the next highest body of governance, at the county, which in turn would send delegates to the state level, which finally, would send delegates to the national governance level.

The delegates at the various levels of governance were not to be career, professional or permanent politicians. They would come for deliberations directly from their various stations of life in the USA communities within which they lived and built their lives.

This political schema holds similarities to the institutions of the Paris Commune, which was established much later, after the popular revolt in France. Karl Marx - admired in the Paris Commune the elements that Jefferson proposed in the ward schema: *active participation, local autonomy and a pyramid of delegation.* Both Jefferson and Marx saw this system of participatory governance as an anti-dote to the undemocratic caste or class run form of parliamentary representation.

Marx wrote that the measures of the Commune had;

> *"...Instead of deciding once every three to six years which member of the ruling class was to misrepresent the people in Parliament...*
> *"...betoken the tendency of a government of the people by the people..."*

Jefferson whose position preceded, but anticipated Marx's formulation, noted that the experience of participation in governance is transformative of the people; because it creates conditions:

> *"...Where every man is a sharer in the direction of his ward/republic, or of some of the higher ones, and feels that he is a participator in government affairs, not merely at an election one day in the year, but every day; when there shall not be a man in the state who will not be a member of some one of its councils, great or small, he will let his heart be torn out of his body sooner than his power be wrested from him by a Caesar or Bonaparte..."*

He would defend that system of participatory or popular self-governance with his own life.

In Jefferson's view, participatory self-rule not only stands opposed to the sham democracy that merely legitimates authority through class or caste limited electoral mechanisms, but more importantly, it creates people who will fight against any form of authority that tries to take power from them.

The most important aspect of participatory democracy is how it changes and, or transforms the people. It is a transformative education experience without equal, which trains the masses of people in skills and capacities it needs to rule itself.

These necessary capacities for popular self-governance are not inherent in human societies.

Jefferson, with Lenin, and other theoreticians such as Zizek, Laclau, Gramsci, etc., understood that people who have been forced to exist in subjection to social and personal abuses and amidst gross adversities in un-liberated social and political formations, if not slave social systems, cannot successfully immediately or spontaneously rise to meet the challenge of popular democratic self-rule instantly upon liberation.

Along with Lenin, Zizek, Laclau, etc., Jefferson recognised that, in that malign situation of social adversity, people have to be transformed and that 'a new people' must be created through democratic education, training and capacitation for popular democratic self-rule.

Requisite capacitation for popular self-governance or democratic self-rule, can be achieved and become a result of habit, via long incessant training over time.

Creating new human nature, for Jefferson as for Lenin, is a result or matter of sustained democratic education and training and acquired necessary habits.

This new humanity is not the prerequisite on which political liberation or revolution takes place, but rather the outcome of liberatory and revolutionary processes.

The long processes requisite to create or mould *"a people"* able to self-govern without a local or foreign master – have never been anywhere easy; and have often been difficult and complex, bloody and painful.

For Jefferson, the goal of democratic self-rule has to be achieved no matter the cost – because true sustainable human progress is dependent on the actualisation of the system of popular democratic self-rule. That;

> *"...The tree of liberty must be refreshed from time to time with the blood of patriots and tyrants, if need be..."* –

was Jefferson's unabashed position.

The relevant fact for politics is that human nature is susceptible to change, that humans can become different and transformed.

The revolutionary or liberatory process which should end in democratic self-rule of the people requires a remaking of human nature that destroys the old habits of servitude and develops capacities for novel, innovative and creative popular democratic self-governance, or self-rule.

Along with these capacities grow the political liberatory horizon, imagination and desires, which can press continuously, far beyond the contemporary or current political situations and into the wider universe.

Indeed liberatory processes are not a one-time affair, but incessant processes of continuous becoming, based on the progressive transformation of humanity and constant democratic self-making and capacitation of the masses of people.

People get transformed by practicing political autonomy and active participation in self-governance.

In this regard - it makes little sense for transition; which takes place from the time of the political triumph of liberation, to be ruled by a hegemonic figure or force which stands above the heads of or holds down the masses of people.

Can popular democracy result from what is its opposite?

Transition which is centred around democratic education and training is a process, if ruled by a hegemonic figure - a dictatorial organisation, party, individual, or any such formation - would not teach the people about self-rule, but rather would only reinforce the imposed habits of subservience, blind obedience of the master, political lethargy and passivity.

People only learn democratic self-governance by doing it or in its practice.

The necessary transformation - learning how to self-govern without a master - can best be achieved through practice, in doing and in action - i.e. in practical education for liberation and popular democratic self-rule.

Often in liberatory and revolutionary processes, the democracy aimed at is in continuous development, which makes transition into a process of infinite becoming.

In revolutionary transition within which self-training in the capacities to self-govern takes place, relevant skills and knowledges get acquired, while habits that are developed in these processes generate the rise of a new humanity – which further expands its horizon of self-rule.

In Cuba and Vietnam, the transition processes took place in the complex situation of the then cold war. In effect, for Cuba it was forced transition when the USA and its allies put that country under siege and economic sanctions. From these experiences it is evident that the nature and character of transition is often defined by the internal situation of a country and it's setting in the international power relations system.

The contentions of powers engaged in the *"cold war"* from the 1950's to the late 1970's – generated globalised push and pull factors which doubtless posed difficulties that affected how the two countries that had asserted their independence and sovereignty, transitioned from the old social orders to new ones.

The Chinese who organised their transition processes after the defeat of the old order regime of Gen. Chiang Kai-shek, organised a most imaginative transition under Chairman Mao Tse Tung. The liberatory forces constituted a **Peoples Consultative Conference/Council (PPC)** – representing all democratic, civil and patriotic forces that were active in the liberation struggle.

This alliance of liberatory forces – forged a popular political, constitutional, socio-economic developmental programme, with Chinese civil societies: peasant leagues, workers and youth organisations, associations of patriotic intellectuals and workers in culture, prominent progressive Chinese personages, etc.; to guide the conference and the development of a **New Peoples Democratic China (NPDC)**. The Chinese Peoples Consultative Council, worked to manage the transition to a Peoples Democratic China amidst the then very acrimonious international post Second World War situation – when the victorious powers were in the processes of reorganising the world.

The problem the Chinese transition faced, was that of movement from the remnant influences of the old Chinese civilizations, layered by the fascist dictatorship of Gen. Chiang Kai-shek – to the then unknown rising phenomenon of a liberated, united, new China. It was a time of great and often costly experimentation. Definitive lack of knowledges of building a new economy, a new popular defence system, a new social system, etc. on a planned basis without the possession of much relevant statistics – led to the adoption of trial and error, criticism and self-criticism and stiff political struggles amongst the new Chinese leadership, which had to discard the old mentalities they had grown in. The Communist Party, which emerged as the leading force and arbiter in post liberation China, had equally limited experiences in construction of a new state and its political and economic systems.

It was as if the millions of the then unlettered, but politically conscious Chinese – had to take advantage of their physique and carry the many physically wounded and disabled, but clear sighted leaderships on their backs in the forward movement to a new China.

China became a huge arena of forward mass movement while questioning everything, and a big theatre of participatory resolution of problems. Hence the policy representation of that experience and experiment by Chairman Mao Tse Tung:

> "...to let a hundred flowers blossom and a hundred schools of thought contend..."

It became a tumultuous affair of conceptual contestations, and cross fertilisation and pollination of ideas leading all the way to the Chinese cultural revolution, and its fall out in triggering yet the most dynamic capital driven modernisation in human history.

Will the Chinese inaugurate another transition when that country ceases to be the workshop of the world for the non-Chinese global capital?

The movement from the old to the new order is in essence an immanent process, a learning of democratic self-governance by doing, which is at the same time a process of self-transformation.

Transition, however, is dependent upon the political defeat and removal of the political power of the old social order, which event and, or process creates the necessity to constitute and access a new autochthonous political process.

Where there occurs, an insufficient rupture or break with the past order as in Africa – the old demons of the capitalist colonial system remain destructively active.

The late Mwalimu Julius Nyerere[74] of Tanzania was once, questioned by a Western journalist as to what could be the cause(s) of general

---

[74] Renowned Tanzanian independence leader, pan-Africanist and first President of the Republic of Tanzania.

political turbulence that had arisen in the then immediate post-independent Africa.

After some minutes of thought, the Mwalimu[75] answered to the amazement of the journalist that;

> *"...There is a devil in Africa..."*

The devil in effect has been preying on Africa and is doing everything within its power to resist the emergence and actualisation of independent sovereign autochthonous popular political processes whose programmes do not rhyme with the interests of capital and imperialism.

That devil, alien capital – has since in real terms not only more profoundly than before subordinated Africa to the orbit of its systems and control, but has globalised its operations, motivated by risen multinational capital and finance.

In Africa – this subsumption and, or subordination to processes of accumulation by dispossession, is generating significant social, economic and political turbulences, volatility and general instabilities in and across African polities.

Africa is adrift in the on-going turbulent processes of international capital flow and in the dynamics of ruthless capital accumulation.

Billionaire George Soros, founder of *"Open Society,"* once asserted at The Davos World Economic Forum, which is an assembly of the world's economic and financial *'high and mighty,'* in respect of post-apartheid South Africa, that:

> *"...South Africa (sic Africa) is in the hands of international capital..."*

In short, Soros meant that a *"democratic"* South Africa, like most of African polities governed by political elites, is held as a slave of international capital. Given this position, the African National Congress[76] (ANC) Freedom Charter, which had set out principles for the South African liberation struggle and a programme for reconstructing post-apartheid South Africa, was abandoned except perhaps as a mobilisation tool. Consequently, only superficial transition could be effected in South Africa. In effect, structurally, the old capitalist social order of apartheid has held in place.

---

[75] Ibid 50; Swahili for 'Teacher' – a reverence that was bestowed on Julius Kambarage Nyerere.

[76] Was the main political driver to remove apartheid rule in South Africa; thereafter took the political steering and governance following a democratic election.

The African polities are subjected to the capitalist structural imperative – in which profit and economic surpluses have in the end to be produced and availed to international capital interests, i.e. to the devil in Africa as the Mwalimu Julius Nyerere had observed.

The African agent governing classes have to be obedient to the logic of capitalist rationality and the calculus of capital.

Africans, who are victims of this evil system, hold in opposition and resistance to this slave system under which their fruits of labour as well as natural and bio resources are robbed by ruthless fortune hunters and bio pirates.

In Africa – many geographical and political spaces however, stand beyond the blanket/total control or authority of any local, alien or multinational capitalist force or associated political power.

It is practically impossible to put police personnel or soldiers under every tree, in the shadow or at the top of every hill, or sand dune or at every creek or river valley, etc. to safe guard the alien interests in African lands.

The reality across Africa – across the lands of the Sahel, the lands of African Sahara, the lands in African equatorial forests, in the polities of the Nile River valleys and Basin, in the Congo River valleys and Basin, in the valleys/Basins of the Shebelle and Juba rivers, of the Cunene, Okavango, Limpopo or the Orange, Senegal, Niger rivers, etc.; in the tribulated polities of Libya, Chad, Somalia, Central African lands; in the Horn of Africa region, etc. – is the ever spiralling turbulence, volatilities and instabilities. Multinational capital and finance-in-action, and their forces of extreme greed and spoliation; that have been set loose on to Africa to reduce the continent into their looting and killing fields just further exacerbate these situations of great turbulence, social and political instabilities.

These global lords of misrule, however, largely only control and hold on to given islands of extractive activity in agriculture, mining, bio-piracies, etc. and their immediate environs.

Their necessary control of these islands of loot is tenuous as that of the local or area governmental authorities.

The deficit in political support that they are faced with significantly reduces and, or emasculates their capacities to assert control of and over these vital spaces in Africa. Their foreign helpers like US Africa Command/US Africom, etc. who extend to them military and other assistance, do operate intermittently in the like of fire fighters.

Though multinational capital and finance have structurally subsumed Africa and its lands, multinational capital/finance interests and their political alliances, cannot assert robust control of or over the difficult and hostile hitherto un-accessed African terrain, nor over the ocean shipping lanes or vital straits in the oceans around Africa which are bedevilled by armed pirates of all kinds.

Naval, air and military bases of world powers, that dot the sad Third World, exist in isolation as sitting ducks that are liable to attacks by the dark forces that have arisen as the bi-products of the dehumanising imperial systems, and now roam the world.

The reconfiguration of global control points that have proliferated since the collapse of the former socialist bloc and the disintegration of polities associated with or attached to it, and the impossible chaotic state of things in the energy-rich middle-eastern countries and tribulated African lands; have in essence made the control of this land by capital-in-action more difficult and daunting.

Without a new historical compromise on a global scale such as that which occurred in the world after World War II between capital/finance, and producers/ labour in the industrial northern European systems across capitalist political and economic formations whose effect defused the then most implosive situation at the time, no force however powerful will be able to assume due control over the social turbulence that is bound to rise in many parts of the world.

The fact of obtaining economic stagnation, regress and desolation across the world and massive financialisation of the global economy and overall financial speculation there arising, perhaps even makes the idea of a future historic compromise fictitious.

Already the world is in the absurd situation, in which capital, finance, goods are mobile, but not labour or human *'capital'*. This situation ignores the negative and endless change and reconfigurations that capital and finance/profit-based systems are inherently bound to undergo in the world.

Yet capital, as a motor of production and definitive social relations, has not only generates transformative change and effected the endless dissolution of all life forms necessitated by processes of capitalist reproduction, but is in itself whenever socially instrumentalised proven to be the greatest revolutionising force in human history. The consequences of its global reconfigurations will doubtless continue to be earth shaking.

The peoples of the world cannot however just continue to be driven by capitalist global forces of extreme greed and avarice to the destruction of the world, and the suffocation of all human life and those of other living organisms and, or to the irreversible ruin of related living ecologies and habitats.

The fundamentals of the terrible obtaining global political economy, and the resource based and geo-political contestations of contemporary and emergent globalising powers – are bound to doubtless remain without necessary substantial change with which to make possible the rise of a more human centred world.

Necessary reconfiguration of power systems and realignments of interests and powers that favour equity in global relations must in this regard, take place if the world is not to be pushed to a point where it gets irreversibly destroyed.

Africa which is squarely caught up in this maelstrom, must work to rise to the challenges that are emergent in the situation and self-redeem.

For the African masses of people across the continent, who have long been held as slave victims of imperialism and its allied fascist dictatorships – the historic call of *"physician heal thyself"* or of *"rise to self-salvation,"* which the detractors of Jesus The Christ, otherwise Prophet Issa in Islam, mocked and tormented him with, while helplessly crucified on the cross; has to be seriously taken up. This is perhaps the only way to move out of, and forward and upwards from the prevailing and terrible predicament within which millions of enslaved Africans still remain entrapped.

African political, social and national liberatory efforts with which its masses of people can leverage the continent from its current state of socio-economic backwardness to dynamic modernity and sustainable development, will have the effect of generating an impact with a magnitude which could positively roll across the world, for the benefit of all people who have for so long suffered extreme oppression, exploitation and sustained dehumanisation under the globalised slavery of finance capital.

Indeed the rise of a new human centred world, which is worthy of the humanity, made in the image of God Almighty; is not only possible, but necessary for the good of all.

Despite the odds against it, humanity, though at great cost and sacrifice, will ride and tame the destructive tempests that finance capital has generated in the world, for the human aspirations and hopes for freedom can like the human soul never get destroyed.

While held in apartheid jail – with his many gallant comrades and hundreds of South African freedom fighters – the unforgettable Nelson Rolihlahla Mandela, leader of South African liberatory struggles, communicated at a most grave moment in their history an unforgettable message to the oppressed and exploited South African people – in a note smuggled out of Robben Island jail through the hands of comrade Mac Maharaj. This message not only spoke for itself, but also finds echo even in the contemporary times of tribulated African humanity- the note began:

> *"...The gun has played an important part in our history..."*

After giving an overview of the then obtaining and developing situation in South Africa, it concluded:

> *"...We who are confined within the grey walls of Pretoria regime's prisons reach out to our people...*
>
> *"...With you we count those who have perished by means of the gun and the hangman's rope...*
>
> *"...We face the future with confidence...*
>
> *"...For the guns that serve apartheid cannot render it unconquerable...*
>
> *"...Those who live by the gun shall perish by the gun...*
>
> *"...UNITE! MOBILISE! FIGHT ON!...*
>
> *"...Between the anvil of united mass action and the hammer of armed struggle we shall crush apartheid and white minority racist rule..."*

And it so happened; apartheid fascist dictatorship as a most destructive tool of multinational capital and finance in South Africa; was felled.

Apartheid was a fascist dictatorship and system, which was destructive of all freedoms and democratic values. It was best countered by liberatory actions for an inclusive peoples democracy, as distinct from caste and class minority rule that is subservient to imperialism.

After apartheid was felled, and democratisation of governance was effected, Nelson Mandela, recognising that a new inclusive popular social order was yet to be built, cautioned the African National Congress (ANC) as a liberation movement in the following words:

> *"...If the ANC does not deliver the goods, the people must do to it what they have done to the apartheid regime..."*

Nelson Mandela had recognised that even the ANC with its sterling record of freedom struggle was not infallible.

Indeed, fascism and its dictatorships in Africa have everywhere to be brought to timely ends, so that the doors to a new history with all its possibilities of human progress are opened to enable African peoples re-assert and restore the fullest ownership of their God-given ancestral lands; take control and command of their destinies and those of their lands, build autochthonous and autonomous popular democratic political, social and economic systems; attain prosperity, institute social justice and legality, and foster Africanity – which is the process of the humanisation of African society, the African youths, women and men, build solidarity with all other oppressed and exploited peoples of the world, and make due progress in the mutual and common interests in the company of the free of the world.

African people animatedly look forward to the *"after fascism"* in the continent, to a time of general freedom, i.e. freedom to be and to win freedom from ideological constraints, from the now stale predominant ways of thinking and dreaming. These are the true conditions of liberation – that shall usher in a time of popular democratic self-governance and self-rule of the African masses, and a time of coalescing necessary capacities for African self-becoming and self-determination, and the recovery of Africa's powers of self-renewal for progress.

CHAPTER 7

THE FUTURE: GUARANTEEING NATIONAL FREEDOM AND BUILDING NILE AFRICA'S POPULAR NATIONAL DEMOCRACY

"...The dogmas of the quiet past are inadequate to the stormy present...

"...The occasion is piled high with difficulty and we must rise with the occasion...

"...As our case is new so we must think anew and act anew...

"...We must disenthrall ourselves, then we shall save our country..."

Abraham Lincoln

At this historical point, the fundamental concern of oppressed and exploited Nile African masses of people is much less about the depiction and interpretation of Nile African peoples long march to national freedom, but much more about actualising political, social and national liberation, and the active transformation of the obtaining reality in the country to make possible the self-becoming and self-determination of the Nile African people.

The poet Bertolt Bretch[77], himself an outstanding fighter for freedom, human and peoples rights, encouraged people in similar situations of slavery thus:

"...Today everywhere, from the hundred storied cities...

"...Over the seas, cross-ploughed by teeming liners,...

"...To the loneliest villages, the word has spread...

"...That mankind's fate is man alone...

"...Therefore...

"...We now ask you, the actors...

"...Of our time - a time of overthrow and boundless mastery...

"...Of all nature, even men's own - at last...

"...To change yourselves and show us mankind's world...

"...As it really is: made by men and open to alteration..."

---

[77] Bertolt Bretch - Collected Poems, Methuen Edition, p.234/ 35-43

The responsibility for securing a worthy future lies in the hands of the oppressed and exploited Ugandan/Nile African people.

Throughout the period of captivity of the country by at first British capital, then by multinational and finance capital, and their domination of economic, production and trade systems - i.e. from the time of the country's colonisation to its new colonisation in political-independence times - the structural framework of the socio-economic system imposed on the country has manifested two related and enjoined sides; on the one hand, the side of capital driven economic *"growth without development"* which is to the benefit of alien capital and finance interests and their local agents and collaborators, and, on the other hand, the inhibiting endless pauperisation or untold impoverishment and exclusion of the majority of Nile Africans from the full ownership and benefit of their fruits of labour.

These contradictory realities favour the appropriation by alien capital interests and the idle and parasitic privileged minority in governance of the country, of a large part of wealth in the country as well as the benefits created by science and culture.

On the other hand this privileged minority and alien capital and finance interests are responsible for the poverty of a large majority of people, who incidentally are much aware of being left out, as their growing aspirations for liberation, justice and popular self-rule, get blocked and thwarted.

His Holiness, the late Pope John Paul-II - took public note of similar grave crises that have entrapped the peoples of the sad Third World thus:

> *"...The growing influence of a few people, parallels the growing poverty of the masses..."*

Further analysing this situation, The Holy Father added,

> *"...We discover that this poverty is not a passing phase...*
>
> *"...Instead it is a product of economic, social and political situations and structures, though there are also other causes for the state of misery...*
>
> *"...In many instances, the state of poverty within our countries finds its origin and support in mechanisms which, because they are impregnated with materialism rather than any authentic humanism, create a situation on the international level where the rich get richer at the expense of the poor, who get poorer..."*

"...The impoverished...

The Holy Father further asserted,

> *"...have a right to have the barricades of exploitation*
> *removed..."*

These grave injustices stemming from mechanisms of oppression and exploitation necessitate the liberation of the poor from the unjust social, political and economic structures within which they are entrapped.

The vast majority of the poor lack the most elementary material goods and services to sustain life.

This is in contrast to the accumulation of wealth in the hands of a small greedy and ravenous parasitic minority, the price being often, extreme poverty of the majority.

The poor however, do not simply lack material goods. They also miss, on the level of human dignity, full participation in socio-political life from which they get excluded.

This is particularly the fate of the African indigenous peoples, peasants, manual labourers, impoverished intellectuals and professionals, artisans, petty traders, marginalised urban dwellers, all the socially excluded and discriminated, the unemployed and the never-shall-be-employed youths, and, in particular, the women of these groups who are multiply oppressed and marginalised most because they are not only poor, but truly the last among the impoverished of God Almighty's humanity.

Penury, which exists side by side with, and because of ill-gotten wealth and injustice, constitutes an already activated fuse of social bombs that generate implosions. The cry for liberation, which rises from these hells on earth, and for the realisation of a new humanist society, can no longer be muffled in contemporary times.

The late Pope Paul-VI in his 1967 pastoral guide illuminated these demands:

> *"...It is not just a matter of eliminating hunger, not even*
> *reducing poverty...*
> *"...The struggle against destitution, though urgent and*
> *necessary, is not enough...*
> *"...It is a question, rather of building a world where every*
> *man, no matter what his race, religion or nationality, can live a*
> *fully human life, freed from servitude imposed on him by bitter*

*men or natural forces over which he has no sufficient control
and a world where freedom is not an empty word and where
the poor man, 'Lazarus', can sit down at the same table with
the rich man...*

*"...We must repeat once more that the superfluous wealth of
rich countries should be placed at the service of poor nations...*

*"...The rule up to now, held good for the benefit of those
nearest to us, must today be applied to all the needy of this
world..."*

This 1967 pastoral guide and admonition of His Holiness Pope Paul-VI holds as a compass and projection for the realisation of a humane world for the oppressed, exploited and struggling peoples of the world – who seek to build a humanist and caring future in the service of the humanity made in the image of God Almighty.

Pope Francis has continued to amplify the humanist concern of his predecessors – noting that life for the ordinary people in the Third World; has in contemporary times deteriorated and become worse as well as for a sizeable number in industrialised and developed countries.

This down trodden and tribulated humanity is entrapped in the most difficult social conditions. They aspire and hope for redemption.

In the Holy Father's Evangelli Gaudium (The Joy of the Gospel) of November 26, 2013, on the Church primary mission of evangelisation in the modern world; he notes the following at paragraph 187:

"... the old question always returns...

*"...How does God's love abide in anyone who has the world's
goods and sees a brother or sister in need and yet refuses to
help?..."*

1 John 3-17

Let us recall how James speaks of the cry of the oppressed:

*"...The wages of the labourers who mowed your fields, which
you kept back by fraud, cry out and the cries of the harvesters
have reached the ears of the Lord of Hosts...*

James 3-4

At paragraph 188, the Holy Father notes, that the church has realised that the need for this plea is itself born in liberating action of grace within each of us, thus it is not a question of a mission reserved for a few.

"... It means working to eliminate the structural causes of poverty and to promote the integral development of the poor, as well as small daily acts of solidarity in meeting the real needs which we encounter..."

The word *"solidarity"* is a little worn and at times poorly understood, but it refers to something more than a few sporadic acts of generosity. It presumes the creation of a new mind-set which thinks in terms of community and priority of life of all, over the appropriation of goods by a few.

At paragraph 189, the Holy Father defines the essence of

"...solidarity..."

Which

"...must be lived as the decision to restore to the poor what belongs to them..."

These convictions and habits of solidarity, when they are put into practice, open the way to other structural transformations and make them possible. Changing structures without generating new convictions and attitudes will only ensure that these same structures will become, sooner or later, corrupt, oppressive and ineffectual.

At paragraph 190: The Holy Father, further points out that; sometimes it is a matter of hearing the cry of the entire peoples, the poorest peoples of the earth, since:

"...peace is founded not only in respect for human rights, but also in respect for the rights of peoples...

"...To speak of our rights, we need to broaden our perspective and hear the plea of other peoples and other regions...

"...We need to grow in solidarity which would allow all peoples to become the artisans of their destiny, since every person is called to self-fulfilment..."

The Holy Father asserts the urgency of the necessity of resolving the outstanding question of the entrapment of the structural causes of poverty, which mass dehumanise God Almighty's humanity.

Paragraph 202 of the Evangelli Gaudium reads:

"...The need to resolve the structural causes of poverty cannot be delayed, not only for pragmatic reason of its urgency for the good of society, but because society needs to be cured of a

sickness, which is weakening and frustrating it, and which can only lead to new uses...

"...Welfare projects, which meet certain urgent needs, should be considered merely temporary responses...

"...As long as the problems of the poor are not resolved by rejecting the absolute autonomy of markets and financial speculation and by attacking the structural causes of inequality, no solution will be found for the world's problems or, for that matter, to any problems. Inequality is the source of social ills..."

It is evident that the humanist and just world that secures the wellbeing, welfare and dignity of all humankind made in the image of God Almighty can only get to be built when the structural causes of poverty in the world are collectively overcome, effaced and transcended.

The people who are destined to effect this odyssey to the end, cannot of course be from amongst those whom the profound Bolivian peasant theologian, one Paz Jimenez Paz, defined before a summit of Latin American Catholic bishops as pagan and, or atheist.

For

"...an atheist..."

Jimenez said,

"...is some one who fails to do justice toward the poor..."

The position stated by Jimenez Paz reflects in this regard the positions and practices of the prophets of God Almighty. All prophets of God Almighty for instance, welcomed and gave sanctuaries/refuge to the poor and oppressed of their time: widows, orphans, poor women, slaves, the hungry and the infirmed.

Hitherto, since modern slavery got imposed upon Africa, as processes organised and instituted to abduct its humanity to provide slave labour in the Americas and elsewhere in the world, over half a millennium ago, African humanity has been made to labour and work, first to feed and meet the needs of the interests of others, and then in exhaustion to seek to labour and self-provide in the effort to keep body and soul together.

The struggles to win a free, independent and sovereign *"African Africa"*, theorised by among others by Kobina Sekyi of Ghana (1892 –

1956), one of those forgotten African geniuses, still hold in their validity. African humanity or African Africans first have to work for their own self development and benefit, well-being and welfare, before it works for others, let alone for those interests that have long preyed on its fruits of labour and on the African natural and bio resource bounties.

The Ugandan peoples are, like all other oppressed African humanity, today forced by their terrible conditions of existence to visualize the past in a new light, analyse the present critically, and face up to the challenge of accessing a future of national freedom, justice, shared prosperity, self-becoming and self-determination, and progress in the company of the free of the world.

The end of the fascist military dictatorship in Uganda upon liberation will hence have to be the beginning of a new beginning for the masses of people of the country.

It will be the act of opening of doors to a new history of open possibilities, buoyed up by the dynamic for progress, which shall be founded in the processes for the realisation or assertion of national freedom and sovereignty.

The path to and for transition to the future in the country will be paved by the democratic drive of systems of peoples self-governance and, or self-rule that shall arise in the country at the demise and end of fascist dictatorship.

These systems of popular and democratic African self-governance and self-rule - have to be owned, commanded and controlled by the masses of people, who hitherto have been forced to exist merely as objects of the power of fascism instead of subjects of self-governance. These systems shall constitute the means with which to invent the long desired *'African African'* future of the country.

The *'network'* of the organs of peoples self-governance and systems of self-rule, shall hold the responsibility to organise a popular sovereign conference of the elected delegates of all the African clusters of peoples, nationalities and communities of the country, the historically disenfranchised and marginalised native and indigenous peoples of the country and active patriotic social, civil, political groupings of the country; cognisant of the imperative need for the equality of the country's nationalities in the face of the division historically imposed on them and other sectionalist prejudices and disadvantages to which they have been subjected.

The democratic institution of this autochthonous popular assembly will mark the beginning of the end of the misrule and political mythology still propagated by the parasitic *"Omuzungu Agambye"*[78] political classes in Nile Africa that the people cannot self-govern nor represent themselves, but have to be represented and governed by others and those from the schooled political classes.

This momentous political feat shall mark the end of the history of slave governance systems in the country and the beginning of truly autochthonous systems of popular self-governance in the country.

The people must self-govern, instead of being manipulated once every five years as to which member of the *"Omuzungu Agambye"*[79] political classes is to be seconded to lord it over the people under the obtaining systems of oppression, exploitation and degradation. The laws and class discriminatory political practices that hold against the self-representation of the unschooled or unlettered and un-certificated persons from the clusters of oppressed Nile African peoples, communities and nationalities, shall no longer obtain.

The hitherto excluded from class minority based governance systems, shall thereafter hold centre stage in the politics, economics, political power systems, and foreign relations of their God-given country.

History and the sterling struggles of the oppressed and exploited peoples of the world to self-representation and self-democratic governance have much to teach all who seek to realise liberty and popular democratic self-rule.

The example of the oppressed and exploited British common people, in this regard, presents a good example. The 17th century English radical democrats[80], faced with a similar dilemma on representation, issued a historical declaration on this matter to the effect that:

> *"...It will never be a good world, while they (knights and gentlemen) make us laws that are chosen for fear and do but oppress us, and do not know the peoples sores...*
>
> *"...It will never be well with us till we have Parliaments of countrymen like us that know our wants..."*

---

78 Ibid 4
79 Ibid 4
80 Christopher Hill, *'The World Turned Upside Down'* (Penguin, 60/70 – quoting 17th century English radical democrat's declaration)

This claim to self-representation has remained valid over time. It is an idealist position, which did not take into account, the constraints and imperatives of the then emergent capital driven socio-economic system of Britain.

The English radical democrats were defeated in the subsequent power contestations by the class alliance of the British aristocracy and the then rising bourgeoisie, both of whom feared and opposed - the rise of the poor to political power and the possible radical transformation of Britain by and under radical democrats and their 'alliance of the poor'.

In defeat, as one British leveller pamphlet stated; the outstanding remaining question in their defeat was;

> "...Whose slaves shall the poor be, the King's or Parliament's?..."

Yet it is not only the victorious bourgeoisie that have contributed to the rise of democratic governance, but the "defeated" too have, in respective ways, endowed or contributed to democratic political development.

Since the triumph of *'capital'* in England and Britain, and globally over a myriad of other socio-economic systems, the essence of political representation has been redefined - in social formations in which the capitalist imperative holds dominant, which demand for the creation of political power systems that work on the basis of the continuous realisation of profit and other economic surpluses, which 'capital' appropriates.

Representative governance, in this context, holds no real challenge to capitalist rule nor does it even pose a potential challenge to capital.

Representative democracy is hardly opposed to dominant capital - rather it serves as a subtle facilitator and servitor to the mediated and silent, or hidden rule of capital.

Representation here builds its relevance upon the reality of atomisation of society from whose individual members, capital extracts labour-power for set uses to generate economic surpluses and profit, which it appropriates and grabs.

Representation under the system driven and dominated by capital, separates representatives from the represented and leaders from the led, and imposes in place hierarchical structures in social and political power relations and organisation.

The very process of representation under socio-economic and political systems that exist subject to the demands of the capitalist structural and profit imperative, are hence class and socially limited. This aborts all well-meaning attempts to assert the general entitlements of the people and their rights, which are made illusory.

What is often involved in the processes of representation?

Representation as a tool in bourgeois democratic governance has continued over time to be used to animate vigorous, but inconclusive debates in the struggles for political power and hegemony.

One, Edmund Burke, in his *"Speech to the Electors of Bristol"* delivered as far back as 3rd November 1774, stated a position on the nature of representation which has since prevailed in democratic politics under bourgeois class hegemonies.

Burke unequivocally rejected any idea of *"a mandate or instructions"* from the constituents as to what lines the elected representatives should take in the exercise of their mandates in elected assemblies.

Burke[81] asserted that,

> *"...Your representative owes you, not his industry only, but his judgment and he betrays, instead of serving you, if he sacrifices it to your opinion..."*

Parliament, he noted, was

> *"...not a congress of ambassadors from different hostile interests ... but ... a deliberate assembly with one interest, that of the whole, where not local purpose, not local prejudices ought to guide, but the general good; resulting from the general reason of the whole..."*

The British levellers on the other hand asserted popular sovereignty, i.e. supremacy of the people, including over elected Assemblies and Parliaments. Thus the author of 'Aremonstrance of Many Thousand Citizens'[82] - reminded the House of Commons in 1646 that,

> *"... we are your Principals, and you our Agents...*
> *"...we are possessed you with the same Power that was in our selves...*
> *"... For we might justly have done it ourselves without you, if we had thought it convenient ..."*

---

81   [Edmond Burke on Government, Politics and Society - ed., B.W. Hill, Glasgow, Fontana, 1975, pp. 157-8]

82   [Don M. Wolfe, ed. Leveller Manifestoes of the Puritan Revolution - New York, Tomas Nelson, 1944, p.113]

In between these two positions - stand the liberal democrats and the idealists.

Aneurin Bevan[83], a lead labour party politician and UK parliamentarian reflected this position in his book:

> "...A representative person is one who will act in a given situation in much the same way as those he represents would act in that same situation...
> "...In short, he must be of their kind...
> "...Election is only one part of representation...
> "...It becomes full representation only if the elected person speaks with the authentic accents of those who elected him...
> "...he should share their values; that is, be in touch with their realities..."

In these systems it is evident that a true representative doubtless is surely someone who is authorised to speak and act on behalf of those she or he represents, and who has been so authorised by them.

A true representative in other words is a delegate, carrying a mandate and acting under instructions.

Yet there still exist a myriad of problems inherent in the very principle of representation.

To Jean-Jacques Rousseau and Thomas Paine, sovereignty that belongs to the people, cannot be transferred by them to any other body or person. In short to both men, sovereignty is inalienable.

Further, Thomas Paine[84], in his contention in, *"The Rights of Man"* asserts the point that:

> "...Every age and generation must be free to act for itself, in all cases, as the ages and generations which preceded it ...
> "...Man has no property in man; neither has any generation a property in the generation which are to follow..."

Thus in this regard, the right of every generation to decide for itself how it should be governed, is inalienable and bars such generation from willing away that right on behalf of its successors. One generation that may consent to limited democracy or to authoritarianism or dictatorship should not handicap the successor generation that have absolute right to revoke such constraining decisions. In this regard popular

---

[83] In Place of Fear, London, Quartet Books, 1978, p.35.
[84] Thomas Paine, The Rights of Man, pp.41-2.

sovereignty has hence to be inalienable; if it is to remain as a fountain of popular liberatory initiatives.

It is in this regard that democratic governance means that government shall do what the people want and not, that the people shall consent to what the government proposes or manipulates a people to agree to.

African humanity has since the times of political independence or in post-colonial times, fallen victim to the nefarious political machinations and manipulations of the African political and governing classes.

The question of popular democratic self-rule of the African masses of people can in this regard hardly be avoided.

Conceptually, representation is *'a fictio juris'*, that some person is present in a place from which he or she is materially or physically absent.

Representation is the process by which somebody else – the representative – *'substitutes for'* and at the same time is supposed to 'embody' the represented.

In social and political systems, which exist in Africa today, perfect representation is a logical impossibility.

But perhaps the conditions for perfect representation could be met, when representation is a direct process of transmission of the will of the represented, when the act of representation is a fully transparent reflection of that will.

But the will to be transmitted, is never fully constituted, and is often subject to continuous change. It exists subject to the vagaries of imprecision.

The conditions of a perfect representation do not obtain in either the side of the representative, or that of the represented.

The processes of representation are subject to the endless cycle of continuous composition, decomposition and re-composition of wills.

Perpetual change and the struggles for continuous becoming in human society are endless, even in situations in which the objectives of the latter are, but a pipe dream.

The critical point here to keep in mind is that the popular political drive in Africa remains aimed at realising the self-becoming and self-determination of African peoples, nationalities and communities.

These processes like emancipation, which are self-acts, cannot be effected by representative 'action' carried out on behalf of those who are supposedly meant to benefit from the processes that lead to the self-becoming, and self-determination of peoples, nationalities and communities in Africa.

The efforts that impel African humanity to struggle for the attainment of the state or condition of freedom and securing sovereign spaces requisite to unfold the march of the African masses of people towards their desired goals of self-becoming and self-determination, redefines the relevance of the idea and matter of representation in the political systems of a continent of polities that are not, in aspiration, let alone practice, in movement towards the self-becoming and self-determination of peoples.

This situation calls for a critique of representation in the perspective of the objectives of winning and securing national freedom and sovereignty for the self-becoming and self-determination of African peoples, nationalities and communities.

Representation as it stands today, involves elements of definition, exclusion and separation in governance systems.

In this process, the representative and the represented have to be defined as well as the period of time for which the representative shall act or acts on behalf of the represented.

These specifications that are set out in definitions are exclusive in nature. In the elections of the representatives many other categories stand disqualified – by law and operational practices and, or lack of necessary resources to facilitate one's participation in elections, hence suffer exclusion. In essence, representation means that someone is chosen to *'speak on behalf'* of the represented whose place they take, which in effect exclude the represented over a given period of time.

There exists a definitive separation that is imposed between those who represent and those who are represented.

This divide is frozen in time, for a specific duration, excluding all others except as objects of representation, until the next election of other representatives.

A different world of politics is hence created, that is separate from the daily life of society, which is occupied by a distinct class, and caste of persons – who get acculturalised to communicate and speak in their own parliamentarised-lingua or language while they operate within the confines of the logic of state power that is subservient to the capitalist imperative of surplus/ profit making and their appropriation by capital.

The representatives get transformed into social and cultural aliens who exist and float above the terrible social realities in which their people are forced to exist.

They get blinded to all happenings except those from which they benefit or gain.

Their language of operation and the reality of assimilation to state power systems ensure that they become mere appendages of the state executives, which compromise them with moneys and other largesse.

Theirs is a world of power illusions, in which separation between on the one hand, politics and power, and, on the other, society – is cynically and subtly constructed in the like of the *'Wall of China'* which was built or erected to separate the Chinese social system and power from the then alleged threatening *'hordes of barbarians'* from outside China.

The representative political systems in effect only represent the interests of their lords and masters, local and foreign, and of the ruinous socio-economic systems which global and multinational capital has forced Africa to host since colonisation and despite de-colonisation.

Representative democracy is not opposed to the dominance of Africa by capital or the reproduction of systems that serve the capitalist imperative of profit and economic surplus generation and appropriation by capital. In effect, it is the responsibility of representative governance systems in capitalist dominated Africa not only to secure these *'nyampala'*[85] systems, but also to facilitate their sustenance into the future in the continent.

Representative democracy in this situation, works and is used as the means to open up whole spaces – for the operation of capital and its systems. Capital intrudes into the African polities sometimes stealthily, and, other times, violently and brutally.

In Africa, representative systems of governance perhaps would have a different positive meaning and effect in situations of truly autochthonous development in the spaces within which political independence and sovereignty thrive, full political freedom, social, economic and political equity abound; and where the drive for African self-becoming and self-determination of peoples, nationalities and communities is accompanied by truly responsible and accountable, open

---

[85] Ibid 2

transparent, participatory and shared processes of societal management and governance.

In the said context – representative democracy and governance could in tandem with participatory, consultative, deliberative and monitory democratic processes be utilised to raise self-motivated mass actions to open up vistas to a new developmental future, of shared prosperity, of equity and of social justice, where in the processes of self-becoming and self-determination of the peoples, nationalities and communities of Nile Africa - the processes for the humanisation of society and Nile African youths, women and men, shall be accomplished in solidarity with and in the company of the free or free humanity in the world.

The drive towards self-becoming and self-determination of African peoples, nationalities and communities implies the assumption of mutual respect and shared responsibility amongst popular political leaderships and in their systems of activity and operations.

Mutual respect and shared responsibility in the knowledge based drive towards self-becoming and self-determination; and movement towards the creation of a society of equality, equity, and social justice based on the mutual recognition in dignity, is necessarily a process of endless searching, question asking, enquiry, analyses and interrogations of obtaining and emergent dynamic realities in the world.

These processes cannot actively and fruitfully operate except on the basis of dialogue of equals, researching and prodding/analysing given realities, of listening before talking or listening – talking. Monologues, hereby, get excluded, including one-sided talking at persons, instead of dialogue as equals who communicate with other persons in the realisation of common objectives.

In this regard, no person, however capacitated, can singly assume to have *"the"* answer to given problems. The resolution of problems here becomes a common endeavour and pursuit – a movement forward via questioning, developing and the further posing of necessary questions and problems that have to be resolved in the common interest.

It becomes an imperative in such processes that forward movement in the resolution of problems has to involve as many question askings and interrogations as the movement forward is effected. Here commandist practices of issuing directives from the *"top"* or *"above"* downwards have to be abandoned.

Such commandist and directive practices – inhibit the otherwise necessary free expression and open discussion of problems whose solutions have to be democratically arrived at. Popular democratic movement into the future, which is a movement into the unknown, is doable. It is about inventing ways forward together – in a team made up of a myriad of teams, to win the self-becoming and self-determination of African peoples, nationalities and communities. It is a forward movement of the African masses of people that is best motored by not only the elected delegates democracy, but by mass participatory, consultative, monitory and deliberative democratic processes.

These are processes of collective self-emancipation and liberation, and collective participatory forward march of African peoples, nationalities and communities towards African self-becoming and self-determination.

Oppressed and exploited African masses of people, all over the continent, are groping their ways to liberation which is the means by which to open up new doors for their self-becoming and self-determination.

It is hence, also a time of intelligent imagination and experimentation on, and innovation and invention of, the way forward.

All over the continent, Peoples Assemblies/Parliaments/Baraza's/ *Bunge's/Mbongi a nsi's/etc.*, or peoples talking, debating and deliberative points, are emerging and operating under trees, in parks, schools yards, streets, outside temples, churches and mosques, in deprived rural and urban slums, zones and areas.

This humanity has little time for caste and class representative systems – based on representations on *"the behalf of"* formula of class rule. The talk points are arena of direct political intervention and participation by all concerned.

From here, there is a crossing to be made to transform these arena and fora from mere public talk- and debating-points or even points of altercations; into spaces within which the assumptions of popular political responsibility over freed autonomous spaces, takes place.

With more programmed self-organisation, the talk arena can be transformed into points of political decision making and engagement in public affairs, including local, area, zonal and national matters that can be articulated within a workable network or chain of equivalents. They can thereby be further developed and consolidated as the nerve points in the animation of the entire country network.

What shall thereafter emerge is a networked system of political responsibility and accountability in which the popular self-governance points of popular control and command further develop in the new political dynamic.

After liberation and the political defeat of the fascist military regime, a national gathering of the entire people of the country, has to be organised encompassing delegates from; every part of the country and its clusters of peoples, nationalities and communities, the native and indigenous peoples, workers and people of labour, oppressed youths, students and women, the country's intelligentsia, those Ugandan/Nile African communities in diaspora, faith communities, patriotic professionals, etc.

This shall be the first autochthonous national popular gathering of the genuine delegates of the oppressed and exploited masses of the people of Uganda/ Nile Africa, since colonisation.

The composition of this *"Great National People's Delegate Assembly" (GNPDA),* must not only negate the type of representation in which the country's intermediary bourgeoisie and political elite that is dominant, but must ensure the permanent entry of the masses of the people onto the centre stage of Uganda's politics. This demands the formulation of the type of delegate representation that has to overcome political careerism and mock parliamentarianism, which has been used to effectively exclude the common people from participating as equal subjects in the governance of the country. In the Ugandan people's experience, parliamentarisation of governance under the country's politicals has meant thinly disguised despotism and dictatorship presided over by the parasitic *'nyampala'*[86]/agent false-bourgeoisie and the schooled *'Omuzungu Agambye'*[87] intermediary elite.

Being the ravenous local parasites that prey and live on society and its poor as opposed to the creators of the country's sustenance and wealth, the intermediary bourgeoisie cannot be easily integrated into the democratic process that shall emerge from national liberation, which seeks to end the social system of exploitation and parasitism and the imperialist domination of Uganda. They are a servant class to the

---

[86] Ibid 2
[87] Ibid 4

alien interests that have for very long enslaved the people. They owe their ultimate loyalty to this alien cluster of interests.

The parasitic existence of this class, makes it play a most degenerate role that is geared at working together with their masters to sustain the basis for the continued existence of the sorry reality of deep poverty, rampant illiteracy, disease and hunger that is imposed on the people, in the malign context of the country's general socio-economic backwardness.

The intermediary bourgeoisie play the role of covering up this reality with all types of divisive and sectionalist guises: religious, ethnic, nationality, etc. - in order to maintain the destructive divisions amongst the people. In this way, they slow down the evolving unity of the people so that the disadvantageous economic system which is based on the excessive pillage of the country's national resource endowments, the export of raw materials and the import of luxury goods largely for the country's false-bourgeoisie, and technology and production techniques that are central to their profligate existence, is maintained and perpetuated. The involvement of the intermediary bourgeoisie in the politics of the New Uganda/Nile Africa which seeks autochthonous and, or autonomous and auto-centred development and the unity of the people; is thus unsuited.

Hence, it is necessary that the new popular representative, participatory, consultative, monitory and deliberative democratic system of the country be founded on the basis of delegate representation of the producers of sustenance and wealth, all their democratic, nationalist and patriotic political movements and parties, genuine mass organisations, representatives of all nationalities and communities, patriotic countrymen and women resident overseas, and other democratic and patriotic youths, men and women, so that people's national democratic power shall become the instrument of the will of the whole people of Uganda. This great national democratic and patriotic gathering of people's delegate representatives, shall there by constitute the much needed fulcrum to heave Uganda forward to peace and justice, stability, shared prosperity and progress.

Fighting for a new, just, and democratic Uganda/Nile Africa therefore demands that, those countrymen who are *"no-body's"* in the politics of today's Uganda must through their fullest participation in the national liberation process, be enjoined on the basis of equality to participate in the public affairs of the country, in order that all may enter the centre stage of popular Ugandan/Nile African politics that emerges upon the liberation of the country. This popular mass intervention in history, can no longer be averted.

The need to draw participatory delegate representation from patriotic countrymen and women resident overseas is justified in the context of the situation of chronic social, political and economic crises and upheavals, which have expelled Ugandans of all nationalities and races into the diaspora. These people have not only the responsibility, but also a duty to heed the liberatory call and popular developmental aspirations of their motherland. As such, those who actively care for her welfare and practically identify with her well-being should indeed participate in her public affairs and course of development.

The *"Great National People's Delegate Assembly "* will be charged with tasks of paving and, or forging a popular, community, social and national democratic political path for the independent development of a new, just, and democratic Uganda. This new body will have to come up with an all embracing political, socio-economic, popular, community and national security/defence and cultural construction programmes, and set up requisite mechanisms, for their implementation. Without such democratic evolution of the programme to construct the country, a new, just, and national democratic Uganda will not emerge.

The institution by the fascist dictatorship of its infamous National Resistance Army/Movement (NRA/M) ten-point program and its secret political programme for rebuilding militarist dictatorship in a neo-colonial Uganda/Nile Africa, reveals the tragic *'nyampala*[88]' or agent mission that is the basis of its dictatorial imposition on Uganda/Nile Africa.

The political system, which provides fascism, a free hand to impose its destructive programmes and projects on the country and its people has to be brought to an end at the political defeat of the dictatorship.

A new, just, and democratic Uganda/Nile Africa will have to follow a popular democratic path in the evolution of its development programmes for popular, community and national construction.

The *"Great National People's Delegate Assembly "* as a body which is representative of the entire people, shall be the most suitable organ to constitute an interim or provisional people's national unity authority for the democratic and devolved administration of popular self-

---

[88] Ibid 2

government in a new, just democratic Uganda. It shall also prepare grounds of ushering in national democratic power through a new, independent, national democratic system that is based and fulcrumed on the countrywide-networked system of popular self-governance units.

This new popular, community and national democratic self-governance system and, or state will have to sustain itself on the foundation, strength and power of; organised, co-ordinated and allied producers of sustenance and wealth in Uganda/Nile Africa, i.e. labouring youths, men and women, and all other popular, community, national democratic, patriotic and revolutionary categories which consistently reject dictatorial and minority class systems of authoritarian governance. These are the people who can be organised to fight and collectively guarantee, for themselves and all the country's diverse peoples, broad democratic rights and genuine freedom (freedom of speech, press, assembly, demonstrations, association, establishment of democratic, patriotic and anti-imperialist political movements, parties and social organisations etc.).

It is this popular, community and national democratic rule and self-administration of the masses that shall constitute the foundation that secures the future of national freedom and popular sovereignty of the country. The majority, who have been previously ruled by others, will have to transform themselves into self-rulers for the benefit of all.

It shall be the paramount duty of the people's emergent national liberation movement to find ways to promote the higher development and advancement of this popular exercise of national sovereignty. It shall equally be necessary to forge a suitable, less costly, autochthonous and, or home grown system of devolved administration which does not, in costs and wasted opportunities, overburden the country. The direct involvement of the people in their own administration and exercise of power shall constitute a good foundation for creating such a system of affordable self-government in which careerism and bullying by bureaucracy is overcome, and honesty, competence, and achievement are enabled to flourish for the common good.

At the same time, it shall be necessary to support this popular, community, and democratic power by adopting economic policies, which can lay the foundation for balanced national economic development. Only in this way can Uganda/Nile Africa be transformed into a modern and developed country with a viable nationally rooted dynamic market and into a country with the necessary vision and strength to relate beneficially with the other economies in the broader international division of labour and market.

Hence, in time, the new popular, community and national democratic Uganda will have to forge ways and means which enable it to relate effectively to the capitalist market, as well as the entire world market on terms which are in the circumstances most beneficial to its economic and development needs.

On this basis, Uganda will be able to seek out appropriate niches in the world market in order to exploit whatever possibilities there may be, to realise the necessary accumulation of capital for generating higher productivity in priority sectors of her economy.

With the implementation of such economic strategies, Uganda can in time establish a path for economic construction in which a home-rooted industrialisation process is put in place. This will have the twin objectives of bringing about a revolution in agriculture and the development of a viable economic system of production based, on producer capital and the manufacture of mass consumer goods. Under such model of development, agriculture rooted on secure land tenure systems that favour the majority of producers who are involved in it, must be encouraged to overcome its historic backwardness, and modernised through popular, community and nationally based processes of development. Agriculture can thereby further contribute to a healthy accumulation of capital for national industrialisation and provide a basis for a modern food and raw materials production sector.

In the sphere of politics, as in the economic sphere; conditions shall be fostered that encourage research and innovation, creativity and experimentation that are promotive of economic, scientific, technological and general development. This type of conscious and targeted development shall equally then ensure sustained protection and regeneration of the natural ecology and environment in the country.

The implementation of such a model of planned economic development is absolutely necessary to lay the foundation for an economy which meets the fundamental wants and needs and, or necessities of the people; and popular, community and national developmental requirements. Only such an economy will be strong and viable enough to take the place of the present economic system based on pillage and loot and the production of raw materials for export, and the consumption of imported luxury goods for the ravenous and indolent parasitic elite and false-bourgeoisie – in the country.

In the immediate period after the success of the national liberation struggle, a just and democratic Uganda/Nile Africa must concentrate all its efforts on generating production in the economy, which ensures activities for vigorous sustained capital accumulation and the availability of products and goods for mass consumption. This will, in turn lead to the integration of millions of underemployed and unemployed in production processes that meet the fundamental national developmental requirements and the material, social and cultural needs of the people.

In the beginning, it will be necessary to make the fullest use of the urban and rural private and capitalist economy and revive co-operatives as a priority, to facilitate the regeneration of production. Appropriate policies and measures will have to be adopted and carried out for the production, exchange, and distribution of mass consumption goods, in addition to adoption of flexible policies on taxation, producer and market prices, and suitable labour and work conditions.

In time, it shall be necessary to allow economic activity to develop within the context of democratic national economic planning in order to overcome and transcend the old negative model of resource allocation. A new model of economy that is embedded in society should be constructed to meet its overall needs and necessities, including development and provision of quality education, health services, housing, investment in culture etc. for the people, all of which are of critical importance for genuine societal and human development and advancement.

In essence, producer, consumer, marketing, and credit co-operatives etc., (which are at this stage the only possible collective self-help economic organisations that the labouring people can build) have to be harnessed and given all possible assistance and incentives to play their due role in popular, community and countrywide economic activity and national development.

What is crucial at this stage is the democratic adoption of suitable policies and measures on; sustained quality human capacity development, and capital accumulation, investment, and trade, all of which in the long-term can help promote and foster the country's auto-centred economic development and independence, and afford necessary protection and rejuvenation to the environment which the old socio-economic system wastefully exploited and deeply damaged.

The new sovereign, popular, community and national democratic governance system and, or state which emerges with the success of the political, social and national liberation must therefore focus its concern on the creation of the political and socio-economic conditions necessary to overcome the economic system dominated by foreign finance and multinational capital, and build in its place vibrant popular, community and national democratic socio-economic and power relations systems which ensure the prosperity of the people and country.

In the emergent socio-economic conditions, the objective must be to, establish dynamically interconnected, rural and modern economic installations, that ensure immediate improvements in the conditions of the poor. By using customisable modern techniques, productivity can be enhanced so that the terrible economic situation of the poor is arrested, and reversed, thereby create a climate which frees productive forces for meaningful and mass beneficial development.

Critical to the success of this economic strategy is the sustenance of the all-round quality education, training, skilling, capacitation and development of the human being and society, which is initiated in the national liberation struggle.

In the obtaining conditions of the country, where circumstances have made it impossible to forge an educational system suitable for genuine human development and progress, the character of the new system has to be popular, national, scientific and democratic, so that the people can access and acquire suitable knowledges of natural, physical and social sciences and technologies which are necessary tools with which to develop the required personnel for popular, community, national, technical and scientific construction work as well as for research and development.

The new cultural and educational system has to make possible the eradication of neo-feudal, comprador, fascist, militarist, and anti-democratic ideologies of the old order; introducing in their stead popular, community, national and Africanist democratic outlooks which are promotive of selfless service to the country and African people in their entirety. It is then, that the process of nation formation, (integration, cohesion and unity) begun during the national liberation struggle, falls into place on fertile soil where it can more readily take root. Then, it will be possible to overcome nationality chauvinism and other discriminations practised against and amongst the diversity of the Ugandan/Nile African peoples, thereby denying imperialism and its local Ugandan '*nyampala*[89]', '*Omuzungu Agambye*'[90] agents, the chance to misuse these divisive platforms and practices for mass manipulation, deception and exploitation of the people.

It will then also be possible to pursue with extra vigour, the popular and community educational programmes begun during the process of national liberation for the emancipation of the Ugandan woman. When her own basic leadership and fullest participation in self emancipation are realised and the historical and contemporary disabilities and prejudices that society has unjustly imposed on her are overcome and transcended, the full flowering of her talents will be generated for the benefit of our entire African people. This achievement shall constitute a most significant advance in the popular forward march towards national development and progress.

When national construction is thus given this needed boost, national development, will rest on a solid foundation to anchor national, social, political liberation and independence.

This foundation will be constructed through the efforts of self-motivated youths, women and men, who stand prepared to build a self-reliant Uganda, drawing on the people's creative possibilities and development aspirations which promote their emergence as a free people, giving expression to their creative energies and liberatory enthusiasms.

With the increasing accumulation of material, cultural and 'spiritual' wealth and a democratic political and socio-economic system centred around meeting the genuine needs, wellbeing and welfare of the people, the stage will be set for meeting the people's demands for human centred development, social justice and social progress.

Then, it will be, possible to introduce an unfettered and independent, popular, community, and national democratic legal and justice order endowed with a new body of laws, jurisprudence and appropriate mechanisms and structures for their judicious application. This much needed legal development will ensure the strict observance of legality, furtherance and protection of fundamental peoples and human rights, freedom, personal integrity, and inviolability of the

---

[89] Ibid 2
[90] Ibid 4

person, life, privacy and personal property, community, social, and national endowments.

The African people must not however underestimate the very difficult and hostile, African and international environment in which the national liberation process unfolds and shall triumph. Ugandans must equally be appreciative that the successes recorded by other peoples struggling against imperialism for national freedom and liberation, further extend their own freedom, and serve to weaken the common foe of the world's oppressed peoples, and systems of their exploitation and endless dehumanisation.

Popular, practical and internationalist commitment to the liberatory and freedom cause of all oppressed peoples and requisite active solidarity amongst the anti-imperialist forces in Africa and the world, is an objective and logical necessity for the collective and secure future of the world's rising and self-emancipating peoples.

Hence, the new, independent and national democratic Ugandan polity and state which shall be the instrument for the assertion of Uganda's national and international sovereignty, shall have to work in active solidarity with other oppressed and struggling, rising and free peoples of the world for freedom, progress, peace, equality, democracy and beneficial development.

Success however, in the circumstances, much depends on the type and quality of leadership that emerges and gets developed in the common fight for liberation with the oppressed and exploited people in Africa.

The absence of popular and organic quality leadership has remained a critical question that has most negatively affected the outcomes of many African struggles.

Amilcar Cabral, the African visionary and liberation leader noted that, for Africa's new bourgeoisie to serve the people, they would have to commit *"class suicide"* and reincarnate in the condition of the people. That is to say, they would have to turn their backs on the seductions of power: luxury Mercedes Benz cars in the drive way, the lucrative corporate directorships, the luxury homes in high class estates in Africa, and in the best and highest value land in Europe and abroad, their mock worship by external and white technocrats and experts, who stand in the thrall to the much touted latest advancements in the works of the gods of profit. They would have to give due priorities to meeting the needs and necessities, and ensuring the wellbeing and welfare, and the dignity and happiness of their peoples first, and not the interests of commission agents who work to serve the interests of multinational and, or high capital and finance – but to hold as the true responsible and accountable delegate representatives of the African masses of people.

Before Amilcar Cabral's counsel, the internationalist freedom fighter from the Caribbean, Frantz Fanon[91], issued an admonition and warning to the oppressed and exploited peoples of the sad Third World about the possible ill transformation of the political independence fighters who were bound to get to governmental authority and behave like a caste which:

> *"...Discovering its historic mission: that of the intermediary. Seen through its eyes, its mission has nothing to do with transforming the nation: it consists, prosaically of being the transmission line between the nation and a capitalism, rampant though camouflaged, which today puts on the mask of neo-colonialism...*
>
> *"...The new bourgeoisies will be quite content with the role of the Western business agent, and it will play its part without any complexes in a most dignified manner...*
>
> *"...But this same lucrative role, this cheap jack's function, this meanness of outlook ...*
>
> *"...is in fact beginning at the end..."*

The betrayals of the people by the new African agent governing classes and castes, have been rationalised in many forms.

Questioned by a leading Western journalist, John Pilger[92], whether he recognised that the political settlement in his country by which state governance and management was Africanised, was considered as a betrayal of the South African people – Thabo Mbeki, successor to Nelson Mandela, as state president in post political settlement South Africa replied:

> *"...Had we not made the historic compromises, there would have been a blood bath and great suffering across the land!.."*

May be so, but had the price already paid by the victims of fascist apartheid dictatorship been any less costly? Was this not comparing the

---

[91] Franz Fanon - The Wretched of the Earth/ pp.289-90
[92] John Pilger - Freedom Next Time: Apartheid Did Not Die/ Bantam Press, London, 2007/ pp.294-5

terrible *'known'* or record of the massacres of South Africans, with a new feared *'imaginary'*?

The South African political settlement, may have frozen the popular aspiration and hope that had been articulated in the African National Congress (ANC) Freedom Charter, but perhaps it has not succeeded in killing its spirit of freedom, justice and self-becoming of the South African people. The South African political settlement in effect, marked the victory of the class that had exercised political power in apartheid South Africa.

Given the similarity between the language that was adopted and used by the new empowered governors of South Africans after apartheid rule and that of past apartheid leaders – to explain the realities of the political economy of post-apartheid South Africa; the dominance of multinational capital and finance over South Africa, the real enemy of the oppressed and exploited South African masses, had by the sleight of the hand won definitive victory.

For, true victory is when the enemy comes to talk one's language.

Is it not true victory, a victory in political defeat, which occurs when one's specific message is accepted as a universal ground and couched in commonly accepted language, even by the enemy?

Like in matters of faith or belief verses natural science, the true victory of science begins to unfold when faith, the church, temple or mosque, starts to defend, project and portray itself in the language of science.

The leadership of the ANC, after the South African political settlement, began to define its socio-economic programmes and explain the nature and character of the South African political economy in the language of multinational capital and finance – which became the common lingua with former apartheid rulers and bureaucrats since the political settlement for a democratic South Africa! In fact Thabo Mbeki, in another interview baptised himself a Thatcherite[93].

Circumstances which indeed change people, positively or negatively should not be let to compromise the great and high goals of the African masses of people for liberation and freedom from the slave systems of multinational capital and finance.

---

[93] Ibid 45; A supporter of the political and economic policies of the former British Conservative Prime Minister Margaret Thatcher, particularly those involving the privatization of nationalized industries and trade union legislation.

At the fall of fascist apartheid regime in South Africa, Thabo Mbeki had come face to face with, *"the dilemma"* that the imaginative American novelist Mark Twain, had once had the occasion to comment upon; as that matter which has for long faced and much troubled humanity and its ability to make choices whose outcomes had varied and definitive consequences. Mark Twain wrote:

> *"...There were two 'reigns of terror' if we could but remember it and consider it; the one wrought murder in hot passion, the other in heartless cold blood; the one lasted mere months; the other lasted a thousand years; the one inflicted death upon a thousand persons; the other upon a hundred millions; but our shudders are all for the 'horrors' of minor terror; the momentary terror, so to speak; whereas, what is the horror of swift death by the axe compared to the lifelong death from hunger, cold insult, cruelty, and heartbreak?...*
>
> *"...What is swift death by lightning compared with slow death by fire at the stake...?*
>
> *"...A city cemetery would contain the coffins filled by the brief terror which we all have been diligently taught to shiver and mourn over; but all France could hardly contain the coffins filled by the older and real terror - that unspeakably bitter and awful terror which none of us has been taught to see in its vastness or pity it deserves..."*

Chairman Mao Tse Tung, the leader of the struggles to liberate China in the 20th century, was once asked whether he was in fear of a possible atomic world war whose destruction would be massive.

His answer was that;

> *"...We stand for peace and against war. But if the imperialists insist on unleashing war, we should not be afraid of it...*
>
> *"...Our attitude on the question is the same as our attitude towards any disturbance: first we are against it; second, we are not afraid of it..."*

Chairman Mao's basic message in essence was; we should not be afraid.

In facing up to great hazards in the world, His Holiness the late Pope John Paul-II, had taken a similar position in his advice to believers; *"...Be not afraid..."* he admonished.

One brilliant intellectual commented on this line of thought and attitude;

> *"...Is this not the only correct attitude a propos of war? First we are against it, second - we are not afraid of it..."*

There is definitely something terrifying about this attitude; however, terror is nothing but the condition of freedom!!

Perhaps history will prove President Thabo Mbeki right. Even so, will history - given the incalculable direct and indirect social and human cost incurred since the South African political settlement for a democratic South Africa - absolve him and his colleagues who took the convenient political line that they adopted in fear of possible consequent violent conflagrations and maelstrom arising in South Africa, if the alternative path not taken had been adopted?

The positions of the African National Congress (ANC), and that of Thabo Mbeki, pre-political settlement in South Africa, had certainly changed from those prescribed by the ANC Freedom Charter. Their new positions on the fundamentals of the political economy of South Africa now rhymed with those of multinational capital and finance, which had backed the cruel rule of fascist apartheid regime in South Africa.

Jesus The Christ pre-crucification and pre-resurrection, could hardly be taken to be the same Christ after crucification and resurrection. After the sacrifice of crucification and upon resurrection, Jesus The Christ had attained a qualitatively new level of being. Indeed in history, sacrifices have had to be made to attain qualitatively higher goals. Africa still has to make sacrifices in order to achieve the high goals of its salvation and win a new qualitative being.

When Africa's genuine resurrection and, or real reincarnation occur? Is Africa's struggle for redemption going to be a process like that of a snake which sheds its old skin and acquires a new one, but remains the same poisonous reptile?

A poem by the Ghanaian Albert Kayper Mensah, read on radio[94] on Ghana's independence day in 1957, problematises the matter of Africa's resurrection and reincarnation in the following words:

> *"...And as I walked, I saw Lazarus...*
> *"...Emerge from a tomb, his dead-clothes o'er his shoulders..,*
> *"...His powerful body freed from bandages...,*
> *"...A rising flame of life, from the night of death...,*
> *"...Uncertain yet how long the ravages...,*
> *"...The germs and the million killing ways of earth...,*

---

[94] Voice of Ghana, Accra, 1958; In Swanzy (ed), p.204

"...Will spare his new-found life, his radiant grace...
"...And as he walked past me, I saw my face..."

In the vision of the Ghanaian poet, Jesus The Christ, had brought back Lazarus from the state of death into that of dynamic life. To Kayper Mensah, the true meaning of independence is Africa's resurrection and reincarnation for renaissance.

The rise of the free in history, will be achieved as humanity's long dreamt odyssey; to become master of its own life and destiny is realised, and its societies and communities self-become as it comes to assert their due role in history and the right to live in dignity amidst the free in the world who stand imbued with truly high caring human values.

In the words of the renowned Iranian sage, Sheikh Moslehadin Sa'adi (1213-1293), which are engraved on the wall of the main building of the United Nations Headquarters; this shall be a world of caring humanity, which he depicted in a most memorable poem:

"...All Adam's children are members of the same frame...:
"...Since all, at first from the same essence came...,
"...When by hard fortune, one limb is oppressed...;
"...The other members lose their wonted rest...
"...If though feel's not for others misery...;
"...A child of Adam is no name for thee..."

[Sheikh Molehadin Sa'adi]

The minimal, perhaps ephemeral change that Africa has undergone, since its struggles in modern times to resurrect and self-become, has been in fundamentals *'change without transformative change'* and perhaps only the nominal psychological uplift and triumph of the oppressed African masses of people.

Imposed co-existence of the oppressor and the oppressed, of the exploiters and their victims in neo-colonies as has happened throughout post-colonial and independent Africa, is at best perhaps only a pause in the on-going African struggles to at last win true freedom to enable African people to self-become and self-determine in the company of the free of the world.

In this regard, the African masses of people have to overcome all obstacles that yet blur their vision of reality as the poet said of

'*Lazarus*' and hence determine to begin anew, the struggles to be free, self-become and self-determine their destinies and those of their lands in the world.

The triumph of Africa's liberatory processes will consequently open necessary vistas to transition to a new history of free African humanity.

Commenting on the direction of Africa's future, the late unforgettable Osagyefo Kwame Nkrumah said that Africa would go neither West nor East, but forward. This position remains valid in our times.

Kwame Nkrumah's position rhymed with that of Marcus Garvey, who had appealed to African humanity in the following words;

> "*...Let us not try to be the best or the worst of others, but let us make the effort to be the best of ourselves...*"

The late lamented President Thomas Sankara of Bourkina Fasso, one of the principal protagonists of African liberation and revolution, boldly called upon Africa to take the courage and abandon old formulas which did not serve its liberatory interests, but instead strive to work to win the age of open possibilities and dare invent it's a new future that it commands. Otherwise, Africa would be reduced to accepting the wretched slave present.

Can the future then perhaps be that which one intellectual of the people Vernon Venable, in his book "Human Nature", projected as that in which a free individual;

> "*...is no longer history's pawn, no longer condemned by the blind mechanics of social and economic forces to the mere suffering of history, but one who is a maker of history, who, knowing the nature of these forces, becomes, by choice and action, a part of them, thus changing them, and changing too, himself, thus guiding both along those paths where each may live its fullest fruitfulness and history becomes at last appropriate to the best that human nature can become!...*"

If man and woman is an end in themselves and not mere means to an end, and thus the highest beings for man and woman, are men and women themselves, then it becomes imperative to remove all relationships within and by which man and woman are humiliated, enslaved, taken undue advantages of, abused, despised, oppressed, exploited and dehumanised.

The struggle for freedom, the wellbeing, welfare and self-becoming of humanity is a common endeavour of human kind. The great late, lamented African writer, poet and cinematographist and philosopher, Ousmane Sembene of Senegal, long saw the struggles for freedom of the world's oppressed and exploited as one.

Sembene[95] wrote a poem called *"Fingers"* in which he illustrates the necessity of solidarity in the liberation struggles of the world's oppressed and exploited. The poem is directed against the finger of the oppressors and enslavers of humanity who hold the trigger of a gun that is aimed at the destruction of the lives of the world's oppressed people:

> *"...Fingers, skilled at structure...*
> *"...At modelling figures on marble...,*
> *"...At translation of thoughts...*
> *"...Fingers that would impress...,*
> *"...Fingers of artists...*
> *"...Fingers, thick and heavy...*
> *"...That dig and plough the soil...*
> *"...And open it up for sowing...,*
> *"...And move us...,*
> *"...Fingers of land tillers...*
> *"...A finger holding a trigger...*
> *"...An eye intent on a target finger...*
> *"...Men at the very brink...*
> *"...Of their lives, at the mercy of their finger...*
> *"...The finger that destroys life...*
> *"...Across the rivers and languages...*
> *"...Of Europe and Asia...*
> *"...Of China and Africa...,*
> *"...Of India and the Oceans...,*
> *"...Let us join our fingers to take away...*
> *"...All the power of their finger...*
> *"...Which keeps humanity in mourning..."*

A glorious future for Uganda/Nile Africa is within the reach of her African peoples.

---

[95] Ousmane Sembene, "Finger" - quoted in Lotus Awards 1971, published by the Permanent Bureau of Afro-Asian writers.

With; the support of God Almighty, the liberatory momentum of history and justice on the side of the people, their firm liberatory resolve and commitment, Ugandans/Nile Africans shall win national freedom and national democratic liberation from imperialism, build necessary capacities and acquire innovative developmental knowledges with which to invent a new future in the dynamic of the emergent modernities in the world within which they shall self-become and win self-determination.

It is imperative that in the situation, all those who struggle for human emancipation in the face of the wrath of imperialism take counsel of the poet, Percy Bysshe Shelley[96], into account, to:

"...Rise like lions after slumber...
"...in unvanquishable number - ...
"...shake up your chains to the earth like...
"...dew...
"...which in sleep had fallen on you...
"...ye are many - they are few..."

In Nile Africa, the fascist dictatorship has continued to live a lie and hold in self-denial in the tragic social and political, economic and ecological conditions that entrap the country over which it has presided for decades.

Nonetheless, even in the face of mounting mass opposition to its cruel rule, the fascist dictatorship continues to overestimate its strength and underestimate its vulnerabilities.

This foolhardy position is largely a replay of the old story of the decline and fall, and the demise and perdition of systems of dictatorship in history.

Fascism and its dictatorship can however only continue in vain to attempt to obstacle and delay, but not forever block, the rise of the long aspired for and awaited truly sovereign and democratic commonwealth of equal peoples, nations and communities of Nile Africa.

Indeed history which has been and remains the process for struggle for freedom and social justice holds progressive possibilities yet to be realised.

---

[96] Poet Percy Bysshe Shelley In *"The Mask of Anarchy"*

Popular memory and consciousness, native African genius and imagination stand as critical factors with which Ugandans/Nile Africans can leverage themselves to freedom, a new beginning and a new history of open possibilities.

It is the experience of human kind in history that all things that have a beginning logically, have to have an end.

History, shall have the last word.

Appendices:

A RE-READING OF AND RETHINKINGS ON THE COMMON MAN'S CHARTER

At the end of the turbulent twentieth century one great historian Eric Hobsbawn, in his book, *"The Age of Extremes"*, summed the outcome of that century thus:

> *"...The historic forces that shaped the century, are continuing to operate...*
>
> *"...We live in a world captured, uprooted and transformed by the titanic economic and techno-scientific process of the development of capitalism...*
>
> *"...We know, or at least, it is reasonable to suppose, that it cannot go on ad infinitum ...*
>
> *"...There are signs...*
>
> *"...that we have reached a point of historic crisis...*
>
> *"...The forces generated by the techno-scientific economy are now great enough to destroy...*
>
> *"...the material foundations of human life...*
>
> *"...The structures of human societies themselves...*
>
> *"...are on the point of being destroyed...*
>
> *"...Our world risks both explosion and implosion...*
>
> *"...The alternative to changed society is darkness..."*

The world has certainly moved on since 1970, the year of adoption of the Common Man's Charter.

The Charter's last paragraph - posed the fundamental and historical challenge which still holds relevance, i.e. to:

> *"...provide an opportunity to the common man for the realisation of the full fruits of his labour and social justice..."*

Is it too much today to say that the common man after the long wait from the politicals of the country, within which time he/she has been further politically disabled and crippled – shall now have to self-avail and self-realise that cardinal right to actualise or secure for self, *"the realisation of the full fruits of his labour and social justice?"*

"...It is modern folly to alter a corrupt ethical system, Its
constitution and legislation, without changing the religion, to
have a revolution without a reformation..."

George Wilheim Friedrich Hegel

"... Changing structures without generating new convictions and
attitudes will only ensure that those same structures will
become sooner or later corrupt, oppressive and ineffectual..."

[Pope Francis, Evangelli Gaudium 2013, para.189]

THE COMMON MAN'S CHARTER
BY MILTON OBOTE

Proposals for document No. 1 on "THE MOVE TO THE LEFT"

By

Dr A MILTON OBOTE
President of the
Uganda Peoples Congress
to the Annual Delegates' Conference
of the

UGANDA PEOPLES CONGRESS

FOREWORD BY THE PRESIDENT

In June, 1968 the Annual Delegates' Conference of the Uganda Peoples Congress passed a number of far-reaching Resolutions. The National Council, the Central Executive Committee and the officials of the Party, were directed by the Conference to implement those resolutions.

As President of the Party I have made a detailed study of the implications behind the Resolutions passed in June, 1968 the Party Conference and the methods of carrying them out. As a result, officials of the Party and I have produced a document - Proposals for National Service (Document No. 2 on "The Move to the Left") to implement some aspects of the Conference Resolutions.

It is my sincere belief that in June, 1968 the Party Conference clearly indicated that the Party and Uganda as a whole must take initial steps, as early as possible, to move ideologically and practically to the left. The practical steps for and the degree of commitment by Party members to such a move were not defined at the Conference. It has been my responsibility as the President of the Party to codify all the Party stands for and principles, which have been basic characteristics of the Party since its foundation. In this exercise, officials of the Party, members of the Party and other persons have been of the greatest assistance in enabling me to interpret the Party Resolutions.

I hereby present to the Central Executive Committee, to the National Council and to the Annual Delegates' Conference, these same principles and the strategy for the implementation of the June, 1968 Resolutions. Similarly, I commend this document to the people of Uganda and all our well wishers.

A MILTON OBOTE
President
Uganda People's Congress

THE COMMON MAN'S CHARTER[97]

FIRST STEP FOR UGANDA TO MOVE TO THE LEFT

1.   We the members of the Annual Delegates' Conference of the Uganda Peoples Congress (UPC), assembled on this Twenty-Fourth Day of October, 1969, in an Emergency Meeting in Kampala; being the body charged under the Constitution of the UPC with the responsibility *"to lay down the broad basic policy of the Party"* and being conscious of our responsibility and of the fact that the Government of the Republic of Uganda, District Administrations and Urban Authorities are currently run by our Party and on policies and programmes adopted by our Party and recognising our responsibility to the people of Uganda as a whole and to the association of Uganda, Tanzania and Kenya in the East African Community and to Uganda's Membership of the Organisation of African Unity, do hereby adopt this Charter for the realisation of the real meaning of Independence, namely, that the resources of the country, material and human, be exploited for the benefit of all the people of Uganda in accordance with the principles of Socialism.

2.   We hereby commit ourselves to create in Uganda conditions of full security, justice, equality, liberty and welfare for all sons and daughters of the Republic of Uganda and for the realisation of those goals we have adopted the Move to the Left Strategy herein laid as initial steps.

3.   We subscribe fully to Uganda always being a Republic and have adopted this Charter so that the implementation of this Strategy prevents effectively any one person or group of persons from being masters of all or a section of the people of Uganda, and ensure that all citizens of Uganda become truly masters of their own destiny.

4.   We reject, both in theory and in practice that Uganda as a whole or any part of it should be the domain of any person, of feudalism, of Capitalism, of vested interests of one kind or another, of foreign influence or of foreigners.   We further reject exploitation of material and human resources for the benefit of a few.

5.   We reject, both in theory and in practice, isolationism in regard to one part of Uganda towards another, or in regard to Uganda as a whole to the East African Community in particular, and Africa in general.

6.   Recognising that the root of the UPC have always been in the people right from its formation, and realising that the Party has always commanded us that whatever is done in Uganda must be done for the benefit of all, we

---

[97] https://books.google.co.uk/books/about/The_common_man_s_charter.html

hereby re-affirm our acceptance of the aims and objectives of the UPC, which we set out in full:

(i)   To build the Republic of Uganda as one country with one people, one Parliament and one Government.

(ii)   To defend the Independence and Sovereignty of Uganda and maintain peace and tranquillity, and to preserve the republican Constitution of Uganda.

(iii) To organise the Party to enable the people to participate in framing the destiny of our country;

(iv)   To fight relentlessly against Poverty, Ignorance, Disease, Colonialism, Neo-Colonialism, Imperialism and Apartheid;

(v)   To plan Uganda's Economic Development in such a way that the Government, through Parastatal Bodies, the Co-operative Movements, Private Companies, Individuals in Industry, Commerce and Agriculture, will effectively contribute to increased production to raise the standard of living in the Country;

(vi)   To protect without discrimination based on race, colour, sect or religion every person lawfully living in Uganda and enable him to enjoy the fundamental rights and freedom of the individual, that is to say:

Life, Liberty, Security of the person and Protection of the Law; Freedom of Conscience, of expression and association; Protection of Privacy of his home, property and from deprivation of property without compensation.

(vii) To ensure that no citizen of Uganda will enjoy any special privilege, status or title by virtue of birth, descent or heredity;

(viii) To ensure that in the enjoyment of the rights and freedoms no person shall be allowed to prejudice the rights and freedoms of others and the interests of the State;

(ix)   To support organisations, whether international or otherwise, whose aims, objects and aspirations are consistent with those of the Party;

(x)   To do such other things that are necessary for the achievement of the aims, objects and aspirations of the Party."

7.   Republicanism in Uganda, just like the political Independence of Uganda, is now a reality, but the demand and struggle for *Uhuru*[98] has no end. This is part of life and part of the inalienable right of man. It is also the cornerstone of progress and of the liberty of the individual, the basis of his prosperity and the hallmark of his full and effective participation in the

---

[98] Ibid 21

affairs of his country. October 9, 1962, therefore, was the beginning of a much greater struggle of many dimensions along the road of full *Uhuru*[99]. During the last seven years the UPC, by action and exhortation, has shown to the people of Uganda that it is wrong and deceitful to treat and regard the October 9, 1962, as the end of the road; or the day on which the people of Uganda as a whole reached a stage in their development when all that remained was to divide the spoils on the principle of the survival of the fittest; or that the well-to-do, the educated and the feudal lords must and should be allowed to keep what they have, and get more if they can, without let or hindrance.

The Party has always made it clear to the people that the only acceptable and practical meaning of October 9, 1962, is that the people of Uganda must move away from the ways and mental attitudes of the colonial past, move away from the hold of tribal and other forms of factionalism and the power of vested interests, and accept that the problems of poverty, development and nation-building can and must be tackled on the basis of one Country and one People. The Strategy laid down in this Charter aims at strengthening the fundamental objective of the Party. We do not believe that any citizen of Uganda, once freed of the mental attitudes of the colonial past, freed of the hold of tribal and other forms of factionalism, and freed of the power of vested interests, will find himself or herself at a disadvantage. On the contrary, it is our firm belief that such a citizen will gain that part of his/her freedom which has so far been in the hands of others, and which enabled those others to exploit for their own benefit not only the wealth of the country, but also the energy of our people, thereby arresting the mental development of our people.

8.   Less than ten years ago the most prominent and explosive political issues, which faced the people of Uganda, had in reality, and in practical terms, nothing to do with the people as such. The issues were "...*The form of government suitable for an independent Uganda...*" and "...*Who was to be the Head of State on the achievement of Independence?...*" These issues were made to appear as of national importance, not because the when solutions were found they would advance the lot of the common man, but because the feudalists, on account of their hold on the people, saw Independence as a threat to their then privileged positions and sought to make these positions synonymous with the interests of the common man. It cannot be denied that the then privileged positions of the feudalists were a barrier to the full and effective participation of the common man in the Government of Independent Uganda. The feudalists wanted to continue to rule as they used to before the coming of the British and they did not want the common man to have a say in the shaping of the destiny of an independent Uganda. That situation,

---

[99] Ibid 22

however, is no longer with us Uganda is now a Republic. We hold it as the inalienable right of the people that they must be masters of their own destiny and not servants of this or that man; that they must, as citizens of an Independent Republic, express their views as freely as possible within the laws of their country, made, not in separate Parliaments, but in one Parliament in which the people as a whole have an equal say through their representatives.

9.   The republican status, therefore, has taken Uganda further towards the goal of full *Uhuru*[100]. It must not be accepted, however, that our new status by itself is sufficient, or that it has removed exploitation and has brought full Uhuru[101]. We realise that it is, by itself, an advance towards the goal of full Uhuru[102], but because we are also convinced that more has yet to be done, this Charter has been adopted, and its strategy is in our view a logical development from the fact that we have been moving away from the hold of feudal power since1966. For so long as that feudal power was a factor in the politics and economy of Uganda it could not be disregarded. Thus the reason for this Charter. It must also be noted that in a society in which feudalism is an important and major political and economic factor, that society cannot escape being Rightist in its internal and external policies. With the removal of the feudal factor from our political and economic life, we need to do two things. First we must not allow the previous position of the feudalists to be filled by neo-feudalists. Secondly, we must move away from circumstances, which may give birth to neo-feudalism or generate feudalistic mentality.

The move to the Left is the creation of a new political culture and a new way of life, whereby the people of Uganda as a whole – their welfare and their voices in the National Government and in other local authorities – are paramount. It is, therefore, both anti-feudalism and anti-capitalism.

10.   In 1968, the UPC Delegates' Conference passed the following resolution on the important matter of nation-building:

(a)   "NOTE with deep satisfaction the liquidation of anti-national and feudal forces, and the introduction of the Republican Constitution;

(b)   THANK the leaders of the Party and the Government on initiating the revolution for economic, social and political justice;

(c)   RECOGNISE that the most important task confronting the Party and the Government today is that of nation-building;

(d)   RESOLVE that its entire human and material resources be committed in that task of nation-building;

---

[100] Ibid 21
[101] Ibid 21
[102] Ibid 21

(e)   DIRECT that the National Council of the Party do examine ways and means for active involvement of all institutions, State and private, in joint endeavour with the Party to achieve and serve a nation united and one."

11.   We have no doubt whatsoever about the high priority which must be given to nation-building, and we are fully aware that there may be many people in this country who are either uninformed or misguided, who have not yet come to appreciate the importance of nation-building. We, therefore, consider it our responsibility to inform the uninformed, and to guide the misguided. It is also our responsibility to enlighten the people about the necessity of all the institutions in this country and the people as a whole being actively involved in the joint endeavour to serve the Nation.

12.   When the UPC proposes a policy or programme on behalf and for the benefit of the people of Uganda, the meaning of the phrase *"people of Uganda"* is always clear and definite. It is, One People under One Government in One Country. Accordingly, over the seven years of Independence the Party has indicated more than sufficiently that to belong to a clan, tribe, a linguistic group, a region or a religion, is neither an advantage nor a disadvantage to any citizen of Uganda. The fact of being a citizen of Uganda, however, is a decided advantage which gives him fundamental rights and freedoms, and affords him full opportunity to exercise his social duties and obligations to his clan, tribe, region or religion, save as forbidden by laws passed by Parliament. These laws, as it is clearly stated in Principle 6 of the UPC Aims and Objects, and in the Republican Constitution, are desirable so as to enable all citizens to enjoy their fundamental rights and freedoms without infringing upon the rights and freedoms of any other citizens to do the same.

13.   In seven years of independence we have experienced that the mass of people are law-abiding citizens, who believe in the security of their families, stable conditions around their homes and throughout Uganda; who appreciate the need for expanding economic and social services, and who are desirous to work hard to improve their conditions of living and participate fully in political control of governmental institutions. This experience is in contrast to another, namely, the desire of foreign powers and institutions to choose leaders for us, to influence the policies of the Government of Uganda to the benefit of foreign interests, and to use the sons and daughters of Uganda to advance these interests. In our experience we have not found a single instance where foreign interests have sought to use the masses of the people to serve the interests of foreigners. We have, however, had abundant instances where the well to do, the educated and the feudal elements have been bought to serve the interests of foreigners. This kind of corruption of the intentions and frustrations of the wishes of the people may be tolerated in countries

where nationhood has been firmly established, illiteracy is almost unknown and other factional issues do not play any important part in elections or in the formulation of Government policies. Uganda has not yet reached that stage of development; but even when we eventually reach that stage we will not tolerate, on principle, the corruption of the intentions and the frustration of the wishes of the people.

14. One of the most important considerations facing the people of Uganda, in the view of the UPC is the future of the youth. We have only to look at the figures of all the young men and women in the Universities, in the Secondary Schools, in other institutes of learning and in Primary Schools, to speak nothing of those who are at home, to realise that these are citizens of Uganda who are being prepared to shoulder responsibilities of consolidating further the political independence now have, and to open more and more avenues which will lead the people of Uganda to real economic and social independence.

15. If here in Uganda, we adopt the policy of developing our country and preparing our youth within the confines of tribal Governments, tribal Parliaments and traditions, and as tools of sectionalism and factionalism of any kind, we would neither be making a contribution to the African Revolution, nor would we be giving these young people what is within our power to give them – that is, the broadening of their horizon to look at the whole of Uganda and not just a part of it as the centre and platform of their operations. It is our duty and responsibility to accept these young people irrespective of the corner of Uganda, which may be their birthplace. The whole of Uganda is their inheritance and we must not deny either all of them or a majority of them or even a minority of them, their heritage. They are growing in a different world – a world very different from the world in which those who faced the British when they first imposed colonial rule in Uganda lived. Young people are growing in a world which is becoming smaller and smaller, and for us to make that world even smaller by inducing them, directly or indirectly, to become exponents of tribal Herrenvolk principles[103], religious bigotry and fanaticism and feudalistic selfishness, and capitalistic rapacity's would be to do a disservice that Africa will never forget, and a disservice that will certainly reduce the mental capacities of our young men and women. Uganda cannot afford to be so heartless to her youth.

16. It is not only the youth whom we must think about. Those who are grown up are equally important. Even the old and the infirm are important. The tribal confines and security are no longer strong enough to give them the requirements of modern times, or to protect their lives and property or to

---

[103] A concept/driver of the German Nazi Ideology of a master race. It is inferred here as a system that offers democratic participation to a dominant group.

give that important recognition of human dignity and citizenship of a sovereign state.

17. We reiterate the fact that the struggle for Independence was not a struggle confined to people professing one religion. The colonial power heard voices from all corners of Uganda. The struggle, however, was not that different parts of Uganda should return to the days of tribal quarrels, disunity and wars but to move to the new era wherein all people of Uganda are one and the country is one, and to regain our dignity as human beings.

18. We recognise that ours is a society in transition. We want to bring it our considered assessment of the present situation as the starting point for our adoption of the move to the Left Strategy set out in this Charter. Uganda is a country, which is already independent politically. It is that status that makes it the responsibility of the people of Uganda to shape their destiny. Before the October 9, 1962, the people of Uganda did not have the responsibility of power. The sixty-nine years of colonial rule, during which an alien way of life was not only planted but also took root, resulted in the phenomenon of developing our human and material resources to bear the imprint of this factor in our society. What was planted in Uganda during the era of British protectorate appeared in the eyes and minds of our people as the final word in perfection regarding the development of our material resources and human relationship. Consequently, both before and after Independence, our people have been living in a society in which an alien way of life has been embedded. The result has been that most of our people do not look in to the country for ideas to make life better in Uganda, but always look elsewhere to import ideas, which may be perfectly suitable in some other society but certainly unfitting in a society like ours. The more we pursue that course, the more we artificially organise our society, our material resources and human relationship, and the more we perpetuate a foreign way of life in our country.

19. We cannot afford to build two nations within the territorial boundaries of Uganda: one rich, educated, African in appearance but mentally foreign, and the other, which constitutes the majority of the population, poor and illiterate. We do not consider that all aspects of the African traditional life are acceptable as socialistic now. We do not, for instance, accept that belonging to a tribe should make a citizen a tool to be exploited by and used for the benefit of tribal leaders. Similarly, we do not accept that feudalism, though not inherently something peculiar to Africa or Uganda is a way of life, which must not be disturbed because it has been in practice for centuries. With this background, we are convinced that Uganda has to choose between two alternatives. We either perpetuate what we inherited, in which case we will build on a most irrational system of production and distribution of wealth based on alien methods, or we

adopt a programme of action based on realities of our country. The choice adopted in this Charter is the latter. We must move away from the ways of the past to the avenues of reality, and reject travelling along a road where the signpost reads: *"Right of admittance is belief in the survival of the fittest."* To us, every citizen of Uganda must survive and we are convinced that Uganda has to move to the Left as a unit. Conditions must be creates to enable the fruits of Independence to reach each and every citizen without some citizens enjoying privileged positions or living on the sweat of their fellow citizens.

20. The emergence and growth of a privileged group in our society, together with the open possibilities of the group assuming the powers of the feudal elements, are not matters of theory and cannot be disregarded with a wave of the hand. Nor should the same be looked at from a doctrinaire approach. It is for this reason that in this Charter we do not intend to play with words, even if those words have meanings, such as *"Capitalism"* or *"Communism"*. We are convinced that from the standpoint of our history, not only our educational system inherited from pre-independence days, but also the attitudes to modern commerce and industry and the position of a person in authority, in or outside Government are creating a gap between the well-to-do on the one hand and the mass of people on the other. The move to the Left Strategy of this Charter aims at bridging the gap and arresting this development.

21. We identify two circumstances in which the emergence of a privileged class can find comfort and growth. First, there is our education system, which aims at producing citizens whose attitude to the uneducated and their way of life lead them to think of themselves as the masters and the uneducated as their servants. Secondly, the opportunities for self-employment in modern commerce and industry and to gain employment in Government and in other sectors of the economy are mainly open to the educated few; but instead of these educated few doing everything possible within their powers for the less educated, a tendency is developing where whoever is in business or Government looks to his immediate family and not to the country as a whole in opening these opportunities. The existence of these circumstances could lead to actual situations of corruption, nepotism and abuse of responsibility. It is unrealistic for anyone to believe that the answer to such situations lies in the strict application of the laws. Much as the laws might assist in preventing such crimes being committed against the nation, it is our view that the answer lies in tackling the roots of the problems, namely to generate a new attitude to life and to wealth, and new attitudes in exercising responsibilities. Our country is fortunate in that these problems have not taken deep roots and the crimes, which they generate and the crimes, which they generate, are universally condemned by the society. If

do not take initial effective measures to change the course of events at this stage of our history, it may be too late to avoid violence in future years. It is because we are convinced that this is the right moment to re-orient our course that we have adopted the measures set out in the move to the Left Strategy of this Charter.

22. The ordinary citizen of Uganda associates economic development of this country with a rise in his own private real income. The income may accrue to him from self-employment, i.e., farming, fishing, cattle-keeping, or paid employment. What is of crucial importance to the ordinary citizen is that Government should provide him with certain social services free and that his income should rise faster than the cost of living, so that he can afford more goods and services for his own use. But there are also three other major dimensions of economic development, which must concern our Government. These are the distributions of the national income, the structure of the economy and the creation of institutions conducive to further development and consistent with the Socialist Strategy outlined in this Charter.

23. Let us begin the examination of the distribution of income in our country. It is obvious that for development to take place there should be a rise in the average income per head (per capita). This can only occur if the rate of growth of national income exceeds the rate of population growth. For this reason our Government must always place great emphasis on the fast rate of growth of the economy and the national income. Indeed, increased production and wealth is one of the three major goals of the current Plan *("Work for Progress")* 1966-71. We are fully convinced that this emphasis is not misplaced, since raising the standard of living of the Common Man in Uganda must be the major aim of our Government. It is possible, however, for the overall rate of growth to rise without affecting large masses of the population. This is a danger we must guard against. We must not either because of inertia, corruption or academic love for the principle of the theory of free enterprise fail to take bold corrective measures against this danger.

24. There is also the danger that economic development could be unevenly distributed as between regions of the country. The fact is that there is no automatic mechanism within our economic system to ensure an equitable distribution of the national income among persons, groups of persons or regions. We need only to stretch our eyes not to the distant future but to the years immediately ahead of us, taking into account the fact of our present expanding economy, to recognise that if no new strategy is adopted now, inequalities in the distribution of income will change dramatically the status of millions of our people, and might result in our having two nations – one fabulously rich and living on the sweat of the other, and the other living in abject poverty – both living in one country.

In such a situation political power will be in the hands of the rich and the maximum the Government will do for the poor will be paternalism, where the lot of the masses will be not only to serve the well to do, but to be thankful on their knees when opportunity arises to eat the crumbs from the high table.

25. The nature of our economy today is such that the resources are not allocated by a central authority. The reality of the situation is that allocation of resources in Uganda is directly proportionate to the distribution of income. The practical fact, which emerges from this can be illustrated in this way. If 15 per cent of the population receive, say, 50 per cent of the national income among them, this small minority possesses the power to command at least half of the productive resources of the country. With so much wealth at their disposal their consumption habits will affect the whole economy. As it happens, these habits will be characterised by the consumption of luxurious goods not produced in the country but imported from outside, or produced in the country at extremely high cost. If the goods have to be imported then the bulk of the population must produce export in order to pay for the import of such luxurious goods. Our argument for a change to make it impossible for such a situation to develop as a feature of Uganda, is that consumption habits of the very rich not only impinge directly on the disposal of one of the important resources of the country, namely foreign exchange, but also constitute a negation of the real meaning of our Independence. The crucial point here is that inequitable distribution of income leads directly to non-development of resources which could cater for the consumption needs of the poor, since the masses cannot afford to pay for the goods which would be produced, and instead the economy becomes dependent on exports of primary commodities in order to pay for imports of luxurious goods for the rich. The end result is a constant problem of unfavourable balance of payments and external debts, and a neglect of the welfare of the Common Man.

26. We must examine the argument in another way. A redistribution of income, which puts more purchasing power in the hands of the Common Man, who constitutes the greatest proportion of the population, would give an impetus to the development of local industries. This is because the needs of the masses are unlikely to be of the luxurious type. As the mass of the people of Uganda begin to acquire higher and higher incomes, they would in all probability acquire more and more goods produced in their country; but to open the door only to the rich to buy at high prices any quantity of imported goods and locally produced goods at high costs, which put them beyond the means of the Common Man, is to disregard the existence of the mass of the population or to acknowledge their servitude to the rich.

27. The heart of the Move to the Left can be simply stated. It is both political and economic. It is the basic belief of the Uganda Peoples Congress that political power must be vested in the majority of the people and not the minority. It is also the fundamental belief of the Uganda Peoples Congress that economic power should be vested in the majority and not in the minority, as is the case at present. It is therefore, our firm resolution that political and economic power must be vested in the majority.

28. The structure of Uganda's economy is characterised by: an excessive dependence on agriculture as a source of income, employment and foreign exchange; a heavy dependence on exports based on two major export crops; heavy dependence on imports, particularly of manufactured products; and the limited participation of Ugandans in the modern industrial and commercial sectors of the economy. It has therefore been the policy of the Party to diversify the economy to make it less dependent of foreign trade, to promote the participation of citizens in all sectors of the economy, and the Move to the Left is intended to intensify these efforts through collective ownership, viz. Co-operatives and state enterprises.

29. Economic development demands, among other things, capital (money). We recognise that a country cannot depend upon capital from outside because this, apart from being unpredictable, is subject to variation by various factors and has always got strings attached to it. We are convinced from experience that this country is capable of generating sufficient capital out of the savings of all the citizens. We therefore propose that a suitable means where the savings of the citizens can be effectively tapped and correctly channelled into further economic development should be introduced.

30. To this effect we propose that the system be based on the present basis of calculation upon which wage earners pay contribution of a fraction of their earnings into the Social Security Fund. The basis of the calculation of that part of the income of the wage earners that goes into contributions to the National Social Security Scheme should apply proportionately to the income earned by all other persons, either by way of salary or other method of determinable income. With the exception of the wage-earner who is already required by law to make contribution to the National Social Security Scheme, all other persons will either pay direct or have it deducted and paid into an approved scheme.

31. The present banking institutions cater mainly for the needs of commerce and industry. It is not possible for the peasants, who constitute the majority of our population, to advance their lot through financial assistance in the form of loans from these commercial banks. Even if they were to do so, they would spend a substantial part of it, if not their entire income, in paying back these loans. It is, therefore, imperative that a

new banking system, to be known as the Co-operative Bank, be established to cater solely for the peasants who are members of the Co-operative Unions. The policy of such a Bank should include a provision to the effect that the Co-operative Union of the person applying for a loan from the Bank gives a guarantee and takes over administration of the repayment of the loan, and that the loan in the majority of cases should be given in relation to what the applicant is already doing.

32. We reiterate the fact that there can be no investment unless somebody first makes a corresponding saving. This applies equally to local and overseas investment.

    (a)   With regard to local investment we have now proposed a scheme for compulsory saving in a number of schemes, and the establishment of Co-operative Banks.

    (b)   With regard to foreign investment we fully realise that foreign investors want guarantees, and we consider that the Foreign Investment (Protection) Act covers this adequately and generously. Much as we appreciate the need to attract foreign investment, we are fully convinced that the economic future of this country depends on local capital formation and local savings and investment.

33. In future we would wish to see foreign investments coming into Uganda under the Foreign Investment (Protection) Act, engaging in priority projects and not projects decided solely on the basis of profitability. Similarly, local investments should be controlled in such a way that they are made in priority projects determined by the needs of the economic development of the country.

34. In our Move to the Left Strategy, we affirm that the guiding economic principle will be that the means of production and distribution must be in the hands of the people as a whole. The fulfilment of this principle may involve the nationalisation of enterprises privately owned.

35. The issue of nationalisation has already been determined and therefore it is a settled matter. It was in the 1962 Constitution, as it is in the republican Constitution of 1967. Therefore no citizen or person in private enterprise should entertain the idea that the Government of Uganda cannot, whenever it is desirable in the interest of the people, nationalise any or all privately owned enterprises, mailo and freehold land and all productive assets or property, at any time, for the benefit of the people. The Party therefore directs the Government to work along these lines.

36. In this Charter we lay emphasis first on the people being given massive education in operating and establishing institutions controlled, not by individuals, but by the people collectively. This massive education should aim at re-orienting the attitudes of the people towards co-operation in the

management of economic institutions, and away from individual and private enrichment. We therefore direct the Government to give education to the people to acquire new attitudes in the management of our economy where collective exploitation of our resources to the benefit of all take the place of individual and private enterprise aimed at enriching a few.

37. We must move in accordance with the principle of democracy. That is the way that brings human progress. Ideas must be generated and sifted, and citizens – educated or not – must be able to think for themselves, learn to work together, and to participate in the processes of governing themselves.

38. The Move to the Left involves government by discussion. This Charter and the principles enunciated herein should be widely disseminated through mass media of communication, and discussed by study groups and individuals all over the country.

39. Principles are a good thing but they are no substitute for hard work. The success of the Charter demands full commitment of leaders to its realisation, acceptance by the mass of the population, and hard work by all.

40. The adoption of the Charter provides an opportunity to the Common Man for the realisation of the full fruits of his labour and of social justice.

SUBJECT INDEX

www.ingramcontent.com/pod-product-compliance
Lightning Source LLC
Chambersburg PA
CBHW062211270326
41930CB00009B/1710